The
Barnabas
Family
Bible

C000286068

Text copyright © Martyn Payne and Jane Butcher 2014
The authors assert the moral right to be identified as the authors of this work

Published by
The Bible Reading Fellowship
15 The Chambers, Vineyard
Abingdon OX14 3FE
United Kingdom
Tel: +44 (0)1865 319700
Email: enquiries@brf.org.uk
Website: www.brf.org.uk
BRF is a Registered Charity

ISBN 978 1 84101 713 6

First published 2014
10 9 8 7 6 5 4 3 2 1 0
All rights reserved

Acknowledgements
Unless otherwise indicated, scripture quotations are from the Contemporary English Version. New Testament © American Bible Society 1991, 1992, 1995. Old Testament © American Bible Society 1995. Anglicisations © British & Foreign Bible Society 1996. Used by permission.

p. 71: Quotation taken from The Holy Bible, New International Version (Anglicised edition) copyright © 1979, 1984, 2011 by Biblica. Used by permission of Hodder & Stoughton Publishers, an Hachette UK company. All rights reserved. 'NIV' is a registered trademark of Biblica. UK trademark number 1448790.

A catalogue record for this book is available from the British Library

Production management by Bible Society Resources Ltd
BSRL/2014/3.9M
Printed in China

The Barnabas Family Bible

Martyn Payne and Jane Butcher

Acknowledgements

Jane and Martyn owe a huge debt of gratitude to their own family networks for their support and encouragement during the writing of this book; and in particular to Katie and to Ruth, who with us know first-hand the challenges and joys of trying to be a Christian family in today's world.

Contents

Introduction 7

Bible story times

The story of creation *Genesis 2:4b–22* 10
The first sin *Genesis 3:1–13* 12
The great flood *Genesis 6:5–22* 14
Abram's choice *Genesis 13:1–13* 16
God's promise *Genesis 15:1–6; 17:1–8* 18
God tests Abraham *Genesis 22:1–14* 20
Jacob and Esau *Genesis 27:1–19* 22
Jacob wrestles with God *Genesis 32:22—33:4* 24
Joseph and his brothers *Genesis 37:14b–30* 26
The king's dreams *Genesis 41:1–16* 28
Slaves in Egypt *Exodus 1:14–16; 2:1–10* 30
The burning bush *Exodus 3:1–12* 32
Escape from Egypt *Exodus 12:31–42* 34
Crossing the Red Sea *Exodus 14:5–7, 10–22* 36
Water from the rock *Exodus 17:1–7* 38
The ten commandments *Exodus 20:1–17* 40
Exploring the land of Canaan
    Numbers 13:1–4a, 21–33 42
Joshua is chosen *Joshua 1:1–9* 44
Rahab and the spies *Joshua 2:1–14* 46
The battle of Jericho *Joshua 5:13—6:8* 48
The time of the judges *Judges 2:6–17* 50
Gideon defeats the Midianites *Judges 7:1–7* 52
Naomi goes home *Ruth 1:1–18* 54
Ruth and Boaz *Ruth 2:1–12* 56
God speaks to Samuel *1 Samuel 3:1–10* 58
Israel's first king *1 Samuel 8:4–22a* 60
David and Goliath *1 Samuel 17:31–40* 62
David lets Saul live *1 Samuel 24:1–11, 16* 64

David is kind to Mephibosheth *2 Samuel 9* 66
David and Bathsheba *2 Samuel 11:2–15* 68
The wisdom of Solomon *1 Kings 3:5–15* 70
Building the temple *1 Kings 5:1–12* 72
The kingdom divides *1 Kings 12:1–16* 74
Elijah stops the rain *1 Kings 17:1–16* 76
The contest on the mountain *1 Kings 18:26–39* 78
Earthquake, fire and whisper *1 Kings 19:9b–18* 80
Naboth's vineyard *1 Kings 21:1–16* 82
Elijah's chariot *2 Kings 2:7–18* 84
Naaman is healed *2 Kings 5:1b–14* 86
Joash repairs the temple *2 Kings 12:1–15* 88
Jonah runs away *Jonah 1:1–15, 17* 90
Jonah is angry *Jonah 4* 92
Hezekiah gets ill *2 Kings 20:1–11* 94
Josiah discovers God's law *2 Kings 22:1–13* 96
Captivity in Babylon *Daniel 1:3–19* 98
The fiery furnace *Daniel 3:13–27* 100
Daniel in the lions' den *Daniel 6:10–22* 102
Nehemiah goes to Jerusalem *Nehemiah 2:1–8* 104
Rebuilding the walls *Nehemiah 4:6–20* 106
The promise of a saviour *Isaiah 40:1–11* 108
Zechariah receives a promise *Luke 1:11–20* 110
An angel visits Mary *Luke 1:26–38* 112
Mary visits Elizabeth *Luke 1:39–56* 114
The birth of Jesus *Luke 2:1–16* 116
Simeon praises the Lord *Luke 2:22–35* 118
Herod and the wise men *Matthew 2:1–12* 120
The escape to Egypt *Matthew 2:13–23* 122
Lost in Jerusalem *Luke 2:41–52* 124
John the Baptist's message *Luke 3:2b–17* 126
Baptism and temptation *Matthew 3:13—4:11* 128

Jesus chooses his first disciples *Luke 5:1–11* 130

The wedding at Cana *John 2:1–12* 132

The paralysed man *Mark 2:1–12* 134

Choosing the twelve apostles *Luke 6:12–19* 136

The soldier's request *Luke 7:1–10* 138

The parable of the sower *Luke 8:4–15* 140

The woman at the well *John 4:3–14* 142

John the Baptist is executed *Matthew 14:1–12* 144

Healing Jairus' daughter *Luke 8:40–56* 146

Feeding the 5000 *Matthew 14:13–21* 148

Walking on water *Matthew 14:22–33* 150

The transfiguration *Matthew 17:1–9* 152

The woman caught breaking the law *John 8:1–11* 154

The good Samaritan *Luke 10:30–37* 156

Mary and Martha *Luke 10:38—11:4* 158

The prodigal son *Luke 15:11–24* 160

A Pharisee and a tax collector *Luke 18:9–14* 162

The death of Lazarus *John 11:17–27, 38–44* 164

A rich young man *Matthew 19:16–30* 166

Blind Bartimaeus *Mark 10:46–52* 168

Zacchaeus in the tree *Luke 19:1–10* 170

The parable of the king's servants *Luke 19:11–24* 172

The tenants of a vineyard *Luke 20:9–19* 174

The sheep and the goats *Matthew 25:31–46* 176

Jesus arrives in Jerusalem *Luke 19:28–40* 178

Cleansing the temple *John 2:13–22* 180

The plot to kill Jesus *Luke 22:1–13* 182

The perfume offering *Mark 14:1–9* 184

The Last Supper *Luke 22:14–23* 186

Gethsemane *Matthew 26:36–46* 188

Peter denies Jesus *Matthew 26:57–58, 69–75* 190

The death sentence *Matthew 27:15–26* 192

The road to the cross *Luke 23:26–37* 194

The crucifixion *Luke 23:38–49* 196

The empty tomb *John 20:11–18* 198

The road to Emmaus
    Luke 24:13–20, 22–23, 25–33a 200

Doubting Thomas *John 20:19–29* 202

At Lake Galilee *John 21:1–14* 204

Jesus ascends to heaven *Acts 1:4–11* 206

Pentecost *Acts 2:1–13* 208

Peter and John heal a lame man *Acts 3:1–10* 210

Stephen is killed *Acts 6:8–15; 7:54–60* 212

Philip and the Ethiopian *Acts 8:26–40* 214

The road to Damascus *Acts 9:1–12* 216

Peter brings Dorcas back to life *Acts 9:36–43* 218

Peter in prison *Acts 12:1–16* 220

Paul at Philippi in Greece *Acts 16:16–31* 222

An accident in Troas *Acts 20:3b–12* 224

Shipwreck on the way to Rome *Acts 27:9a, 11–25* 226

John's vision of heaven *Revelation 21:1–7* 228

Guidance and support

Faith begins at home.. 232

Establishing a time and place 234

Reading the Bible together 236

Handling difficult questions 238

Praying as a family 240

Creating shared memories.. 242

Supporting your child's faith 244

Overview of the Bible... 246

Best-loved Bible passages 250

Further resources 256

Introduction

Jesus asked, 'Who is my mother and who are my brothers?' Then he looked at the people sitting around him and said, 'Here are my mother and my brothers. Anyone who obeys God is my brother or sister or mother.'

MARK 3:33–35

'Family' is a big word. At least, it always used to be. Certainly it was so in Old Testament times, when family included a wide network of more distant as well as immediate relatives. It linked up all those connected not just by DNA but by bonds of friendship, financial obligations and mutual concerns over territory and shared faith. It is only in more recent times that we have limited family to two parents and their biological children in a small home. But times have changed and now once again families come in all shapes and sizes, drawn together by a commitment that does not necessarily depend on the promises of marriage vows.

Family is a big idea and needs to be seen as such. It is for all sorts of families that *The Barnabas Family Bible* has been written. Wherever children are being nurtured in love by significant adults in their lives, there is family. This is the family of those trying to do things God's way. Jesus talked about this when his own immediate family told him to get back home and stop behaving crazily! He had to remind them, as he does us today, that his family was much bigger. In fact, the family of faith—of those who do God's will—was created by the intergenerational community gathered around Jesus. As the Gospels make clear, this included a bunch of young men who were tradesmen and accountants, women who were wealthy and well-connected, and even others of more dubious reputation. It was a family of mothers with their young children, as well as those who were sick, alone and vulnerable. This model is an exciting and relevant one for today, helping us to reclaim and redefine the concept of family.

So however you are gathering to read the Bible together, we hope that this book will become a treasured and valued companion. It includes a selection of passages that will take you right through the story of the Bible from its glorious and hopeful beginnings in the garden of Eden through the very human and often tragic stories of the people of God; from the longing of God's heart to mend the brokenness of the world to the wonder of the story of Jesus and what he did to bring the family of God together again; and it ends with the beautiful description of the new earth and heaven to which all those who have faith in Jesus are travelling. The aim of the authors has been to make these passages accessible for all ages in your family as you take time to focus on these stories together.

The translation used is the Contemporary English Version (CEV), which is easy for both adults and children to read. Following each **Bible passage**, there is a **commentary** that starts to unpack each story, with regard to both its place within the wider narrative of the Bible and its relevance for us today. Although this is designed primarily for adults to read, we hope that the language will also be accessible to older children.

What follows is an opportunity to engage with the story in a number of creative ways. The **questions** that follow the commentary are designed to get everyone talking. They are not just for the children but, we hope, will stretch everyone's minds and imaginations. And, recognising that it is always helpful to have a focus, a suggestion for a **visual aid** is made. This will be an item that can be found easily around the home, so that it can be on display as the story is read and talked about.

We learn most by doing things, of course, and there is therefore an **activity idea** too, providing an engaging and memorable way to touch the theme of the story. Christians believe that the stories of the Bible can teach us more about ourselves and about God, and therefore, as we open up its pages, we are drawn closer to God himself, to which the natural response is to pray. Again, picking up on the contents of the story, there is always a **prayer idea** to help you do this.

From each passage we have also picked out a **key verse** which is a headline for that story and points to a Bible truth that can become an anchor for both adults and children as they read the story together.

Sadly, space was limited, and this has meant that we have had to miss out some really good stories. We would have loved to explore the ups and downs of Samson's volatile life, the bravery of Esther, the patience of Job, the wisdom of Solomon, more from the poetry of the Old Testament prophets and the teaching from Paul's epistles, but we couldn't cover everything. Nevertheless, we hope you will enjoy what is here so much that you will want to go on and read more for yourselves. To help you with that, for every single story we have provided a **story link** passage to somewhere else in the Bible, which should encourage you to continue exploring this amazing book.

After the Bible story times is a section of **guidance and support**—a series of short articles with practical advice about how to grow faith in the home, handle difficult questions and establish patterns for praying together. Unless faith takes root in the home, all the best efforts of our work on Sundays (or whenever churches meet) are liable to flounder. The strength of the Bible's understanding of family is that faith is rooted in the everyday, in a family's experiences of festivals and celebrations, when everyone comes together. This was the way faith grew in the early history of the church, where households of faith came together to worship God in gatherings that included a wide range of people of different ages and in different relationships. Once again we're back to a much wider and more exciting definition of 'family' than perhaps churches have tended to promote.

Finally, there is a short **overview of the Bible** and a selection of **best-loved Bible passages** to provide a regular reference point for your inspiration and encouragement.

It is as young and old rub shoulders together alongside God's word that faith can really grow effectively. The young need the older members, to hear and learn from their experience of what it means to trust God through all the circumstances of life; but the old also need the younger members of the family, who bring a lively spirituality and sense of adventure when it comes to exploring the wonders of God's creation and what faith in Jesus means. Faith grown in this sort of soil is much more likely to put down deep roots and produce beautiful fruit.

It is our prayer that you will find this book useful and, as you turn its pages together, you will meet with more than just good ideas and thought-provoking insights; rather, we hope, far more importantly, that you as a family will be drawn closer to God himself as part of the family that Jesus talks about—the family of those who discover God's ways and God's will in today's world.

Bible story times

³Praise the God and Father of our Lord Jesus Christ for the spiritual blessings that Christ has brought us from heaven! ⁴Before the world was created, God had Christ choose us to live with him and to be his holy and innocent and loving people. ⁵God was kind and decided that Christ would choose us to be God's own

The story of creation

4b When the LORD God made the heavens and the earth, 5 no grass or plants were growing anywhere. God had not yet sent any rain, and there was no one to work the land. 6 But streams came up from the ground and watered the earth.

7 The LORD God took a handful of soil and made a man. God breathed life into the man, and the man started breathing. 8 The LORD made a garden in a place called Eden, which was in the east, and he put the man there.

9 The LORD God placed all kinds of beautiful trees and fruit trees in the garden. Two other trees were in the middle of the garden. One of the trees gave life— the other gave the power to know the difference between right and wrong.

10 From Eden a river flowed out to water the garden, then it divided into four rivers. 11 The first one is the Pishon River that flows through the land of Havilah, 12 where pure gold, rare perfumes, and precious stones are found. 13 The second is the Gihon River that winds through Ethiopia. 14 The Tigris River that flows east of Assyria is the third, and the fourth is the Euphrates River.

15 The LORD God put the man in the Garden of Eden to take care of it and to look after it. 16 But the LORD told him, 'You may eat fruit from any tree in the garden, 17 except the one that has the power to let you know the difference between right and wrong. If you eat any fruit from that tree, you will die before the day is over!'

18 The LORD God said, 'It isn't good for the man to live alone. I need to make a suitable partner for him.' 19–20 So the LORD took some soil and made animals and birds. He brought them to the man to see what names he would give each of them. Then the man named the tame animals and the birds and the wild animals. That's how they got their names.

None of these was the right kind of partner for the man. 21 So the LORD God made him fall into a deep sleep, and he took out one of the man's ribs. Then after closing the man's side, 22 the LORD made a woman out of the rib.

The LORD God brought her to the man.

GENESIS 2:4b–22

Commentary

The Bible begins with two parallel stories of creation, of which this is the second. In this version the focus is on how special human beings are. Although formed from the raw material of the soil, the man is special because God breathes life into him. God gives him a special place to live—a beautiful garden called Eden—and a special role as caretaker of a world full of beauty, with 'pure gold, rare perfumes, and precious stones'. This specialness is also seen in the way God gives the man the freedom to make his own choices. The warnings about the tree of knowledge of good and evil are clear, but God graciously leaves it up to the man to decide whether to listen to them or not. Finally, God gives him a special friend, because being alone is not in his plan for human beings. Togetherness is something we all need, and it also seems to be part of God's own character.

Questions

▶ If you could create your own perfect world, what would it be like?

▶ How can you play your part in caring for God's world?

▶ Why do you think God put such a dangerous tree in the garden?

▶ Why do you think human beings are so special to God?

Visual aid

Blow up a number of balloons with your own 'breath of life' and draw faces of people on them. Maybe you could also try some animal balloon modelling. Check the internet for instructions and the appropriate balloons to use.

Activity idea

Play an alphabet creation game, choosing words for different parts of creation—for example, **A**ntelope, **B**utterfly, **C**amel, **D**affodil, and so on. Talk about how you can best look after each part of God's world. This Bible story also underlines how special God thinks each one of us is. Play a second alphabet game celebrating people and places—for example, **A**dam, **B**razil, **C**anada, **D**iana, and so on.

Prayer idea

Using a blow-up globe, big picture atlas, nature calendar or images from the internet, look at the variety of this world—human, animal and plant life, as well as the colours and shapes of the mountains, valleys, rivers and oceans. Let each person choose his or her favourite part of creation and make up a special prayer to say 'thank you' to God for it.

Key verse

'The LORD God put the man in the Garden of Eden to take care of it' (Genesis 2:15).

New Testament story link

Revelation 21:1–7: Here is a word picture of the new Eden that God will give us all one day, because of what Jesus Christ has done to mend our broken world.

The first sin

¹ The snake was more cunning than any of the other wild animals that the Lord God had made. One day it came to the woman and asked, 'Did God tell you not to eat fruit from any tree in the garden?'

² The woman answered, 'God said we could eat fruit from any tree in the garden, ³ except the one in the middle. He told us not to eat fruit from that tree or even to touch it. If we do, we will die.'

⁴ 'No, you won't!' the snake replied. ⁵ 'God understands what will happen on the day you eat fruit from that tree. You will see what you have done, and you will know the difference between right and wrong, just as God does.'

⁶ The woman stared at the fruit. It looked beautiful and tasty. She wanted the wisdom that it would give her, and she ate some of the fruit. Her husband was there with her, so she gave some to him, and he ate it too. ⁷ Straight away they saw what they had done, and they realised they were naked. Then they sewed fig leaves together to make something to cover themselves.

⁸ Late in the afternoon a breeze began to blow, and the man and woman heard the Lord God walking in the garden. They were frightened and hid behind some trees.

⁹ The Lord called out to the man and asked, 'Where are you?'

¹⁰ The man answered, 'I was naked, and when I heard you walking through the garden, I was frightened and hid!'

¹¹ 'How did you know you were naked?' God asked. 'Did you eat any fruit from that tree in the middle of the garden?'

¹² 'It was the woman you put here with me,' the man said. 'She gave me some of the fruit, and I ate it.'

¹³ The Lord God then asked the woman, 'What have you done?'

'The snake tricked me,' she answered. 'And I ate some of that fruit.'

GENESIS 3:1–13

Commentary

If God made such a beautiful world, then why is there so much wrong with it now? This is the big question that this story begins to answer. However, it is too easy, like the woman, to blame the snake; or, like the man, to blame the woman. They both knew the warnings that God had given about the dangerous tree. It was their own choice to ignore God's words, and, of course, from then on things began to go wrong. Suddenly they were more concerned about how they looked than about who God is. They felt ashamed of the bodies that God had given them, and were even so frightened of God, who loved them, that they hid behind the trees. Shame, fear, blame and lies now poisoned the atmosphere of Eden. It was as if a great, ugly crack had appeared in the masterpiece that was creation, and it was all the fault of human beings. God's world was spoiled, and there must have been great sadness in God's voice when he called out, 'Where are you?' One of the Bible words for all this brokenness is 'sin'.

Visual aid

Find some pictures of road signs from the Highway Code or the internet, particularly those that give a warning (signs in a red triangle). Talk about what these signs mean, why people sometimes break these rules, and what can happen if they do. Can you design your own warning sign to be placed in the Garden of Eden near to the tree of knowledge of good and evil?

Activity idea

The snake sowed doubts into Eve's mind about God's instructions. Perhaps it wouldn't matter if they ate the fruit? Play an 'excuses game' in which each of you comes up with a reason why you won't do something, such as going shopping for a neighbour who is not well, or giving some of your pocket money to a charity collector on the street. Talk about why people make excuses to avoid doing the right thing. You could also try playing a game of 'Would I lie to you?' where one person gives a fact about themselves and the others have to decide whether it is true or false.

Questions

▶ Who do you blame for what happened in the story? The snake? Eve? Adam? God?

▶ What was it, do you think, that most tempted Eve to go against God's instructions?

▶ Do you think that God knew all this would happen? If so, why didn't he stop it?

▶ Adam and Eve did not die immediately. So what did God mean by saying that they would?

Prayer idea

The fruit from that tree looked 'beautiful and tasty'. Take a shiny piece of fruit. Would you still be tempted to eat it if you'd been told by someone you trusted that it was dangerous—possibly poisonous or rotten at its core? Between you, name some of the tempting choices you might face each day and ask God to help you do the right thing—for example, the choice not to hand in some money that you have found, or to blame someone else for something you've done, or to break the rules when no one is looking.

Key verse

'The man and the woman heard the Lord God walking in the garden. They were frightened and hid behind some trees' (Genesis 3:8).

New Testament story link

Matthew 4:1–11: Jesus faces temptations but chooses to do things God's way.

The great flood

⁵ The LORD saw how bad the people on earth were and that everything they thought and planned was evil. ⁶ He was very sorry that he had made them, ⁷ and he said, 'I'll destroy every living creature on earth! I'll wipe out people, animals, birds, and reptiles. I'm sorry I ever made them.'

⁸ But the LORD was pleased with Noah, ⁹ and this is the story about him. Noah was the only person who lived right and obeyed God. ¹⁰ He had three sons: Shem, Ham, and Japheth.

¹¹⁻¹² God knew that everyone was terribly cruel and violent. ¹³ So he told Noah:

Cruelty and violence have spread everywhere. Now I'm going to destroy the whole earth and all its people. ¹⁴ Get some good timber and build a boat. Put rooms in it and cover it with tar inside and out. ¹⁵ Make it one hundred and thirty-three metres long, twenty-two metres wide, and thirteen metres high. ¹⁶ Build a roof on the boat and leave a space of about forty-four centimetres between the roof and the sides. Make the boat three storeys high and put a door on one side.

¹⁷ I'm going to send a flood that will destroy everything that breathes! Nothing will be left alive. ¹⁸ But I solemnly promise that you, your wife, your sons, and your daughters-in-law will be kept safe in the boat.

¹⁹⁻²⁰ Bring into the boat with you a male and a female of every kind of animal and bird, as well as a male and a female of every reptile. I don't want them to be destroyed. ²¹ Store up enough food both for yourself and for them.

²² Noah did everything the LORD told him to do.

GENESIS 6:5–22

Commentary

If something precious that you had made got broken, might you not want to repair it by starting all over again? This is how God felt about his creation, as things went from bad to worse following the first sin. There is great sadness in this story, as God even says he is sorry that he ever made people because of the way they are now behaving to one another. God's anger at cruelty and injustice is also expressed in this story, because his people no longer reflect his image.

The solution is a drastic one, but there is hope. When God finds Noah living a good life, he is ready to help him escape; and this rescue will include Noah's whole family. The beauty and variety of the animal life that God has created won't be lost either. So Noah is instructed to build a huge boat to house a floating zoo that will survive the great flood.

This familiar story is

certainly one of terrible judgement, but it is also about a God who rescues and will always provide a safe place for those who trust in him. It is about a God who offers the world and those in it a second chance, with the opportunity to start over again.

Visual aid

Take a blow-up globe and cover it with sticky notes showing words that sum up what is spoiling our planet. Include things like war, pollution, greed and so on. These are the sorts of things God saw as he looked down on the world he loved. But he also saw a good man. Replace each of the negative sticky notes with others that mention the good things God is doing in the world through people today.

Activity idea

Choose an old toy, or maybe a small piece of household furniture that needs a good clean. Share the pleasure of washing it so that it sparkles like new. Talk together about how this could be done for a world that gets spoiled and dirty. How can bad thoughts, jealousy and anger be washed away from inside people?

Questions

▶ What sorts of things do you think made God sorry that he had created people?

▶ How do you think Noah pleased God?

▶ What do you imagine his friends and neighbours said about Noah as he started building the boat?

▶ Do you think Noah's family had as much faith in God as he had?

▶ How easy would it be for you to trust in God if you were asked to do something strange, as Noah was?

Prayer idea

Using some washable felt tip pens, make random marks on your hands as a sign of the mess we all get into; alternatively, get hands muddy or messy in some other way. Now have a great clean-up together and turn this into prayer as you thank God with spotless hands for the deep cleaning he offers through Jesus Christ.

Key verse

'Noah did everything the Lord told him to do' (Genesis 6:22).

New Testament story link

Mark 1:1–8: John the Baptist prepares the way for Jesus, and people are washed clean through baptism as a sign that they want to make a new beginning.

Abram's choice

[1] Abram and Sarai took everything they owned and went to the Southern Desert. Lot went with them.

[2] Abram was very rich. He owned many cattle, sheep, and goats, and had a lot of silver and gold. [3] Abram moved from place to place in the Southern Desert. And finally, he went north and set up his tents between Bethel and Ai, [4] where he had earlier camped and built an altar. There he worshipped the LORD.

[5] Lot, who was travelling with him, also had sheep, goats, and cattle, as well as his own family and slaves. [6-7] At this time the Canaanites and the Perizzites were living in the same area, and so there wasn't enough pastureland left for Abram and Lot with all of their animals. Besides this, the men who took care of Abram's animals and the ones who took care of Lot's animals started quarrelling.

[8] Abram said to Lot, 'We are close relatives. We shouldn't argue, and our men shouldn't be fighting one another. [9] There is plenty of land for you to choose from. Let's separate. If you go north, I'll go south; if you go south, I'll go north.'

[10] This happened before the LORD had destroyed the cities of Sodom and Gomorrah. And when Lot looked around, he saw there was plenty of water in the Jordan Valley. All the way to Zoar the valley was as green as the garden of the LORD or the land of Egypt. [11] So Lot chose the whole Jordan Valley for himself, and as he started toward the east, he and Abram separated. [12] Abram stayed in the land of Canaan. But Lot settled near the cities of the valley and put up his tents not far from Sodom, [13] where the people were evil and sinned terribly against the LORD.

GENESIS 13:1–13

Commentary

The ability to make choices in life is a precious freedom recognised by people everywhere. The trouble is that we never make choices in isolation. What we do affects others, and choosing what may be best for us could possibly upset or even damage other people. God gave human beings the gift of 'free will', and it was a risk. Already in the book of Genesis bad choices have meant that people have hurt themselves and others. In this story, Abram graciously allows his nephew Lot to choose which part of the land he wants, even though God had promised it all to Abram. He does this to put an end to a growing quarrel between the two family groups and, like God, takes a risk. Lot chooses the land that looks most attractive. It is the choice in the Garden of Eden all over again!

Lot's choice leads to disaster for his family, played out in the next chapter; but, again just like God, Abram comes to his rescue. God longs for us to make good choices each day, but even when we don't he never gives up on us because he loves us so much.

Visual aid

From the Highway Code, find a picture of a traffic sign with a lot of exit choices (see www.gov.uk/highway-code). Use this as a way to talk about the choices you face on your journey through each day.

Activity idea

Make up a story together in which each person adds a new line. The hero of the story should have lots of choices to make, but each time things should go badly wrong and there has to be a way out. For example:

Kate decides to take a short cut to school…
But down one street she meets an angry, barking dog…
Then its owner comes out and drags the dog away…
Then she decides to delay her journey by visiting a sweet shop…
But she drops her money and it rolls under the counter…

Questions

▶ What are the most important choices you make each day?

▶ What helps you decide how to choose?

▶ Is it easy to let someone else have first choice in order to avoid an argument?

▶ How can we involve God in the choices we make?

Prayer idea

Find a picture of some traffic lights where all three colours are clearly visible. Use this as a pattern for prayer when making choices about the way ahead. Use the red 'stop' signal to be quiet before God for a moment; use the amber 'get ready' signal to talk through possible ways forward; then 'go green' with your prayer to God, asking him to show you the way to go. Work this through with some big choices facing you and your family.

Key verse

'We are close relatives. We shouldn't argue… There is plenty of land for you to choose from' (Genesis 13:8–9).

New Testament story link

Matthew 7:7–14: Jesus promises that God is like the best father ever, always ready to help us make good choices.

God's promise

[1] Later the Lord spoke to Abram in a vision, 'Abram, don't be afraid! I will protect you and reward you greatly.'

[2] But Abram answered, 'Lord All-Powerful, you have given me everything I could ask for, except children. And when I die, Eliezer of Damascus will get all I own. [3] You have not given me any children, and this servant of mine will inherit everything.'

[4] The Lord replied, 'No, he won't! You will have a son of your own, and everything you have will be his.' [5] Then the Lord took Abram outside and said, 'Look at the sky and see if you can count the stars. That's how many descendants you will have.' [6] Abram believed the Lord, and the Lord was pleased with him...

17 Abram was ninety-nine years old when the Lord appeared to him again and said, 'I am God All-Powerful. If you obey me and always do right, [2] I will keep my solemn promise to you and give you more descendants than can be counted.' [3] Abram bowed with his face to the ground, and God said:

[4-5] I promise that you will be the father of many nations. That's why I now change your name from Abram to Abraham. [6] I will give you a lot of descendants, and in the future they will become great nations. Some of them will even be kings.

[7] I will always keep the promise I have made to you and your descendants, because I am your God and their God. [8] I will give you and them the land in which you are now a foreigner. I will give the whole land of Canaan to your family forever, and I will be their God.

GENESIS 15:1–6; 17:1–8

Commentary

I wonder what your definition of a best friend would be. Maybe it is someone who always keeps a promise. In other words, he or she is completely trustworthy and will never let you down. This is the sort of friend that God offers to be to Abram in the story, and in this friendship God makes an amazing commitment to Abram. He promises lifelong protection and a great future for his family, with the gift of a child. Abram and Sarai are old and childless at this point and are frightened about what will happen when they die. But God has a plan for them—a plan that, in fact, reaches right through the Bible and on into our own time. Abram's family will one day be like stars in the sky, completely beyond counting, and this family will make history right across the globe. It must have seemed like an impossible dream to Abram, but his name change would always remind him of the God who made that promise; and God's promises never fail.

Visual aid

Find some luminous stars that will glow in the dark. Decide where you are going to stick them in your

Questions

▶ How do you feel when someone breaks a promise to you?

▶ Why do you think Abram felt he could believe what God promised him?

▶ What promises have you made recently? Have you managed to keep them?

▶ What sort of promises does God make and keep for each one of us every day?

home as a reminder each night that God has kept and will always keep his promises to us.

Activity idea

Together, cover a large piece of black card with as many stick-on stars as you can, to create a beautiful, bright night sky scene. Whenever Abraham saw the stars in the sky, he remembered God's great promises to him. What promises from God can they remind you of? For example: God will always love us; God will never leave us; God will always hear our prayers, and so on.

Prayer idea

It is as if God breathed a new syllable into Abram's name to help him remember that God had made this special friendship with him forever. He was now to be called

Abra*ha*m. God's breath is his Spirit. As you pray for your family and friends, write out the word S P I R I T several times, with spaces between the letters, and then add the names of the people you want to pray for, as a way of asking God to breathe his Spirit into them, to help them and keep them safe, just as he has promised.

For example: **S** *p* **P** *e* **I** *t* **R** *e* **I** *r* **T**

Key verse

'I will always keep the promise I have made to you' (Genesis 17:7).

New Testament story link

Galatians 3:6–9 and 14: Paul reminds us that the promises made to Abraham are now promises for us too, all because of Jesus.

God tests Abraham

¹ Some years later God decided to test Abraham, so he spoke to him.

Abraham answered, 'Here I am, Lord.'

² The Lord said, 'Go and get Isaac, your only son, the one you dearly love! Take him to the land of Moriah, and I will show you a mountain where you must sacrifice him to me on the fires of an altar.'

³ So Abraham got up early the next morning and chopped wood for the fire. He put a saddle on his donkey and left with Isaac and two servants for the place where God had told him to go.

⁴ Three days later Abraham looked into the distance and saw the place. ⁵ He told his servants, 'Stay here with the donkey, while my son and I go over there to worship. We will come back.'

⁶ Abraham put the wood on Isaac's shoulder, but he carried the hot coals and the knife. As the two of them walked along, ⁷⁻⁸ Isaac said, 'Father, we have the coals and the wood, but where is the lamb for the sacrifice?'

'My son,' Abraham answered, 'God will provide the lamb.'

The two of them walked on, and ⁹ when they reached the place that God had told him about, Abraham built an altar and placed the wood on it. Next, he tied up his son and put him on the wood. ¹⁰ He then took the knife and got ready to kill his son. ¹¹ But the Lord's angel shouted from heaven, 'Abraham! Abraham!'

'Here I am!' he answered.

¹² 'Don't hurt the boy or harm him in any way!' the angel said. 'Now I know that you truly obey God, because you were willing to offer him your only son.'

¹³ Abraham looked up and saw a ram caught by its horns in the bushes. So he took the ram and sacrificed it in place of his son.

¹⁴ Abraham named that place 'The Lord will Provide'. And even now people say, 'On the mountain of the Lord it will be provided.'

Genesis 22:1–14

Commentary

Even after over 20 years of living by faith, Abraham still has something new to learn about God. Being asked to set out into the unknown to find a promised land and having to wait patiently in old age for the gift of a child were surely challenges enough, but now he faces a test like no other. Who will come first in his life? Will it be his much-loved son Isaac or his God? This story is both fascinating and disturbing. How could a loving God put Abraham through such an ordeal? But Abraham does remain faithful. He exercises the sort of faith that becomes an example to future generations. When he shows that he really is prepared to go through with it, he is in effect demonstrating his belief that God can bring Isaac back to life again, if he wants to.

The hope of resurrection is here in this story, as well as its being a signpost to Good Friday, when God the Father provided a substitute sacrifice in order to rescue not just one person but the whole human race.

Visual aid

Find or make a 'first prize' medal on a ribbon, or perhaps a rosette. What or who has first place in our lives? What would show others that God takes first place?

Questions

- Why do you think God decided to test Abraham in this dramatic way?
- What do you think young Isaac felt about what was going on?
- What might the servants have thought was going to happen? (They knew there was no animal to sacrifice.)
- What does Abraham learn from all this?
- What does God discover about Abraham?

Activity idea

Work together to create a soundtrack for this well-known story: there's the chopping of wood and the saddling of the donkey, the three-day journey (with donkey noises), the hard slog up Mount Moriah, the making of the bonfire, the angel's shout and the sound of the ram caught in the bush. Perhaps you could include some human speech too. What else would be heard in this sound drama?

Prayer idea

Most people have things that are precious to them, and there is always a danger that they can come to love those objects more than God. Collect some examples of what is special to you and your family—either the objects themselves or something that represents them—for example, a favourite toy, a picture of a holiday destination or even the names of friends or of each other. Place them on the open palms of hands held out in prayer and thank God for these gifts. Ask God to help you put him first, because he is the one who gave you the gifts in the first place.

Key verse

'Abraham named that place, "The LORD will Provide"' (Genesis 22:14).

New Testament story link

Romans 4:18–25: Abraham's faith in a God who can raise the dead stands as a pattern for us and shows us how we can be accepted by God.

Jacob and Esau

1 After Isaac had become old and almost blind, he called in his firstborn son Esau, who asked him, 'Father, what can I do for you?'

2 Isaac replied, 'I am old and might die at any time. 3 So take your bow and arrows, then go out in the fields, and kill a wild animal. 4 Cook some of that tasty food that I love so much and bring it to me. I want to eat it once more and give you my blessing before I die.'

5 Rebekah had been listening, and as soon as Esau left to go hunting, 6 she said to Jacob, 'I heard your father tell Esau 7 to kill a wild animal and cook some tasty food for your father before he dies. Your father said this because he wants to bless your brother with the Lord as his witness. 8 Now, my son, listen carefully to what I want you to do. 9 Go and kill two of your best young goats and bring them to me. I'll cook the tasty food that your father loves so much. 10 Then you can take it to him, so he can eat it and give you his blessing before he dies.'

11 'My brother Esau is a hairy man,' Jacob reminded her. 'And I am not. 12 If my father touches me and realises I am trying to trick him, he will put a curse on me instead of giving me a blessing.'

13 Rebekah insisted, 'Let his curse fall on me! Just do what I say and bring me the meat.' 14 So Jacob brought the meat to his mother, and she cooked the tasty food that his father liked. 15 Then she took Esau's best clothes and put them on Jacob. 16 She also covered the smooth part of his hands and neck with goatskins 17 and gave him some bread and the tasty food she had cooked.

18 Jacob went to his father and said, 'Father, here I am.'

'Which one of my sons are you?' his father asked.

19 Jacob replied, 'I am Esau, your firstborn, and I have done what you told me. Please sit up and eat the meat I have brought. Then you can give me your blessing.'

GENESIS 27:1–19

Commentary

Here begins a Bible story full of family feuding, deception and out-and-out lies! These 'heroes of faith' are far from perfect, but make mistake after mistake, just as we do. Esau and Jacob are not only twins but rivals. Their parents, Isaac and Rebekah, each show favouritism; and before this part of the story, Esau has already shown that he is more interested in a full stomach than his position as the senior of the two brothers. It seems strange that God should choose to use such a messed-up family to bless the world, when all they can do is plot and scheme over who gets the blessing of the family inheritance. They are each as bad as the other, but God does not give up on them, just as he never gives up on whatever's going on in our family life. As Jacob starts to lie to his 'old man', encouraged by his mum, it doesn't seem possible that one day God will bring good out of all this. However, God does do just that.

Visual aid

Play the card game 'Happy Families', but play it differently, as 'Unhappy Families'. In this version, each player has to collect a totally mixed-up set of unrelated people. Who will be first to make an unhappy family, like Isaac's?

Activity idea

List together all the words that describe things that tear families apart—for example, jealousy, disrespect, lying, favouritism and so on. Talk about how they can creep in, even between people who love each other, and how we can stop them. You could make a list of golden rules or maybe use symbols such as an ear for listening, a clock for spending time together, scales for being fair or a speech bubble with 'sorry' in it for being the first to say 'I'm sorry'.

Prayer idea

Fold a long strip of paper as a concertina and then, on the top, draw the outline of a person, making sure the arms stretch out

Questions

▶ 'You've always been Mum's favourite!' … 'It's not fair!' … 'It's my turn!' must have been phrases regularly heard in Isaac's home. Are you ever tempted to say something similar?

▶ Who do you think is most to blame for how things turned out? Isaac? Rebekah? Esau? Jacob?

▶ If you were asked to help sort out this family mess, where would you start?

▶ Why do you think God didn't just step in and put an end to all the rows, the hurt and the lying?

and touch each side at left and right. Cut out the figure without cutting through where the hands touch the sides, and unfold your people chain. On each figure write the name of a person in your immediate or extended family (tape two or three chains together as necessary). Use this prayer chain as a reminder of who to pray for, turning over one person in the concertina at a time.

Key verse

'What can I do for you?' (Genesis 27:1).

Use Esau's question as you look for ways to bless others today.

New Testament story link

Luke 12:13–21: Jesus tells a special story about what really matters to two brothers who were quarrelling over a family inheritance.

Jacob wrestles with God

22–23 Jacob got up in the middle of the night and took his wives, his eleven children, and everything he owned across to the other side of the Jabbok River for safety. 24 Afterwards, Jacob went back and spent the rest of the night alone.

A man came and fought with Jacob until just before daybreak. 25 When the man saw that he could not win, he struck Jacob on the hip and threw it out of joint. 26 They kept on wrestling until the man said, 'Let go of me! It's almost daylight.'

'You can't go until you bless me,' Jacob replied.

27 Then the man asked, 'What is your name?'

'Jacob,' he answered.

28 The man said, 'Your name will no longer be Jacob. You have wrestled with God and with men, and you have won. That's why your name will be Israel.'

29 Jacob said, 'Now tell me your name.'

'Don't you know who I am?' he asked. And he blessed Jacob.

30 Jacob said, 'I have seen God face to face, and I am still alive.' So he named the place Peniel. 31 The sun was coming up as Jacob was leaving Peniel. He was limping because he had been struck on the hip, 32 and the muscle on his hip joint had been injured. That's why even today the people of Israel don't eat the hip muscle of any animal.

33 Later that day Jacob met Esau coming with his four hundred men. So Jacob made his children walk with their mothers. 2 The two servant women, Zilpah and Bilhah, together with their children went first, followed by Leah and her children, then by Rachel and Joseph. 3 Jacob himself walked in front of them all, bowing to the ground seven times as he came near his brother.

4 But Esau ran towards Jacob and hugged and kissed him. Then the two brothers started crying.

GENESIS 32:22—33:4

Commentary

Jacob's life story is full of drama. After cheating his brother and lying to his dad, he is forced to run for his life, spends years working long hours for his uncle Laban, and is then cheated over his choice of marriage partner. All this time, he believes that his brother is out to kill him, which explains the preparations at the beginning of this story.

Jacob is definitely already someone who has wrestled his way through life, and now he wrestles with a stranger who turns out to be God. God's commitment to Jacob has been remarkable, and perhaps this wrestling match is a picture of the way God has never given up trying to bring out the best from Jacob. Maybe it is also a way to understand Jacob's own wrestling with his worst self, of which he is bitterly reminded when he hears that Esau is coming. But God has the last word, changing his name and leaving his mark.

Jacob, now known as Israel, meets with forgiveness from his brother, not hatred. No wonder the Bible often describes God as 'the God of Jacob'—the man who saw God face to face and was changed.

Visual aid

Use some play dough to make a person, and then push and pull that shape before remaking it into a person again. This is a bit like God's 'remaking' of Jacob in the story.

Activity idea

Have a go at some playful arm wrestling with each other. Maybe introduce some simple handicaps to even things up, such as making the adults use their weaker arm. Whose tussle lasts the longest? Do you feel weak and exhausted after it all? How does it feel to win or to lose? Who 'gave up' first?

Prayer idea

This story is often used by Christians to encourage them not to give up on prayer, especially when praying about something big and difficult. Explore some different ways of interlocking hands for prayer to match the wrestling theme, such as clenching fingers tightly together or pushing knuckles up against each other. Use these different shapes when you pray for something especially big that is worrying you as a family. Maybe name that thing out loud, put your hands together in the chosen 'wrestling' way and then count down from 10 to 0 to make a big 'knock-out prayer' to God for that important thing.

Questions

▶ God knew that Jacob was haunted by the fear of meeting Esau again. Why do you think God decided to help him face his fear in this strange way?

▶ What signs can you find in the story that Jacob had already begun to change for the better?

▶ Why did it take Jacob so long to recognise who was wrestling with him?

▶ Is there anything in our lives that God is wrestling with us about at the moment?

Key verse

'Don't you know who I am?' he asked. And he blessed Jacob (Genesis 32:29).

New Testament story link

Luke 18:1–8: Jesus tells a story to encourage us never to give up in our prayers.

Joseph and his brothers

14b Joseph was near Shechem 15 and wandering through the fields, when a man asked, 'What are you looking for?'

16 Joseph answered, 'I'm looking for my brothers who are watching the sheep. Can you tell me where they are?'

17 'They're not here any more,' the man replied. 'I overheard them say they were going to Dothan.'

Joseph left and found his brothers in Dothan. 18 But before he got there, they saw him coming and made plans to kill him. 19 They said to one another, 'Look, here comes the hero of those dreams! 20 Let's kill him and throw him into a pit and say that some wild animal ate him. Then we'll see what happens to those dreams.'

21 Reuben heard this and tried to protect Joseph from them. 'Let's not kill him,' he said. 22 'Don't murder him or even harm him. Just throw him into a dry well out here in the desert.' Reuben planned to rescue Joseph later and take him back to his father.

23 When Joseph came to his brothers, they pulled off his fine coat 24 and threw him into a dry well.

25 As Joseph's brothers sat down to eat, they looked up and saw a caravan of Ishmaelites coming from Gilead. Their camels were loaded with all kinds of spices that they were taking to Egypt. 26 So Judah said, 'What will we gain if we kill our brother and hide his body? 27 Let's sell him to the Ishmaelites and not harm him. After all, he is our brother.' And the others agreed.

28 When the Midianite merchants came by, Joseph's brothers took him out of the well, and for twenty pieces of silver they sold him to the Ishmaelites who took him to Egypt.

29 When Reuben returned to the well and did not find Joseph there, he tore his clothes in sorrow. 30 Then he went back to his brothers and said, 'The boy is gone! What am I going to do?'

GENESIS 37:14b–30

Commentary

Although Joseph turns out in the end to be the hero of this family story in Genesis, he is by no means an attractive character—at least not at the beginning. As his dad's favourite, born to his favourite wife after waiting many years, Joseph was clearly spoilt and it went to his head. No wonder his eleven brothers got fed up with him showing off his splendid coat and boasting of dreams in which he turned out to be the most important member of the family. Nevertheless, the plot to kill him off comes as a shock, and his eldest brother's plan to rescue him is foiled when he is sold as a slave to passing traders.

This is a sad but maybe recognisable tale of family jealousy, rivalry and hatred. Even so, God still has his eye and hand on all that happens. There is irony here too in the fact that Jacob, who in his day had experienced favouritism and had himself been a liar, now falls victim to his own foolishness and is lied to by his own children. The poison of bad choices seems to be spread from one generation to another, but so too is the grace of God, who will, we shall discover, turn all this to good in the end.

Visual aid

Ask each member of the family to go and fetch his or her favourite item of clothing—something kept for special occasions only. Let everyone talk about why they like it and why they wouldn't use it for everyday activities. Joseph always had his best clothes on and it made the others feel second best.

Activity idea

Find a CD of the musical *Joseph and the Amazing Technicolor Dreamcoat*. You will probably be able to find one in your local library. Listen and sing along to this catchy and colourful interpretation of the whole story.

Prayer idea

Joseph's long-sleeved fine coat is often imagined to have been made from a variety of materials in different colours: name as many colours as you can together and note them down. Now go through some of them and link each one with an object of that colour, or a place, person or mood associated with it, and turn your ideas into a prayer. For example:

- Green: thank God for forests and fields.
- Blue: pray for people who are in cold places or who are feeling sad.
- Red: ask God to forgive you for times when your temper has got the better of you.

Questions

▶ How would you react if someone in your family started having dreams which suggested they were more important than the rest of you?

▶ Who do you blame for what went so badly wrong in this story? Joseph for aggravating everyone? The brothers for hatching the plot? Reuben for not acting more quickly? Jacob for being unfair?

▶ What would you have said to Joseph or the brothers to make them behave differently?

▶ How and where do you see God at work in this story?

Key verse

'For twenty pieces of silver, they sold him to the Ishmaelites who took him to Egypt' (Genesis 37:28).

New Testament story link

Luke 22:1–6: Here, Jesus is also about to be sold to his enemies for money, but it isn't the end, for God is in control.

The king's dreams

[1] Two years later the king of Egypt dreamed he was standing beside the River Nile. [2] Suddenly, seven fat, healthy cows came up from the river and started eating grass along the bank. [3] Then seven ugly, skinny cows came up out of the river and [4] ate the fat, healthy cows. When this happened, the king woke up.

[5] The king went back to sleep and had another dream. This time seven full heads of grain were growing on a single stalk. [6] Later, seven other heads of grain appeared, but they were thin and scorched by the east wind. [7] The thin heads of grain swallowed the seven full heads. Again the king woke up, and it had only been a dream.

[8] The next morning the king was upset. So he called in his magicians and wise men and told them what he had dreamed. None of them could tell him what the dreams meant.

[9] The king's personal servant said:

Now I remember what I was supposed to do. [10] When you were angry with me and your chief cook, you threw us both in jail in the house of the captain of the guard. [11] One night we both had dreams, and each dream had a different meaning. [12] A young Hebrew, who was a servant of the captain of the guard, was there with us at the time. When we told him our dreams, he explained what each of them meant, [13] and everything happened just as he said it would. I got my job back, and the cook was put to death.

[14] The king sent for Joseph, who was quickly brought out of jail. He shaved, changed his clothes, and went to the king.

[15] The king said to him, 'I had a dream, yet no one can explain what it means. I am told that you can interpret dreams.'

[16] 'Your Majesty,' Joseph answered, 'I can't do it myself, but God can give a good meaning to your dreams.'

GENESIS 41:1–16

Commentary

Joseph had to wait a very long time for his moment to shine. His experiences first as a slave and then as a prisoner had been far from easy. In one of the Psalms, the writer calls this long wait Joseph's time of testing (105:19). However, God always planned to honour Joseph and, through him, to rescue his whole family, just as his childhood dreams had predicted.

Finally, it was a restless, dream-filled night for the Egyptian king that opened Joseph's cell door to freedom. The gift of understanding the meaning of dreams, which had so annoyed his brothers back home in Canaan, now became his passport to fame and fortune. He knew what the king's dreams about the cows and the corn meant, and as a result he was appointed Prime Minister over Egypt to prepare for the famine that was to come. He had had a long wait, but God was with him; and, as he acknowledges to his brothers at the end of the story, 'God sent me on ahead of you... to save you in this wonderful way' (Genesis 45:7).

Questions

▶ Do you think that God still speaks to people through dreams today?

▶ What do you think kept Joseph going during his long years in prison?

▶ How long are you prepared to wait for an answer to prayer, especially when a situation (like Joseph's) seems hopeless?

▶ Why do you think the king trusted Joseph's explanation of his dreams?

Visual aid

Make a dream-catcher for yourself. Joseph's dreams came true in the end, and he was able, with God's help, to catch the meaning of other people's dreams too. Here is a website with simple instructions: www.dream-catchers.org/make-dream-catchers-kids.php

Activity idea

Being able to have hopes and dreams is a special gift that God has given to people. He wants us to use this ability to inspire others to work for a better world. Cut out some dream bubbles, giving three to each member of your family. Invite everyone to draw or write what his or her dreams are for (a) themselves, (b) the family and (c) the world. Pin the bubbles up on a special family dreams board to remind yourselves what great hopes God has for you all.

Prayer idea

God's plan for Joseph was far bigger than he had ever dreamed. His ability to understand dreams meant that many people, not just his own family, were able to survive the seven years of famine. Find out about an area of the world experiencing famine today, pray for the modern-day Josephs who are trying to help those who suffer, and ask God to show you what you can do.

Key verse

'I can't do it myself, but God can...' (Genesis 41:16).

New Testament story link

Acts 12:5–17: This is the story of Peter, who was also rescued from prison because God still had big plans for him.

Slaves in Egypt

[14] The Egyptians were cruel to the people of Israel and forced them to make bricks and to mix mortar and to work in the fields.

[15] Finally, the king called in Shiphrah and Puah, the two women who helped the Hebrew mothers when they gave birth. [16] He told them, 'If a Hebrew woman gives birth to a girl, let the child live. If the baby is a boy, kill him!' ...

[2] A man from the Levi tribe married a woman from the same tribe, [2] and she later had a baby boy. He was a beautiful child, and she kept him inside for three months. [3] But when she could no longer keep him hidden, she made a basket out of reeds and covered it with tar. She put him in the basket and placed it in the tall grass along the edge of the River Nile. [4] The baby's older sister stood off at a distance to see what would happen to him.

[5] About that time one of the king's daughters came down to take a bath in the river, while her servant women walked along the river bank. She saw the basket in the tall grass and sent one of the young women to pull it out of the water. [6] When the king's daughter opened the basket, she saw the baby and felt sorry for him because he was crying. She said, 'This must be one of the Hebrew babies.'

[7] At once the baby's older sister came up and asked, 'Do you want me to get a Hebrew woman to take care of the baby for you?'

[8] 'Yes,' the king's daughter answered.

So the girl brought the baby's mother, [9] and the king's daughter told her, 'Take care of this child, and I will pay you.'

The baby's mother carried him home and took care of him. [10] And when he was old enough, she took him to the king's daughter, who adopted him. She named him Moses because she said, 'I pulled him out of the water.'

EXODUS 1:14–16; 2:1–10

Commentary

How times change! While Joseph was alive, he was the famous Hebrew who had saved Egypt with his plan to store supplies of corn. But now, hundreds of years later, Joseph's descendants have become slaves, building cities and storehouses for the new king. Egypt's fear of this foreign nation has grown into hatred and, eventually, a terrible plan to wipe them out altogether.

However, although God appears silent and distant, he hasn't abandoned his people. The miraculous way in which baby Moses is saved from the king's death sentence is the first sign that God is still in control. It takes the bravery of two Hebrew midwives (look up Exodus 1:17–22), the patience and skill of Moses' mother to hide a baby for three months, the courage of Moses' sister to speak up in front of enemy royalty, and the unexpected compassion of the king's daughter: all this is God at work and it means that Moses is saved from drowning. Now his mother will even receive payment for looking after her own son and, although he will end up receiving an Egyptian education as the king's adopted grandson, this too will be used as part of God's great plan to rescue his people from slavery.

Visual aid

Collect a few long grasses or reeds from a garden. Use them to remind yourself of the straw that the slaves had to use to make the bricks out of mud, the reeds that Moses' mother used to make the basket, and the grasses that Miriam hid behind, down by the Nile.

Activity idea

Together, make a small Moses basket that can float. Use some chenille wires or art straws to create the frame and then tape over it with black duct tape (to look like tar) to make it waterproof. Can it carry a small weight on the water?

Prayer idea

Moses' family must have prayed hard about how to rescue their beautiful baby boy. Give everyone a small piece of paper or sticky note to hold in their cupped hands. Now invite them to whisper a big prayer of faith secretly into their hands. Fold up the paper 'carrying' this prayer and, each in turn, place it in the floating Moses basket you have made. In a moment of silence, ask God to pull out (this is what Moses' name sounds like in Hebrew) an unexpected answer for each of you in God's time.

Questions

- Why do you think the Egyptians forgot all the good that Joseph had done?
- Why couldn't the Egyptians learn to live at peace with their Hebrew neighbours?
- What must it have been like for the Hebrews, who were shepherds by trade, to end up working on the king's building sites?
- Whose idea was it, do you think, to risk putting Moses in a floating basket—his mum's or his sister's?
- Who do you think was the bravest in this story—the midwives, the mother or Miriam?

Key verse

'At once the baby's older sister came up and asked, "Do you want me to get a Hebrew woman to take care of the baby for you?"' (Exodus 2:7).

New Testament story link

Hebrews 11:23–26: This New Testament writer reminds us how faith was at work in this part of the story of Moses.

The burning bush

1 One day, Moses was taking care of the sheep and goats of his father-in-law Jethro, the priest of Midian, and Moses decided to lead them across the desert to Sinai, the holy mountain. 2 There an angel of the LORD appeared to him from a burning bush. Moses saw that the bush was on fire, but it was not burning up. 3 'This is strange!' he said to himself. 'I'll go over and see why the bush isn't burning up.'

4 When the LORD saw Moses coming near the bush, he called him by name, and Moses answered, 'Here I am.'

5 God replied, 'Don't come any closer. Take off your sandals—the ground where you are standing is holy. 6 I am the God who was worshipped by your ancestors Abraham, Isaac, and Jacob.'

Moses was afraid to look at God, and so he hid his face.

7 The LORD said:

I have seen how my people are suffering as slaves in Egypt, and I have heard them beg for my help because of the way they are being ill-treated. I feel sorry for them, 8 and I have come down to rescue them from the Egyptians.

I will bring my people out of Egypt into a country where there is good land, rich with milk and honey. I will give them the land where the Canaanites, Hittites, Amorites, Perizzites, Hivites, and Jebusites now live. 9 My people have begged for my help, and I have seen how cruel the Egyptians are to them. 10 Now go to the king! I am sending you to lead my people out of his country.

11 But Moses said, 'Who am I to go to the king and lead your people out of Egypt?'

12 God replied, 'I will be with you. And you will know that I am the one who sent you, when you worship me on this mountain after you have led my people out of Egypt.'

EXODUS 3:1–12

Commentary

After running away from life in Pharaoh's palace, Moses had lived many peaceful years as a shepherd, far from his home and his people. But perhaps deep inside him there was a longing to return, if not to his life as a prince, at least to the faith and the community of his real parents. Was it this that drew him that day to take the sheep to the holy mountain of Sinai? God had been waiting many years for this moment. Moses was at last ready to hear God's voice and God caught his attention by a bush on fire—although these were no ordinary flames. Moses' early faith was brought back to life when he heard God speaking to him.

Now, of course it was wonderful that God knew what was happening to Israel and that he had not forgotten his promises; it was also wonderful that he was going to answer their prayers and come down to rescue them, but what most surprised Moses was that this rescue plan would only take place with his cooperation. As so often, God answers prayers by using ordinary people who are willing to work with him. God chooses to work for us by working through us. It took Moses a long time to get that into his head!

Questions

▶ Do you think Moses ever missed his comfortable life as a prince in Egypt?

▶ Why do you think he decided to take his sheep up the holy mountain that day?

▶ Why might Moses have been so afraid to look at God?

▶ What does the story tell us about what God is like?

Visual aid

Find a picture of the shrub known as 'the burning bush'—perhaps from the internet—or use any bright red or yellow flower or plant you can find in the house. Shine a light on it so that it seems to glow like the burning bush.

Activity idea

Pour some sand on to a tray and, with some small stones, a small red plant or shrub, some model sheep and a figure to represent Moses, create a scene to show what it might have looked like up on Mount Sinai. Now retell the story together, imagining it from different points of view—God's, Moses', or even perhaps the sheep's.

Prayer idea

In many parts of the world, taking off outdoor shoes is usual either when people go into someone's home or when they come together to worship God. Collect a pair of shoes for everyone in the household and then arrange them in a pattern on the ground. Then, as you pick up each pair, pray that God will come close and help the person whose shoes you are holding.

Key verse

'God replied, "I will be with you"' (Exodus 3:12).

New Testament story link

Matthew 17:1–9: Once, Jesus went up a mountain with three of his friends and suddenly he shone with the light of heaven. Just like Moses, the friends were afraid, but they heard God speaking. They also saw Moses!

Escape from Egypt

31 During the night the king sent for Moses and Aaron and told them, 'Get your people out of my country and leave us alone! Go and worship the LORD, as you have asked. 32 Take your sheep, goats, and cattle, and get out. But ask your God to be kind to me.'

33 The Egyptians did everything they could to get the Israelites to leave their country fast. They said, 'Please hurry and leave. If you don't, we will all be dead.' 34 So the Israelites quickly made some bread dough and put it in pans. But they did not mix any yeast in the dough to make it rise. They wrapped cloth around the pans and carried them on their shoulders.

35 The Israelites had already done what Moses had told them to do. They had gone to their Egyptian neighbours and asked for gold and silver and for clothes. 36 The LORD had made the Egyptians friendly toward the people of Israel, and they gave them whatever they asked for. In this way they carried away the wealth of the Egyptians when they left Egypt.

37 The Israelites walked from the city of Rameses to the city of Succoth. There were about six hundred thousand of them, not counting women and children. 38 Many other people went with them as well, and there were also a lot of sheep, goats, and cattle. 39 They left Egypt in such a hurry that they did not have time to prepare any food except the bread dough made without yeast. So they baked it and made thin bread.

40–41 The LORD's people left Egypt exactly four hundred and thirty years after they had arrived. 42 On that night the LORD kept watch for them, and on this same night each year Israel will always keep watch in honour of the LORD.

EXODUS 12:31–42

Commentary

This event in Israel's history is so significant that Jews today still remember it at a special annual festival called the Passover. The Egyptian king had refused to release such a large slave workforce, but a series of natural disasters eventually persuaded him to let God's people go free. The final tragedy had included the death of the king's own son, although the sons of the Israelite families had been spared as the angel of death 'passed over' (giving us the word 'Passover') their homes. After this, the Egyptians wanted them to leave their country as soon as possible, and so there wasn't even time to bake bread properly for the journey. This is why, at the Passover festival, flat bread (that is, bread without yeast) is eaten as a way of remembering the day when the Israelites escaped slavery. It was the moment they became a free people again—free to go where they wanted and, even more importantly, free to worship and follow the Lord their God, who had promised to watch over them. This was the beginning of a whole new chapter in the life of God's people.

Visual aid

Use a small suitcase or bag as a focus for the start of the journey of escape that takes place in this story. Think about what you would pack in a hurry.

Activity idea

Flat bread is better known in the Bible as 'unleavened bread'. You can make this as a family, using flour, a little oil and water, following one of the simple recipes on the internet. Talk about how Jews eat this bread every year to remind them of the day they escaped from Egypt. What does the taste make you think of?

Prayer idea

The Israelites had been slaves in Egypt for hundreds of years before this great escape. Many people today do not have freedom: they cannot choose where to go, who to meet or what to do. Pray today as

Questions

▶ What sort of conversations do you think might have taken place when the Israelites got the news that they were going to leave Egypt?

▶ Why was there such a rush to do everything on that one night?

▶ How easy would it have been to get used to being free after so many years of having to do what others told you to do?

▶ Are there special times in your family life that you like to look back to and remember? How can you be sure never to forget them?

a family for those who are trapped because they have no money, no food or no friends. Use a piece of string with three knots tied into it; after each prayer, ask a different member of the family to untie a knot as a way of seeing God bring freedom for the people you are praying for.

Key verse

'On that night the LORD kept watch for them' (Exodus 12:42).

New Testament story link

Luke 22:14–19: Jesus celebrates the Passover with his friends and gives a new meaning to the special bread that they are eating.

Crossing the Red Sea

⁵ When the king of Egypt heard that the Israelites had finally left, he and his officials changed their minds and said, 'Look what we have done! We let them get away, and they will no longer be our slaves.'

⁶ The king got his war chariot and army ready. ⁷ He commanded his officers in charge of his six hundred best chariots and all his other chariots to start after the Israelites...

¹⁰ When the Israelites saw the king coming with his army, they were frightened and begged the LORD for help. ¹¹ They also complained to Moses, 'Wasn't there enough room in Egypt to bury us? Is that why you brought us out here to die in the desert? Why did you bring us out of Egypt anyway? ¹² While we were there, didn't we tell you to leave us alone? We had rather be slaves in Egypt than die in this desert!'

¹³ But Moses answered, 'Don't be afraid! Be brave, and you will see the LORD save you today. These Egyptians will never bother you again. ¹⁴ The LORD will fight for you, and you won't have to do a thing.'

¹⁵ The LORD said to Moses, 'Why do you keep calling out to me for help? Tell the Israelites to move forward. ¹⁶ Then hold your walking stick over the sea. The water will open up and make a road where they can walk through on dry ground. ¹⁷ I will make the Egyptians so stubborn that they will go after you. Then I will be praised because of what happens to the king and his chariots and cavalry. ¹⁸ The Egyptians will know for sure that I am the LORD.'

¹⁹ All this time God's angel had gone ahead of Israel's army, but now he moved behind them. A large cloud had also gone ahead of them, ²⁰ but now it moved between the Egyptians and the Israelites. The cloud gave light to the Israelites, but made it dark for the Egyptians, and during the night they could not come any closer.

²¹ Moses stretched his arm over the sea, and the LORD sent a strong east wind that blew all night until there was dry land where the water had been. The sea opened up, ²² and the Israelites walked through on dry land with a wall of water on each side.

EXODUS 14:5–7, 10–22

Commentary

The miraculous crossing of the Red Sea is a great demonstration of God's power. Not that the people deserved this miracle! When they are trapped by the king's advancing army, all they can do is to say that they wish they'd never listened to Moses—that they would have preferred to stay in Egypt as slaves. But God overrules the weather conditions at just the right time so that the clouds, the winds and the tides change direction to the advantage of the Israelites trapped on the shore. The wind blows back the water and makes a way through the reedy marshes of that part of the Red Sea. The escape from Egypt is complete and soon God's people are safe on the other side of this watery boundary, which later the heavy Egyptian chariots try to cross, only to be trapped and overwhelmed by the returning tide. There is no doubt that God performed a miracle in response to Moses' obedience, but also, more importantly, out of his great love for his people.

Visual aid

Use some blue bedsheets to represent the Red Sea. Practise making them move like water.

Questions

▶ Why do you think the Egyptian king changed his mind and chased after the Israelites?

▶ If you had been Moses, how would you have reacted to all the people's complaints?

▶ Has there ever been a time when you felt trapped in a difficult situation?

▶ Why didn't Moses give up and join in with the complaining?

▶ Imagine how you would have felt walking out across the Red Sea with the water on both sides. Do you think some people might have felt too frightened to go?

Activity idea

Re-enact the crossing of the Red Sea, using the blue sheets. Freeze the action from time to time and try to become the characters in the story, such as the people who complained because they were so afraid; Moses telling them to put their trust in God; the families crossing the Red Sea, looking both over their shoulders at the army and to either side at the water; groups arriving safely on the other side, amazed and relieved.

Prayer idea

It seemed like a dead end for the Israelites. No wonder they wanted to blame God and complain to Moses. But God showed them a way out. There are many times when we do not know what to do or pray for, or even how God can help us. Use the outline of a maze downloaded from the internet and trace your way through it with a finger, using the following simple prayer whenever you reach a dead end and have to backtrack: 'Lord, I don't know what to do next. Please show me the way to go.'

Key verse

'Don't be afraid! Be brave, and you will see the Lord save you today' (Exodus 14:13).

New Testament story link

Luke 8:22–25: Jesus rescues his friends from danger on the water by commanding the waves and the winds to obey him.

Water from the rock

¹ The Israelites left the desert and moved from one place to another each time the LORD ordered them to. Once they camped at Rephidim, but there was no water for them to drink.

² The people started complaining to Moses, 'Give us some water!'

Moses replied, 'Why are you complaining to me and trying to put the LORD to the test?'

³ But the people were thirsty and kept on complaining, 'Moses, did you bring us out of Egypt just to let us and our families and our animals die of thirst?'

⁴ Then Moses prayed to the LORD, 'What am I going to do with these people? They are about to stone me to death!'

⁵ The LORD answered, 'Take some of the leaders with you and go ahead of the rest of the people. Also take along the walking stick you used to strike the River Nile, ⁶ and when you get to the rock at Mount Sinai, I will be there with you. Strike the rock with the stick, and water will pour out for the people to drink.' Moses did this while the leaders watched.

⁷ The people had complained and tested the LORD by asking, 'Is the LORD really with us?' So Moses named that place Massah, which means 'testing', and Meribah, which means 'complaining'.

EXODUS 17:1–7

Commentary

The Israelites had escaped from Egypt and crossed the Red Sea, but this was only the beginning of their new life as a free people. There were many hardships ahead as they crossed the desert towards the mountain where God had first appeared to Moses. The desert was a hostile place with little food or water, and Moses was leading a very large number of people. Just as they had had to trust God for their rescue, they also needed to trust him to provide for their needs, and, most importantly, for water to drink.

Once again the people are quick to complain. No wonder Moses is angry, and he despairs of them in his prayer to God. It is all down to Moses' obedience, using the staff to strike the rock, that water is found. Will the Israelites learn from this and be more faithful in future? Clearly Moses isn't sure that they will. He gives the rocks special names that will remind the Israelites not to give up on God quite so quickly in future. It's not just starting out with God that matters, but staying on track through difficult times. This was proving a real challenge for God's people.

Questions

▶ Have you ever been tempted to give up on a difficult task? What kept you going?

▶ How quick are you to criticise or complain in a crisis?

▶ Moses had learned how to talk to God about everything that happened. How easy do you find this?

▶ How can we learn to trust God better?

Visual aid

Fill a glass with water to the halfway point. Talk together about whether you are an optimistic 'glass half-full' or a pessimistic 'glass half-empty' sort of person. What can we learn from both attitudes?

Activity idea

Finding water in the desert is a matter of life and death. Without water, living things cannot survive very long, so it's not surprising that water is often used in the Bible as a picture of God's generous love for us. As a reminder of God's gift of life, plant some cress seeds on cotton wool and keep them well watered. Watch them grow over the next weeks, and, each time you see them, let them remind you that only as God waters us can we grow to become the best we can be.

Prayer idea

Spend some time thanking God for water and all the many things that it helps us to do. Perhaps you could have some glasses of water available and each member of the family can take a sip each time anyone thinks up a new thank-you prayer for what water can do for us. Take a moment to remember the many people in the world who do not have access to clean water.

Key verse

'Why are you complaining… and trying to put the LORD to the test?' (Exodus 17:2).

New Testament story link

John 7:37–39: Jesus says he will give us life-giving water that will flow from deep inside us.

The ten commandments

[1] God said to the people of Israel:

[2] I am the LORD your God, the one who brought you out of Egypt where you were slaves.

[3] Do not worship any god except me.

[4] Do not make idols that look like anything in the sky or on earth or in the ocean under the earth. [5] Don't bow down and worship idols. I am the LORD your God, and I demand all your love. If you reject me, I will punish your families for three or four generations. [6] But if you love me and obey my laws, I will be kind to your families for thousands of generations.

[7] Do not misuse my name. I am the LORD your God, and I will punish anyone who misuses my name.

[8] Remember that the Sabbath Day belongs to me. [9] You have six days when you can do your work, [10] but the seventh day of each week belongs to me, your God. No one is to work on that day—not you, your children, your slaves, your animals, or the foreigners who live in your towns. [11] In six days I made the sky, the earth, the oceans, and everything in them, but on the seventh day I rested. That's why I made the Sabbath a special day that belongs to me.

[12] Respect your father and your mother, and you will live a long time in the land I am giving you.

[13] Do not murder.

[14] Be faithful in marriage.

[15] Do not steal.

[16] Do not tell lies about others.

[17] Do not want to take anything that belongs to someone else. Don't want to take anyone's house, wife or husband, slaves, oxen, donkeys or anything else.

EXODUS 20:1–17

Commentary

When the Israelites reached Mount Sinai, God gave Moses ten rules for life to teach them how to love God and other people. These 'ten words', as they're known in Hebrew, have since been adopted by many societies as the basis for their own laws. Almost all of them are expressed negatively ('Do not…'), but this isn't because they were designed to tell people off. Rather, these rules called the people to be different from those around them who lived by different standards.

God's people were to be distinct in having just one God who was invisible and could not be likened to anything on this planet. God's people were also to stand out from others because they didn't use his name as a magic formula to control him or as a swear word. God's people needed to live their lives according to the pattern God had given in creation, and God's people were those who treated others with respect and dignity because all people were made in God's image. These commandments are uncompromising and all-embracing, given so that God's people would represent God in the world, and this is still their purpose today.

Questions

▶ Which of these commandments do you think is the most important?

▶ Which of these commandments is the hardest to keep?

▶ Which of these commandments is the easiest to obey?

▶ Are there any of these commandments that you could leave out?

▶ If you could add an eleventh commandment, what might it be?

Visual aid

Choose ten differently coloured pieces of string or wool, which will be tied as ten knots on to one long piece of string. Choose a different colour to represent each 'not' of the ten commandments.

Activity idea

The ten commandments were written on stone and brought down the mountain by Moses. Collect ten flat stones (or you could buy some in a garden centre) on which you can write with a silver pen. Decide together on your own wording for each of the ten commandments.

Prayer idea

Turn each commandment first into a question and then into a prayer to say 'sorry' as you reflect on each of the ten in the list. Use your ten fingers and thumbs to work through the list. For example:

- Have I always put God first? 'I'm sorry for so easily forgetting about you, God.'
- Have we worshipped something else as more important than God? 'We're sorry for letting things get in the way of loving you, Father.'
- Have I really cared for my mum and dad? 'I'm sorry for not loving them as I should.'

Key verse

'I am the LORD your God, the one who brought you out of Egypt' (Exodus 20:2).

New Testament story link

Mark 12:28–34: Jesus sums up the ten commandments.

Exploring the land of Canaan

¹ The Lord said to Moses, ² 'Choose a leader from each tribe and send them into Canaan to explore the land I am giving you.'

³ So Moses sent twelve tribal leaders from Israel's camp in the Paran Desert ⁴ with orders to explore the land of Canaan...

²¹ The twelve men left to explore Canaan from the Zin Desert in the south all the way to the town of Rehob near Lebo-Hamath in the north. ²² As they went through the Southern Desert, they came to the town of Hebron, which was seven years older than the Egyptian town of Zoan. In Hebron, they saw the three Anakim clans of Ahiman, Sheshai, and Talmai. ²³⁻²⁴ When they got to Bunch Valley, they cut off a branch with such a huge bunch of grapes, that it took two men to carry it on a pole. That's why the place was called Bunch Valley. Along with the grapes, they also took back pomegranates and figs.

²⁵ After exploring the land of Canaan for forty days, ²⁶ the twelve men returned to Kadesh in the Paran Desert and told Moses, Aaron, and the people what they had seen. They showed them the fruit ²⁷ and said:

Look at this fruit! The land we explored is rich with milk and honey. ²⁸ But the people who live there are strong, and their cities are large and walled. We even saw the three Anakim clans.

²⁹ Besides that, the Amalekites live in the Southern Desert; the Hittites, Jebusites, and Amorites are in the hill country; and the Canaanites live along the Mediterranean Sea and the River Jordan.

³⁰ Caleb calmed down the crowd and said, 'Let's go and take the land. I know we can do it!'

³¹ But the other men replied, 'Those people are much too strong for us.' ³² Then they started spreading rumours and saying, 'We won't be able to grow anything in that soil. And the people are like giants. ³³ In fact, we saw the Nephilim who are the ancestors of the Anakim. They were so big that we felt as small as grasshoppers.'

NUMBERS 13:1–4a, 21–33

Commentary

After their long journey across the desert from Egypt, Moses and God's people have finally arrived at the borders of the promised land. In fact, this was the very country in which their ancestors had once lived, before they had come down to Egypt—the promised land that Abraham had travelled west to find.

Moses is anxious to spy out the country and plan his strategy for occupation. The twelve spies do a thorough job, noting the cities, the different tribal groups and the land's potential for growing crops. They even bring back a huge bunch of grapes. But they don't come back with a hopeful report. They have looked at Canaan not through the eyes of faith but with fear. They see problems, not possibilities, and only Caleb believes that God will help them take the land.

God's people had a grasshopper mentality before the giants of the land, and this lack of trust in God delayed their eventual arrival in the promised land. The journey from Egypt, which should have taken only months, lasted 40 long years. They had forgotten whose people they were and what a great God they served.

Questions

▶ Can you imagine how excited and nervous the twelve leaders must have been as they set out to explore Canaan? Have you ever felt like this?

▶ What surprises did they find as they travelled about?

▶ What was it, do you think, that frightened them the most?

▶ Why could Caleb take such a different attitude?

▶ The spies clearly lied and exaggerated to make their point at the end. Have you ever been tempted to do that?

Visual aid

Have a bunch of grapes on hand, and, if possible, some figs and pomegranates to taste. These were some of the fruits that the spies brought back from Canaan.

Activity idea

Play 'I spy', or arrange for a number of unusual objects to be left around another room in your house. Send out each member of the family in turn to spy out what they can see in a given time. When everyone has had a look, compare their stories. Who spotted most items? Where were they? What could link them all up? (Use your imagination.) And where there is a difference of opinion, who is most believable?

Prayer idea

Write the words 'But God' on a large circular piece of paper. Put down 2p coins, one at a time, to represent some of the challenges and problems facing you as individuals or as a family. Each time you put down a coin, cover it with the big circle showing the words 'But God' and add a prayer of faith.

Key verse

'Let's go and take the land. I know we can do it!' (Numbers 13:30).

New Testament story link

Acts 18:4–11: Paul faced setbacks and problems in Corinth, but God reminded him in a dream that he was still with him.

Joshua is chosen

¹ Moses, the LORD's servant, was dead. So the LORD spoke to Joshua son of Nun, who had been the assistant of Moses. The LORD said:

² My servant Moses is dead. Now you must lead Israel across the River Jordan into the land I'm giving to all of you. ³ Wherever you go, I'll give you that land, as I promised Moses. ⁴ It will reach from the Southern Desert to the Lebanon Mountains in the north, and to the northeast as far as the great River Euphrates. It will include the land of the Hittites, and the land from here at the River Jordan to the Mediterranean Sea on the west. ⁵ Joshua, I will always be with you and help you as I helped Moses, and no one will ever be able to defeat you.

⁶⁻⁸ Long ago I promised the ancestors of Israel that I would give this land to their descendants. So be strong and brave! Be careful to do everything my servant Moses taught you. Never stop reading *The Book of the Law* he gave you. Day and night you must think about what it says. If you obey it completely, you and Israel will be able to take this land.

⁹ I've commanded you to be strong and brave. Don't ever be afraid or discouraged! I am the LORD your God, and I will be there to help you wherever you go.

JOSHUA 1:1–9

Commentary

Moses had been a great leader, but in the end it wasn't his job to take God's people into the promised land. This work fell to his apprentice and successor, Joshua. Joshua had been Moses' right-hand man for many years, learning from him not only how to be a leader but also how to depend on God. Even so, it must have been a huge weight of responsibility on his shoulders as he stepped into Moses' shoes. He needed all the help and encouragement he could get—and this is exactly what he receives. God reassures him that the promised land is God's gift to the people of Israel, and he tells Joshua that he will be with him just as he was with Moses. He also shares with Joshua the secret of how to be strong and brave. This strength and courage will follow if he makes the Book of the Law his daily companion. Reading God's words and the stories of God's people will give him all the inspiration he needs.

Obeying the law was Moses' secret weapon, and it would be Joshua's too. For us today, the whole story of God as recorded in the Bible is our place to go for the same encouragement and guidance.

Visual aid

Make a Bible available to explore. Invite everyone to share stories that have been important to them and have helped them at some stage in their life.

Activity idea

Using the five letters of the word BIBLE, create together a simple poem or acrostic that attempts to describe how special this book is. It could be five individual words or five sentences, each beginning with a letter from the word BIBLE.

Prayer idea

In this story Joshua is at prayer, but he is listening, not speaking. God has a lot to say to him to prepare him for his new work. Try to spend time in prayer together, listening and not speaking. After a time of silence, share together what you

Questions

▶ Do you think Moses was disappointed that he never got to take the people into the promised land?

▶ Have you ever had to step into someone else's shoes and take over, as Joshua did? How did it feel?

▶ Why was it important that God spoke to Joshua in prayer like this?

▶ What, in the story, makes you think that Joshua might have been just a little bit scared?

▶ Which of God's promises in this passage do you think meant most to Joshua?

think you have heard. Perhaps some words came into your head, or a picture, or a story from the Bible, that could be the way God is encouraging you as a family today. End this time by reading together some of the special promises from this passage, which were spoken to Joshua then but are also in the Bible for us today.

Key verse

'Don't ever be afraid or discouraged! I am the LORD your God, and I will be there to help you wherever you go' (Joshua 1:9).

New Testament story link

Matthew 28:16–20: Here are the last words Jesus spoke to encourage his disciples for the work that lay ahead of them.

Rahab and the spies

[1] Joshua chose two men as spies and sent them from their camp at Acacia with these instructions: 'Go across the river and find out as much as you can about the whole region, especially about the town of Jericho.'

The two spies left the Israelite camp at Acacia and went to Jericho, where they decided to spend the night at the house of a prostitute named Rahab.

[2] But someone found out about them and told the king of Jericho, 'Some Israelite men came here tonight, and they are spies.' [3-7] So the king sent soldiers to Rahab's house to arrest the spies.

Meanwhile, Rahab had taken the men up to the flat roof of her house and had hidden them under some piles of flax plants that she had put there to dry.

The soldiers came to her door and demanded, 'Let us have the men who are staying at your house. They are spies.'

She answered, 'Some men did come to my house, but I didn't know where they had come from. They left about sunset, just before it was time to close the town gate. I don't know where they were going, but if you hurry, perhaps you can catch them.'

The guards at the town gate let the soldiers leave Jericho, but they closed the gate again as soon as the soldiers went through. Then the soldiers headed toward the River Jordan to look for the spies at the place where people cross the river.

[8] Rahab went back up to her roof. The spies were still awake, so she told them:

[9] I know that the LORD has given Israel this land. Everyone shakes with fear because of you. [10] We heard how the LORD dried up the Red Sea so you could leave Egypt. And we heard how you destroyed Sihon and Og, those two Amorite kings east of the Jordan River. [11] We know that the LORD your God rules heaven and earth, and we've lost our courage and our will to fight.

[12] Please promise me in the LORD's name that you will be as kind to my family as I have been to you. Do something to show [13] that you won't let your people kill my father and mother and my brothers and sisters and their families.

[14] 'Rahab,' the spies answered, 'if you keep quiet about what we're doing, we promise to be kind to you when the LORD gives us this land.'

JOSHUA 2:1–14

Commentary

The two spies discovered more than just how strong a city Jericho was when they stayed at Rahab's home. Her words told them that the news of what God had done to rescue, guide and fight for the people of Israel had already spread to nations far away. God's protection of his people in the desert was clearly well known and had already drawn some outsiders, like Rahab, to recognise that Israel's Lord was the one true God. No wonder she was prepared to put her life at risk by hiding the spies on her roof and sending the soldiers off on a wild goose chase.

Rahab's faith in Israel's God must have come as a surprise to the men, but she was one of many people in the Bible from outside Israel who decided to put their trust in the Lord. She asked for protection for her whole family when Joshua eventually took the town, and this request was honoured. This outsider also later married an Israelite and, as is recorded in Matthew's Gospel (chapter 1), she became an ancestor of the family line into which Jesus was born. God's rescue plans clearly include people from every nation, not just Israel.

Questions

▶ How did Rahab put her faith in God into action?

▶ Why might the spies have been surprised by what she told them?

▶ What different reactions might there have been back in Joshua's camp to the news that they already seemed to have a 'friend on the inside'?

▶ Rahab believed that Joshua would take Jericho before it happened. How can we show faith like this?

Visual aid

Use red rope as a focus. Later in the story, the spies tell Rahab to put a red rope at her window so that the invaders will know where she is and won't attack her home. This red rope becomes a sign of her faith in God.

Activity idea

The spies have to hide from the soldiers. As a family, play a simple game of hide and seek. Which place in the home turns out to be the best place to hide?

Prayer idea

The spies had to trust someone whom they had thought of as an enemy, but this enemy turned out to be a friend to whom God had already spoken. Write out the seven letters of the word ENEMIES on separate pieces of card and, on the reverse, write the seven letters of the word FRIENDS. Now, as you pray about different people who, for some reason, make you feel afraid or in danger, turn over each letter of the word 'enemies' and ask God to help you love them as 'friends', just as he does.

Key verse

'We know that the LORD your God rules heaven and earth' (Joshua 2:11).

New Testament story link

Acts 10: Peter discovers that a Roman soldier named Cornelius is not an enemy but a friend.

The battle of Jericho

13 One day, Joshua was near Jericho when he saw a man standing some distance in front of him. The man was holding a sword, so Joshua walked up to him and asked, 'Are you on our side or on our enemies' side?'

14 'Neither,' he answered. 'I am here because I am the commander of the LORD's army.'

Joshua fell to his knees and bowed down to the ground. 'I am your servant,' he said. 'Tell me what to do.'

15 'Take off your sandals,' the commander answered. 'This is a holy place.'

So Joshua took off his sandals.

6 Meanwhile, the people of Jericho had been locking the gates in their town wall because they were afraid of the Israelites. No one could go out or come in.

2–3 The LORD said to Joshua:

With my help, you and your army will defeat the king of Jericho and his army, and you will capture the town. Here is how to do it: march slowly around Jericho once a day for six days. 4 Take along the sacred chest and have seven priests walk in front of it, carrying trumpets.

But on the seventh day, march slowly around the town seven times while the priests blow their trumpets. 5 Then the priests will blast on their trumpets, and everyone else will shout. The wall will fall down, and your soldiers can go straight in from every side.

6 Joshua called the priests together and said, 'Take the chest and have seven priests carry trumpets and march ahead of it.'

7–8 Next, he gave the army their orders: 'March slowly around Jericho. A few of you will go ahead of the chest to guard it, but most of you will follow it. Don't shout the battle cry or yell or even talk until the day I tell you to. Then let out a shout!'

JOSHUA 5:13—6:8

Commentary

God had promised to be with Joshua and to help him. On the eve of the battle of Jericho, Joshua needed to be reassured, and this happened when he met the heavenly soldier. He realised he was in the presence of God and, like Moses at the burning bush, took off his shoes because he was standing on holy ground.

This encounter must have been a great encouragement as Joshua put God's battle plan into action. He knew from the spies how frightened the inhabitants of Jericho already were, and when they saw the daily silent march around the walls, it must have weakened their morale even further. But it also took great faith on Joshua's part and his army's to carry out God's strange instructions. They didn't know what would happen when they finally shouted the battle cry on the seventh day. That shout was the moment when the walls miraculously collapsed and Jericho could be taken, and Joshua's soldiers must have been as amazed by what happened as the people in the city. God chose to give the victory in such a way that no one could say it was achieved by their own cunning or courage. Faith in God had won the day.

Questions

▶ What do you think the heavenly soldier meant when he said he was on neither side?

▶ Can you imagine what some of the experienced soldiers on Joshua's side must have said when they heard the battle plan?

▶ Why was it so important to put the special chest and the priests at the front of the procession?

▶ What do you think everyone expected to happen on the seventh day?

Visual aid

The trumpets in the story were rams' horns that were also used to call people to prayer at special festival times. Make some of your own out of cardboard tubes or use a real wind instrument.

Activity idea

Build some walls from children's wooden blocks or, if you have the space, some cardboard boxes. Walk around these walls silently 13 times in total (once a day for six days and seven on the seventh) and then, with a great shout and the sound of trumpets, shake the foundations so that the walls you have made come tumbling down.

Prayer idea

This battle began with silent prayer, not the traditional sounds of hand-to-hand fighting. It was also persistent, regular prayer (each day for seven days). As a family, compose a special prayer about something important to you all, and write it around the edge of a circular piece of paper. Pin it up and pray it once a day for six days and seven times on the seventh day. Look out for God's answer, which will almost certainly take you by surprise.

Key verse

"'I am your servant,' [Joshua] said. 'Tell me what to do'" (Joshua 5:14).

New Testament story link

Acts 12:1–17: The church prays regularly for Peter in prison, and the answer takes them all by surprise.

The time of the judges

6-9 Joshua had been faithful to the LORD. And after Joshua sent the Israelites to take the land they had been promised, they remained faithful to the LORD until Joshua died at the age of one hundred and ten. He was buried on his land in Timnath-Heres, in the hill country of Ephraim north of Mount Gaash. Even though Joshua was gone, the Israelites were faithful to the LORD during the lifetime of those men who had been leaders with Joshua and who had seen the wonderful things the LORD had done for Israel.

10 After a while the people of Joshua's generation died, and the next generation did not know the LORD or any of the things he had done for Israel. 11-13 The LORD had brought their ancestors out of Egypt, and they had worshipped him. But now the Israelites stopped worshipping the LORD and worshipped the idols of Baal and Astarte, as well as the idols of other gods from nearby nations.

The LORD was so angry 14-15 with the Israelites that he let other nations raid Israel and steal their crops and other possessions. Enemies were everywhere, and the LORD always let them defeat Israel in battle. The LORD had warned Israel he would do this, and now the Israelites were miserable.

16 From time to time, the LORD would choose special leaders known as judges. These judges would lead the Israelites into battle and defeat the enemies that made raids on them. 17 In years gone by, the Israelites had been faithful to the LORD, but now they were quick to be unfaithful and to refuse even to listen to these judges. The Israelites would disobey the LORD, and instead of worshipping him, they would worship other gods.

JUDGES 2:6–17

Commentary

After the exciting stories of Moses and Joshua comes a less attractive period in Israel's history. It was not long before the people forgot all that God had done for them and began to copy those around them, choosing other gods to worship. Both Moses and Joshua had warned them that this might happen, but it seems that faith in the one true God had not been passed on very well to their children and their children's children. Perhaps they imagined that they didn't have to make an effort to pass on the story to those who came after them and that somehow it would just be picked up; or maybe they underestimated the influences from the tribes around them. What happened to Israel stands as a warning to the people of God in every age. Unless we make the effort to tell and retell the true story of God, it will easily be forgotten or corrupted. No wonder their enemies began to defeat them easily and God seemed to have abandoned them. But God did not give up on them. He sent leaders (judges) from time to time to draw them back to the faith, even though, once these leaders died, many people returned to putting their trust in idols.

Visual aid

Use a compass as a focus. No matter which way you turn, the needle will always point north. The people of Israel chose to ignore the compass that God had given them in the ten commandments and in the amazing story of their rescue from Egypt and God's guidance during the days in the desert. No wonder they lost their way, just as we would if we ignored a compass.

Activity idea

There are lots of things today that grab our attention and influence us in our thinking and our actions. Look through a popular magazine together and cut out pictures of some of the so-called 'gods' of today: fashion, speed, money, popularity, good looks, possessions and power. Although these things aren't necessarily bad in themselves,

Questions

▶ Why did people forget all that God had done, after Joshua died?

▶ Why were the Israelites so attracted to worshipping other gods from the tribes around them?

▶ Why didn't God give up on his people?

▶ What keeps you believing, even though many people around you today do not?

they can be bad for us if they lead us to forget to trust in God.

Prayer idea

If the Israelites had remembered the ten commandments, they would have recalled that the one true God cannot be represented by statues of animals or by sacred trees. Remind each other of the commandments (see page 40) and, as you say each one, turn it into a prayer for help—for example, 'Help us remember that you are the one true God; help us not to worship false gods; help us to respect your name,' and so on.

Key verse

'In years gone by, the Israelites had been faithful to the Lord, but now they were quick to be unfaithful and to refuse even to listen to these judges' (Judges 2:17).

New Testament story link

Matthew 6:24: Jesus tells us that we can't worship more than one God.

Gideon defeats the Midianites

¹ Early the next morning, Gideon and his army got up and moved their camp to Fear Spring. The Midianite camp was to the north, in the valley at the foot of Moreh Hill.

² The LORD said, 'Gideon, your army is too big. I can't let you win with this many soldiers. The Israelites would think that they had won the battle all by themselves and that I didn't have anything to do with it. ³ So call your troops together and tell them that anyone who is really afraid can leave Mount Gilead and go home.'

Twenty-two thousand men returned home, leaving Gideon with only ten thousand soldiers.

⁴ 'Gideon,' the LORD said, 'you still have too many soldiers. Take them down to the spring and I'll test them. I'll tell you which ones can go along with you and which ones must go back home.'

⁵ When Gideon led his army down to the spring, the LORD told him, 'Watch how each man gets a drink of water. Then divide them into two groups—those who lap the water like a dog and those who kneel down to drink.'

⁶ Three hundred men scooped up water in their hands and lapped it, and the rest knelt to get a drink. ⁷ The LORD said, 'Gideon, your army will be made up of everyone who lapped the water from their hands. Send the others home. I'm going to rescue Israel by helping you and your army of three hundred defeat the Midianites.'

JUDGES 7:1–7

Commentary

God's choice of Gideon as Israel's new leader had already been a surprise one. Gideon was the youngest in his family and his tribe was one of the smallest in Israel. It seems that, again and again in the Bible, God chooses the most unlikely people, to show the world that everyone is important to him and that with him all things are possible. The principle is at work in this story, where God deliberately reduces Gideon's army from over 30,000 to just 300 to face a huge Midianite force. According to the number of troops mentioned in Judges 8:10, the odds would have been 45 to 1 against Gideon's troops! There was no way that an Israelite victory could be attributed to human skill or to weight of numbers. The battle, described in the later part of this chapter, was initially won not with weapons but with trumpets, torches and clay jars. All the glory for this victory would go to God and therefore it would be a lesson to the Israelites, as for us today, about God's power to save.

Visual aid

Use 46 counters or coins to illustrate the odds of 45 to 1 that Gideon's 300 soldiers faced. This is a good way to see what their faith in God meant in practice.

Activity idea

Gideon's battle cry when they surrounded the Midianite army at night was 'For the Lord and for Gideon!' (Judges 7:20). It was accompanied by trumpet blasts, the smashing of pots and the waving of flames. Recreate all this together by flashing torches, pouring out coins from a jar, putting fists to mouths to make trumpet noises, as well as shouting the battle cry.

Prayer idea

Clearly Gideon had learned that one plus God is always a majority. Pick out some recent newspaper headlines concerning major issues that involve large numbers or overwhelming circumstances—for example, the numbers of people

Questions

▶ Do you think it was just because they were scared that two-thirds of Gideon's army left at the first opportunity?

▶ Why do you think God chose the 300 who scooped up the water?

▶ How would you have felt if you were one of the 300 facing such a huge enemy army?

▶ What was it that made Gideon trust God so completely? (You might like to look back at the last part of Judges 6.)

▶ What overwhelming problems are you facing that need a faith like Gideon's?

without clean water in the world, the numbers who are running away from war, or are short of food, or are facing serious illness. Against each of these issues put a small sticker or sticky note to represent your small but important prayers to God, and, each time you do so, remind yourselves of Gideon's victory.

Key verse

'I'm going to rescue Israel by helping you and your army of three hundred defeat the Midianites' (Judges 7:7).

New Testament story link

John 6:1–11: A young boy's small picnic turns out to be enough food to feed over 5000 people.

Naomi goes home

¹⁻² Before Israel was ruled by kings, Elimelech from the tribe of Ephrath lived in the town of Bethlehem. His wife was named Naomi, and their two sons were Mahlon and Chilion. But when their crops failed, they moved to the country of Moab. And while they were there, ³ Elimelech died, leaving Naomi with only her two sons.

⁴ Later, Naomi's sons married Moabite women. One was named Orpah and the other Ruth. About ten years later, ⁵ Mahlon and Chilion also died. Now Naomi had no husband or sons.

⁶⁻⁷ When Naomi heard that the LORD had given his people a good harvest, she and her two daughters-in-law got ready to leave Moab and go to Judah. As they were on their way there, ⁸ Naomi said to them, 'Don't you want to go back home to your own mothers? You were kind to my husband and sons, and you have always been kind to me. I pray that the LORD will be just as kind to you. ⁹ May he give each of you another husband and a home of your own.'

Naomi kissed them. They cried ¹⁰ and said, 'We want to go with you and live among your people.'

¹¹ But she replied, 'My daughters, why don't you return home? What good will it do you to go with me? Do you think I could have more sons for you to marry? ¹² You must go back home, because I am too old to marry again. Even if I got married tonight and later had more sons, ¹³ would you wait for them to become old enough to marry? No, my daughters! Life is harder for me than it is for you, because the LORD has turned against me.'

¹⁴ They cried again. Orpah kissed her mother-in-law goodbye, but Ruth held on to her. ¹⁵ Naomi then said to Ruth, 'Look, your sister-in-law is going back to her people and to her gods! Why don't you go with her?'

¹⁶ Ruth answered,

'Please don't tell me
to leave you
    and return home!
I will go where you go,
    I will live where you live;
your people will be my people,
    your God will be my God.
¹⁷ I will die where you die
    and be buried beside you.
May the LORD punish me
if we are ever separated,
    even by death!'

¹⁸ When Naomi saw that Ruth had made up her mind to go with her, she stopped urging her to go back.

RUTH 1:1–18

54

Commentary

This story of one Israelite family gives us a glimpse of what life was like during the time of the judges. Crops failed: families had to become migrants looking for food and work, there was intermarriage between cultures, and some people died very young. Naomi's family experienced all this, and when we meet her in the story she is a widow with her two daughters-in-law from another country. News of the good harvest in Bethlehem provides her with an opportunity to return to her home town, but she doesn't expect Ruth and Orpah to come with her. Clearly these two women are loyal to her, but no one would blame them for staying in their own country of Moab. However, Ruth refuses to leave her elderly mother-in-law, even though she herself will become a stranger in a foreign land. Ruth's devotion and love are remarkable, and the Bible includes this story to remind both its first readers and us today that God is at work in the most unexpected people and places.

Visual aid

People often wear a black armband when they are in mourning for someone who has died. Make some black armbands from fabric to help you think yourself into the story. Why do you think people choose this colour for mourning?

Activity idea

This is a story of loss. Collect together some different pieces of dark material from which you can create a collage of sadness or weave together a cord of unhappiness. Now choose one bright piece of material or wool to add to what you have created, as a symbol of the help that Ruth brought to Naomi. This is also a picture of how we might brighten the lives of others who are facing unhappiness.

Prayer idea

On some paper plates, draw a face, with eyes in the centre, a straight line for the nose and a downturned curve for a sad mouth. Talk about those you know who are sad today and pray for them. Now turn the plates around and rework the picture to make a happy smiling face, making the sad mouth into a hairline and adding a smile. Ask God to help you to be someone who brings comfort and help to people, just like Ruth did.

Questions

▶ Can you imagine what it must be like to be forced to leave your home and live in a country far away?

▶ Naomi had experienced tragedy in her life. What could you say or do for someone you met who was hurting like this?

▶ Orpah and Ruth would have had to give up a lot to stay with Naomi. What arguments for and against going with Naomi can you find?

▶ Who inspires you today by the way in which they are living their life?

Key verse

'I will go where you go, I will live where you live; your people will be my people, your God will be my God' (Ruth 1:16).

New Testament story link

Matthew 15:21–28: Jesus is surprised by the faith of a woman who comes from another country.

Ruth and Boaz

1–3 One day, Ruth said to Naomi, 'Let me see if I can find someone who will let me pick up the grain left in the fields by the harvest workers.'

Naomi answered, 'Go ahead, my daughter.' So straight away, Ruth went out to pick up grain in a field owned by Boaz. He was a relative of Naomi's husband Elimelech, as well as a rich and important man.

4 When Boaz left Bethlehem and went out to his field, he said to the harvest workers, 'The LORD bless you!'

They replied, 'And may the LORD bless you!'

5 Then Boaz asked the man in charge of the harvest workers, 'Who is that young woman?'

6 The man answered, 'She is the one who came back from Moab with Naomi. 7 She asked if she could pick up grain left by the harvest workers, and she has been working all morning without a moment's rest.'

8 Boaz went over to Ruth and said, 'I think it would be best for you not to pick up grain in anyone else's field. Stay here with the women 9 and follow along behind them, as they gather up what the men have cut. I have warned the men not to bother you, and whenever you are thirsty, you can drink from the water jars they have filled.'

10 Ruth bowed down to the ground and said, 'You know I come from another country. Why are you so good to me?'

11 Boaz answered, 'I've heard how you've helped your mother-in-law ever since your husband died. You even left your own father and mother to come and live in a foreign land among people you don't know. 12 I pray that the LORD God of Israel will reward you for what you have done. And now that you have come to him for protection, I pray that he will bless you.'

RUTH 2:1–12

Commentary

Although Naomi and Ruth had returned to Bethlehem, their troubles were not yet over. They were desperately poor and had to depend on the charity of others. It was the custom to leave some grain in the fields at harvest time for poor people to pick up. Ruth offers to gather some grain so that she and her mother-in-law won't starve.

God is clearly guiding events that day because the field where she works turns out to belong to one of Naomi's relatives by marriage. Boaz is a kind man who has heard of Ruth's kindness to Naomi. He arranges for Ruth to pick up as much as she needs and also orders his workers to keep an eye out for her safety. It is the beginning of a love story that leads to a new husband for Ruth, a sure future for Naomi and, in time, children and grandchildren. It is into Ruth's family line that King David is born and from David's family that Jesus comes, far in the future. Ruth's beautiful act of loyalty is rewarded and Boaz's prayer that God will bless her is richly answered.

Visual aid

Take a loaf of bread out of its packet and place it in the centre of a large plate. Now empty the crumbs from the packet all around the loaf. These are like the leftovers that Ruth was allowed to take. How much can you pick up?

Activity idea

By leaving some grain in the corner of the field for the poor to pick up, Boaz was obeying one of the harvest laws in the Old Testament. Our loose change is a bit like the leftovers in Boaz's field. As a family, set out to find and collect as many low-value coins as you can find lying around the house. Look down behind the sofa! Add the money together and turn it into a gift to a charity that cares for those who don't have enough to eat, either in your own country or another.

Prayer activity

Boaz's greeting to his workers was 'The Lord bless you'. He also prayed a blessing on Ruth. To bless someone is to want the best for them. Write the words 'May God bless…' in the middle of a sheet of paper and, as a family, add the names of people, places and special situations that come to your minds. Read them out loud together as a prayer.

Questions

▶ Have you ever experienced what it is like to go without food for a while? If not, can you imagine it?

▶ What risks do you think Ruth was taking in offering to go out and pick up the leftover grain in the fields?

▶ What makes you think that Boaz was a kind man?

▶ Why do you think Ruth was surprised to be treated so kindly?

▶ Can you imagine what Ruth said to her mother-in-law when she returned that evening and described the events of the day?

Key verse

'Now that you have come to [God] for protection. I pray that he will bless you' (Ruth 2:12).

New Testament story link

Luke 6:27–38: Jesus tells us of the many ways in which we can bless others, just as Boaz blessed Ruth.

God speaks to Samuel

1-2 Samuel served the LORD by helping Eli the priest, who was by that time almost blind. In those days, the LORD hardly ever spoke directly to people, and he did not appear to them in dreams very often. But one night, Eli was asleep in his room, 3 and Samuel was sleeping on a mat near the sacred chest in the LORD's house. They had not been asleep very long 4 when the LORD called out Samuel's name.

'Here I am!' Samuel answered. 5 Then he ran to Eli and said, 'Here I am. What do you want?'

'I didn't call you,' Eli answered. 'Go back to bed.' Samuel went back.

6 Again the LORD called out Samuel's name. Samuel got up and went to Eli. 'Here I am,' he said. 'What do you want?'

Eli told him, 'Son, I didn't call you. Go back to sleep.'

7 The LORD had not spoken to Samuel before, and Samuel did not recognise the voice. 8 When the LORD called out his name for the third time, Samuel went to Eli again and said, 'Here I am. What do you want?'

Eli finally realised that it was the LORD who was speaking to Samuel. 9 So he said, 'Go back and lie down! If someone speaks to you again, answer, "I'm listening, LORD. What do you want me to do?"'

Once again Samuel went back and lay down.

10 The LORD then stood beside Samuel and called out as he had done before, 'Samuel! Samuel!'

'I'm listening,' Samuel answered. 'What do you want me to do?'

1 SAMUEL 3:1–10

Commentary

We all long to hear God speaking to us. Whether it comes through a Bible story, the advice of a Christian friend or a quiet voice in our head, a word from God can change everything. But sometimes God seems to have his mobile on silent. It felt like that for Eli the priest and the people of God at the time of this story. What a surprise, then, that when God did speak he chose to give a message to a little child! Samuel could hear God's voice clearly, but didn't realise that it was God who was speaking. It took great humility on Eli's part to recognise that God had chosen to speak to his trainee altar boy rather than to him. God often surprises us like this and, like Eli, we need to be ready to receive a message from God, even if it comes in an unexpected way. Eli advises Samuel what to say when he next hears the voice, and so helps him to begin a life of listening to God that will change him and transform the nation.

Visual aid

Use a transistor or digital radio and have fun together tuning into as many different stations as you can along one wave band. Just think how many unheard sounds there are, all around us in the air, once we know the way to listen in!

Activity idea

Play a listening game together. Set a minute on the timer facility of your mobile and all agree to keep completely silent for that time. Everyone should make a mental note of all the sounds they hear. Then talk about what each of you heard. Try this again, but now make it a minute of listening prayer, starting with the words 'We're listening, Lord.' Ask everyone to notice some of the thoughts that come into their heads. What do they think God might have been saying? (Adults, be ready, like Eli, to accept that God might choose to speak to the children rather than you.)

Questions

▶ Why do you think God chose to speak to Samuel rather than Eli?

▶ How do you think God speaks to people today?

▶ Have you ever heard God speak to you?

▶ Do you think that God may be speaking to us through this story?

Prayer idea

Prayer is as much about listening to God as speaking to him. Try making deliberate space for listening when you pray together today. Pause after every short prayer that you say and keep silent for about 15 seconds. Agree that each of you will do this. As the signal for the short silence, you could all say a version of Samuel's words together: 'We're listening, Lord.'

Key verse

'I'm listening, Lord. What do you want me to do?' (1 Samuel 3:9).

New Testament story link

Matthew 11:25–30: Jesus tells his friends that God doesn't always choose to speak to the people we might expect.

Israel's first king

⁴ One day the nation's leaders came to Samuel at Ramah ⁵ and said, 'You are an old man. You set a good example for your sons, but they haven't followed it. Now we want a king to be our leader, just like all the other nations. Choose one for us!'

⁶ Samuel was upset to hear the leaders say they wanted a king, so he prayed about it. ⁷ The LORD answered:

Samuel, do everything they want you to do. I am really the one they have rejected as their king. ⁸ Ever since the day I rescued my people from Egypt, they have turned from me to worship idols. Now they are turning away from you. ⁹ Do everything they ask, but warn them and tell them how a king will treat them.

¹⁰ Samuel told the people who were asking for a king what the LORD had said:

¹¹ If you have a king, this is how he will treat you. He will force your sons to join his army. Some of them will ride in his chariots, some will serve in the cavalry, and others will run ahead of his own chariot. ¹² Some of them will be officers in charge of a thousand soldiers, and others will be in charge of fifty. Still others will have to farm the king's land and harvest his crops, or make weapons and parts for his chariots. ¹³ Your daughters will have to make perfume or do his cooking and baking.

¹⁴ The king will take your best fields, as well as your vineyards and olive orchards, and give them to his own officials. ¹⁵ He will also take a tenth of your grain and grapes and give it to his officers and officials.

¹⁶ The king will take your slaves and your best young men and your donkeys and make them do his work. ¹⁷ He will also take a tenth of your sheep and goats. You will become the king's slaves, ¹⁸ and you will finally cry out for the LORD to save you from the king you wanted. But the LORD won't answer your prayers.

¹⁹⁻²⁰ The people would not listen to Samuel. 'No!' they said. 'We want to be like other nations. We want a king to rule us and lead us in battle.'

²¹ Samuel listened to them and then told the LORD exactly what they had said. ²² 'Do what they want,' the LORD answered. 'Give them a king.'

1 SAMUEL 8:4–22a

Commentary

Samuel was the last of the judges for the people of Israel. He was a great spiritual leader who had guided the nation well and had been a faithful spokesman for God. However, towards the end of Samuel's life, and with no obvious successor to this great man, the people turned away from God and what was best for them and demanded that Israel become a monarchy with a human figurehead. Israel wanted to be a 'grown-up' country like others in the region, and this meant having a king and an army. God had always wanted his people to be different, because God was their king, and in this way to model a different sort of kingdom to those living round about. Samuel warned them of all the dangers there would be when power was in the hands of an earthly ruler, but they refused to listen. God never forces us to do things against our will, so he gave the people what they wanted. Saul was eventually appointed as the first king, but it turned out badly, just as Samuel had predicted.

Visual aid

Turn an ordinary chair into a grand throne for a king or queen. What are the advantages and disadvantages of having someone on the throne of a country?

Questions

▷ The people of Israel wanted what everybody else had got—a king and an army. Why do you think God wasn't enough for them any more?

▷ How do you think Samuel felt when the people demanded a human king?

▷ What did Samuel say were the dangers of having a king?

▷ Why do you think God gave in to the people and let them have what was not for the best?

Activity idea

Play a game together of 'If I were king/queen for the day, I would…', with each member of the family in turn saying what he or she would do if they were in charge. Challenge each other about what their decisions would mean and how they might deal with people who don't do as they're told. Lead on to a conversation about what difference it makes if, instead of this, God is king, every day.

Prayer idea

The people of Israel had let themselves be influenced by what others had, and they had forgotten their special relationship with God as king. Ask God's help to discover his best for each of you without being distracted by what others are saying. Make a simple crown from a circle of card and hold on to it as a way of saying that you want God to be king in every part of your lives—in your use of money and time, your choice of clothes and friends, and in all the big decisions faced by your family.

Key verse

'Samuel was upset to hear the leaders say they wanted a king, so he prayed about it' (1 Samuel 8:6).

New Testament story link

Matthew 6:31–33: Jesus tells us that if we put God's kingdom first, then God will give us all that we really need.

David and Goliath

31 Some soldiers overheard David talking, so they told Saul what David had said. Saul sent for David, and David came. 32 'Your Majesty,' he said, 'this Philistine shouldn't turn us into cowards. I'll go out and fight him myself!'

33 'You don't have a chance against him,' Saul replied. 'You're only a boy, and he's been a soldier all his life.'

34 But David told him:

Your Majesty, I take care of my father's sheep. And when one of them is dragged off by a lion or a bear, 35 I go after it and beat the wild animal until it lets the sheep go. If the wild animal turns and attacks me, I grab it by the throat and kill it.

36 Sir, I have killed lions and bears that way, and I can kill this worthless Philistine. He shouldn't have made fun of the army of the living God! 37 The Lord has rescued me from the claws of lions and bears, and he will keep me safe from the hands of this Philistine.

'All right,' Saul answered, 'go ahead and fight him. And I hope the Lord will help you.'

38 Saul had his own military clothes and armour put on David, and he gave David a bronze helmet to wear. 39 David strapped on a sword and tried to walk around, but he was not used to wearing those things.

'I can't move with all this stuff on,' David said. 'I'm just not used to it.'

David took off the armour 40 and picked up his shepherd's stick. He went out to a stream and picked up five smooth stones and put them in his leather bag. Then with his sling in his hand, he went straight toward Goliath.

1 Samuel 17:31–40

Commentary

David's victory over Goliath is probably one of the most well-known stories in the Bible. It is so encouraging for those who feel they are overwhelmed by impossible challenges or feel bullied by powerful enemies. Teenager David is the underdog, but with God he is a winner against all the odds and to the utter dismay of the Philistine army.

This is more than just a story about the triumph of the weak over the strong, though. David's motivation is the key to what happens. He loves God with all his heart and can't bear to see God insulted by the Philistine champion. It is his faith that makes him strong and able to defeat this giant enemy. He has experienced God's help in the past and knows that God will be with him. As a shepherd for his father's flock, he has discovered God is with him in times of danger, so here on the battlefield he is not afraid. He doesn't need to rely on Saul's heavy armour but, as he tells Goliath later in the story, he comes to the fight 'in the name of the Lord All-powerful'.

Visual aid

Collect five smooth stones just like

Questions

▸ Which part of the David and Goliath story do you like the best?

▸ Can you imagine what the soldiers said about David behind his back before he killed Goliath?

▸ What do you think they were saying about David after he had won?

▸ David could list times when God had helped him in the past. Can you think back to times when God has looked after you as a family?

▸ Saul's armour only got in the way for David. Do you think we sometimes try to trust in other things to help us, rather than simply putting our faith in God?

David's. Can you link each stone to a reason for trusting in God when faced with a big challenge?

Activity idea

As a shepherd boy, David had learned to use his slingshot effectively. He could be sure of hitting the target first time. Using an elastic band and small bits of rolled-up paper, hold a family competition to see who can knock down a target from a given distance.

Prayer idea

David was not only a shepherd but also a musician. Many of the psalms are said to have been written by him. You can find one of the most famous of the psalms, Psalm 23,

at the end of this Family Bible (see page 250). Read it together, pausing after each verse and turning it into a simple prayer, thanking God for his provision, his guidance, his protection, his blessing and the promise of heaven.

Key verse

'The Lord has rescued me from the claws of lions and bears, and he will keep me safe from the hands of this Philistine' (1 Samuel 17:37).

New Testament story link

2 Timothy 4:16–18: Paul writes to Timothy to tell him how God kept him safe, even when he was faced by terrible danger.

David lets Saul live

¹ When Saul got back from fighting off the Philistines, he heard that David was in the desert around En-Gedi. ² Saul led three thousand of Israel's best soldiers out to look for David and his men near Wild Goat Rocks at En-Gedi. ³ There were some sheep pens along the side of the road, and one of them was built around the entrance to a cave. Saul went into the cave to relieve himself.

David and his men were hiding at the back of the cave. ⁴ They whispered to David, 'The LORD told you he was going to let you defeat your enemies and do whatever you want with them. This must be the day the LORD was talking about.'

David sneaked over and cut off a small piece of Saul's robe, but Saul didn't notice a thing. ⁵ Afterwards, David was sorry that he had even done that, ⁶⁻⁷ and he told his men, 'Stop talking foolishly. We're not going to attack Saul. He's my king, and I pray that the LORD will keep me from doing anything to harm his chosen king.'

Saul left the cave and started down the road. ⁸ Soon, David also got up and left the cave. 'Your Majesty!' he shouted from a distance.

Saul turned around to look. David bowed down very low ⁹ and said:

Your Majesty, why do you listen to people who say that I'm trying to harm you? ¹⁰ You can see for yourself that the LORD gave me the chance to catch you in the cave today. Some of my men wanted to kill you, but I wouldn't let them do it. I told them, 'I will not harm the LORD's chosen king!' ¹¹ Your Majesty, look at what I'm holding. You can see that it's a piece of your robe. If I could cut off a piece of your robe, I could have killed you. But I let you live, and that should prove I'm not trying to harm you or to rebel. I haven't done anything to you, and yet you keep trying to ambush and kill me...'

¹⁶ 'David, my son—is that you?' Saul asked. Then he started crying.

1 SAMUEL 24:1–11, 16

Commentary

When David killed Goliath he became a national hero, but this enraged King Saul. David had tried to live peaceably within the king's court, but was finally forced to run away in fear for his life. He is living as an outlaw with others among the rocks and wild places of Israel when the events of this story take place. To everyone else it seems that Saul's arrival in the cave is David's God-given opportunity to get rid of the king and seize the throne, which David knows from Samuel will be his one day. But David is nobler than that. He knows that it would be wrong to murder Saul while he is defenceless. His generosity and self-restraint are a shining example to all of us who feel the need to take revenge on those who have hurt us.

No wonder the discovery leaves Saul almost speechless and in tears. David is truly a man after God's own heart.

Visual aid

This story is as comical as it is powerful. A unused toilet roll could symbolise Saul's reason for entering the cave. You could tear off some tissue, just as David cut away part of Saul's tunic, and you could also use a piece later to wipe away the tears that filled Saul's eyes.

Activity idea

This incident in the wilderness at Wild Goat Rocks is very dramatic. Play a game of hide and seek, adding the 'sardines' factor— namely, if someone finds the one who is hiding, they should join him or her there. How many of you will manage to hide away like David and his men, before being found by the last person?

Prayer idea

Find Psalm 57 (believed to be written by David when he hid from Saul) in a Bible and read it together. Draw the entrance to a cave on a large piece of paper. Around the cave write some of the things that may be worrying you all at the moment and then each put one hand over the cave entrance and say, each time you mention a particular worry, 'Father God, please keep us safe from all danger.'

Questions

▶ Can you imagine how surprised David and his men were when Saul entered the cave where they were hiding? What do you think they whispered to each other in the shadows?

▶ David's decision not to kill Saul also took everyone by surprise. Can you think of a situation in your life where not fighting back, not raising your voice in anger and not taking revenge might be a surprising thing to do?

▶ Do you think it's possible to respect someone even if they hurt you?

▶ Why do you think David acted so generously towards Saul?

▶ Why do you think Saul decided not to continue chasing David?

Key verse

'I pray that the Lord will keep me from doing anything to harm his chosen king' (1 Samuel 24:7).

New Testament story link

1 Peter 2:11–17: Peter writes to Christians about respecting those in authority and not giving in to the temptation to get our own back.

David is kind to Mephibosheth

One day, David thought, 'I wonder if any of Saul's family are still alive. If they are, I will be kind to them, because I made a promise to Jonathan.' ² David called in Ziba, one of the servants of Saul's family. David said, 'So you are Ziba.'

'Yes, Your Majesty, I am.'

³ David asked, 'Are any of Saul's family still alive? If there are, I want to be kind to them.'

Ziba answered, 'One of Jonathan's sons is still alive, but he can't walk.'

⁴ 'Where is he?' David asked.

Ziba replied, 'He lives in Lo-Debar with Machir the son of Ammiel.'

⁵⁻⁶ David sent some servants to bring Jonathan's son from Lo-Debar. His name was Mephibosheth, and he was the grandson of Saul. He came to David and knelt down.

David asked, 'Are you Mephibosheth?'

'Yes, I am, Your Majesty.'

⁷ David said, 'Don't be afraid. I'll be kind to you because Jonathan was your father. I'm going to give you back the land that belonged to your grandfather Saul. Besides that, you will always eat with me at my table.'

⁸ Mephibosheth knelt down again and said, 'Why should you care about me? I'm worth no more than a dead dog.'

⁹ David called in Ziba, Saul's chief servant, and told him, 'Since Mephibosheth is Saul's grandson, I've given him back everything that belonged to your master Saul and his family. ¹⁰ You and your fifteen sons and twenty servants will work for Mephibosheth. You will farm his land and bring in his crops, so that Saul's family and servants will have food. But Mephibosheth will always eat with me at my table.'

¹¹⁻¹³ Ziba replied, 'Your Majesty, I will do exactly what you tell me to do.' So Ziba's family and servants worked for Mephibosheth.

Mephibosheth was lame, but he lived in Jerusalem and ate at David's table, just like one of David's own sons. And he had a young son of his own, named Mica.

2 SAMUEL 9

Commentary

Before he became king, David had been best friends with Jonathan, King Saul's son. It had broken his heart when he learned that Jonathan had been killed in battle along with his father. As friends they had promised to look after each other whatever happened, so now that David was king he made good that promise by seeking out any surviving members of Jonathan's family. Mephibosheth was Jonathan's son, disabled from the time when his nurse had dropped him on hearing the news of Jonathan's death. In those days, people didn't bother much with those who were disabled and couldn't earn a living, so David's kindness was a cultural surprise as well as an act of compassion by a family friend. David's actions on behalf of this disabled man are an example of the way things are in the kingdom of God, where all are welcome and all are valuable.

Visual aid

Use a pair of crutches—either real ones, if you can get hold of some, or perhaps made from upturned brooms—to experience what it's like to have to get about when one foot can't touch the ground.

Questions

▶ What do you think Mephibosheth thought about David, who had once been hated by his grandfather Saul? Might he perhaps have dreaded meeting David?

▶ What prompted David to make good his promise to Jonathan?

▶ Do you know anybody who is differently able? What sort of help do they need and in what ways can they help you?

▶ What difference to Mephibosheth's life did David's kindness make?

▶ What might Mephibosheth have done for David in return?

Activity idea

Talk about what it must be like to have a disability, such as not being able to walk, to use your hands, to see or to hear. Maybe you know someone you could talk to about this, or perhaps there's someone in the family who could share what it's like. Challenge each other to navigate around the room blindfolded, or to work out what people are saying when your ears are blocked, or to be carried when you want to move about, or to be helped to eat because you can't use your hands. Be sensitive, as this is an everyday experience for many people. What do you think is the best way to show concern for those who face challenges like these?

Prayer idea

Losing the use of a limb can often make people more grateful for the other abilities and senses that God has given them. Touch or wave different parts of your body in turn and thank God that you can see… hear… smell… taste… touch… walk. Then wave and move your whole body in one great shake of praise to God.

Key verse

'I will be kind… because I made a promise' (2 Samuel 9:1).

New Testament story link

Acts 3:1–10: Peter and John show kindness to a man who is lame.

David and Bathsheba

¹ It was now spring, the time when kings go to war. David sent out the whole Israelite army under the command of Joab and his officers. They destroyed the Ammonite army and surrounded the capital city of Rabbah, but David stayed in Jerusalem.

²⁻⁴ Late one afternoon, David got up from a nap and was walking around on the flat roof of his palace. A beautiful young woman was down below in her courtyard, bathing as her religion required. David happened to see her, and he sent one of his servants to find out who she was.

The servant came back and told David, 'Her name is Bathsheba. She is the daughter of Eliam, and she is the wife of Uriah the Hittite.'

David sent some messengers to bring her to his palace. She came to him, and he slept with her. Then she returned home. ⁵ But later, when she found out that she was going to have a baby, she sent someone to David with this message: 'I'm pregnant!'

⁶ David sent a message to Joab: 'Send Uriah the Hittite to me.'

Joab sent Uriah ⁷ to David's palace, and David asked him, 'Is Joab well? How is the army doing? And how about the war?' ⁸ Then David told Uriah, 'Go home and clean up.' Uriah left the king's palace, and David had dinner sent to Uriah's house. ⁹ But Uriah didn't go home. Instead, he slept outside the entrance to the royal palace, where the king's guards slept.

¹⁰ Someone told David that Uriah had not gone home. So the next morning David asked him, 'Why didn't you go home? Haven't you been away for a long time?'

¹¹ Uriah answered, 'The sacred chest and the armies of Israel and Judah are camping out somewhere in the fields with our commander Joab and his officers and troops. Do you really think I would go home to eat and drink and sleep with my wife? I swear by your life that I would not!'

¹² Then David said, 'Stay here in Jerusalem today, and I will send you back tomorrow.'

Uriah stayed in Jerusalem that day. Then the next day, ¹³ David invited him for dinner. Uriah ate with David and drank so much that he got drunk, but he still did not go home. He went out and slept on his mat near the palace guards. ¹⁴ Early the next morning, David wrote a letter and told Uriah to deliver it to Joab. ¹⁵ The letter said: 'Put Uriah on the front line where the fighting is the worst. Then pull the troops back from him, so that he will be wounded and die.'

2 SAMUEL 11:2–15

Commentary

This story has all the makings of a modern-day soap opera: unfaithfulness, lying, cheating and a desperate attempt to cover up a scandal that ends with a murder. The real shock is that it is David who is at the heart of all this—David, God's chosen king, a man after God's own heart, the very David who trusted in God and sang his praises so publicly. The Bible doesn't try to cover up the failings of even its greatest heroes. Believing in God doesn't mean that we are immune to temptation or that we will always make the right decisions in life. David should have been out fighting with his armies; instead he is home alone with time on his hands—time that he fills with wrong thoughts that lead to wrong actions. David's desperate attempt to try to hide the truth has terrible consequences.

King David was a flawed human being like the rest of us, and although he did eventually learn more about himself and God from these events, it only happened when he sincerely turned to God and said sorry.

Visual aid

Cover a small box with wrapping

Questions

▶ Why do you think David decided to stay home that spring and not lead his armies into battle?

▶ David gave in to temptation. What temptations do you struggle with?

▶ When Bathsheba told David she was pregnant, he tried to cover up his wrongdoing. What should he have done instead, do you think?

▶ Uriah proved himself to be a more committed soldier than David. Why do you think David went on making matters worse?

paper and write on it 'Private—do not touch'. Put it where everyone can see it. How tempting is it to peek inside? What excuses could you make, just to take a quick look?

Activity idea

In this story David made wrong decisions because he let his head be ruled by his heart. Make a list of some of the decisions that you make every day—for example, what to wear and what to eat; who to talk to and who to avoid; where to go and what to do in your spare time. For each of these, come up with two choices—one that would be very selfish and one that would be the right thing to do. Talk about how to resist temptation each time.

Prayer idea

A key line in the special prayer that

Jesus taught his followers is 'Keep us from being tempted'. Using a large clock face, move the hands to different times of the day. Talk about what each of you might be doing then—going to school, eating lunch, sitting at a desk, watching television—and then pray about each activity by saying, 'Help us to make right decisions and not end up in trouble.'

Key verse

'It was now spring, the time when kings go to war… but David stayed in Jerusalem' (2 Samuel 11:1).

New Testament story link

1 Peter 5:8–11: Peter gives advice to Christians who are facing trials and temptations.

The wisdom of Solomon

⁵ One night while Solomon was in Gibeon, the Lord God appeared to him in a dream and said, 'Solomon, ask for anything you want, and I will give it to you.'

⁶ Solomon answered:

My father David, your servant, was honest and did what you commanded. You were always loyal to him, and you gave him a son who is now king. ⁷ Lord God, I'm your servant, and you've made me king in my father's place. But I'm very young and know so little about being a leader. ⁸ And now I must rule your chosen people, even though there are too many of them to count.

⁹ Please make me wise and teach me the difference between right and wrong. Then I will know how to rule your people. If you don't, there is no way I could rule this great nation of yours.

¹⁰⁻¹¹ God said:

Solomon, I'm pleased that you asked for this. You could have asked to live a long time or to be rich. Or you could have asked for your enemies to be destroyed. Instead, you asked for wisdom to make right decisions. ¹² So I'll make you wiser than anyone who has ever lived or ever will live.

¹³ I'll also give you what you didn't ask for. You'll be rich and respected as long as you live, and you'll be greater than any other king. ¹⁴ If you obey me and follow my commands, as your father David did, I'll let you live a long time.

¹⁵ Solomon woke up and realised that God had spoken to him in the dream. He went back to Jerusalem and stood in front of the sacred chest, where he offered sacrifices to please the Lord and sacrifices to ask his blessing. Then Solomon gave a feast for his officials.

1 Kings 3:5–15

Commentary

This was not the first time that God had spoken to someone in a dream. Abraham, Jacob and Joseph had all heard God's voice in this way; and even though Solomon had been worshipping extravagantly and with all his heart that day, it was only when his conscious mind was resting that he heard God speaking to him.

God's invitation to Solomon is amazing! He can ask for whatever he wants. The very fact that Solomon does not take selfish advantage of this generous offer underlines that he is God's choice and David's true successor. His prayer reveals both humility and a deep sense of responsibility about his new role as king.

Asking for wisdom is not the same as asking for knowledge. Wisdom is about how we use what we know and, in particular, how we make good choices in life. Anyone in authority knows how important this is as they are faced every day with competing requests for their time and attention. God granted Solomon's prayer and a lot more besides. He became one of the richest kings in Israel's history, but, more importantly, he was a man who acted with justice and integrity. 'The wisdom of Solomon'

Questions

▶ What would you ask for if you could have anything you want?

▶ Solomon knew that he was still very young and being a good king would be hard work. What help do you need from God as you face each day?

▶ It is not always easy to decide what is right and what is wrong. Can you think of some choices that are particularly difficult to make?

▶ Solomon is given all he asks for and more. What do you think might have happened if he had asked for riches or long life instead?

has become a byword for the ability to know the right thing to do in the most difficult of circumstances. This sort of wisdom is a gift from God.

Visual aid

Use a pillow as a symbol of rest and dreams. Why do you think God might choose sometimes to speak to us when we are asleep?

Activity idea

Sometimes people keep something particularly precious under their pillow. Take turns to hide something precious under the pillow, then let the others rest their head upon it and try to guess what it might be. For Solomon it was his trust in God that was his most precious possession.

Prayer idea

Traditionally Christians have used special prayers before they go to sleep. A well-known Jewish prayer from the Psalms is one that Jesus himself might have used: 'Lord, into your hands I commit my spirit' (Psalm 31:5, NIV). Work together to compose a goodnight prayer that you can use as a family and say it before you go to bed each night.

Key verse

'Please make me wise and teach me the difference between right and wrong' (1 Kings 3:9).

New Testament story link

James 3:13–17: James describes what wisdom from God is like.

Building the temple

¹ King Hiram of Tyre had always been friends with Solomon's father David. When Hiram learned that Solomon was king, he sent some of his officials to meet with Solomon.

² Solomon sent a message back to Hiram:

³ Remember how my father David wanted to build a temple where the LORD his God could be worshipped? But enemies kept attacking my father's kingdom, and he never had the chance. ⁴ Now, thanks to the LORD God, there is peace in my kingdom and no trouble or threat of war anywhere.

⁵ The LORD God promised my father that when his son became king, he would build a temple for worshipping the LORD. So I've decided to do that.

⁶ I'd like you to have your workers cut down cedar trees in Lebanon for me. I will pay them whatever you say and will even have my workers help them. We both know that your workers are more experienced than anyone else at cutting timber.

⁷ Hiram was so happy when he heard Solomon's request that he said, 'I am grateful that the LORD gave David such a wise son to be king of that great nation!' ⁸ Then he sent back his answer:

I received your message and will give you all the cedar and pine logs you need. ⁹ My workers will carry them down from Lebanon to the Mediterranean Sea. They will tie the logs together and float them along the coast to wherever you want them. Then they will untie the logs, and your workers can take them from there.

To pay for the logs, you can provide the grain I need for my household.

¹⁰ Hiram gave Solomon all the cedar and pine logs he needed. ¹¹ In return, Solomon gave Hiram two thousand tonnes of wheat and four hundred thousand litres of pure olive oil each year.

¹² The LORD kept his promise and made Solomon wise. Hiram and Solomon signed a treaty and never went to war against each other.

1 KINGS 5:1–12

Commentary

King David had always wanted to build a magnificent temple in Jerusalem as a special place for people to worship, but God told him that this privilege would be his son's instead. A period of peace and stability for the nation gave King Solomon the opportunity he needed to begin the enterprise, but he needed friends such as the King of Tyre to make it possible. The tall cedar trees of Hiram's kingdom would provide wood for the floor, to line the walls and as beams for the roof. The whole project employed thousands of people and helped forge strong trading alliances with neighbouring kingdoms. The temple took seven years to build. When it was dedicated, there was a special service of worship where God's presence was powerfully felt and during which Solomon prayed publicly, pledging himself to be a faithful king and the true successor to his father David.

Visual aid

Find a picture of a cedar tree from a book or the internet. There are still cedar trees today in Lebanon, where King Hiram lived. This tree is also part of the design on the Lebanese flag.

Questions

▶ How do you think David felt when he learned that he was not going to be the one allowed to build a temple?

▶ According to the story, what led Solomon to start building the temple?

▶ If you were designing a special building to worship God, what would it look like?

▶ What materials and colours would you choose to create a special place for God?

Activity idea

Using Lego™, Duplo™ or wooden building blocks, build your own model version of the temple together. You can find suggestions of how it might have looked in a Bible encyclopedia or on the internet. There were steps up to the entrance, flanked by two tall pillars. Inside there were two main rooms—a larger one where the people gathered to worship and a special smaller room at the back, called the Holy of Holies, separated off by a curtain. Around the walls were storerooms.

Prayer idea

Pray together this adapted part of Solomon's prayer from the day when the temple was opened: 'There's not enough room in all of heaven for you, Lord God. How could you possibly live on earth in a temple? But we ask you to answer our prayer. Please watch over us day and night and listen when we turn towards you and pray' (based on 1 Kings 8:27–29).

Key verse

'The Lord God promised my father that when his son became king, he would build a temple for worshipping the Lord. So I've decided to do that' (1 Kings 5:5).

New Testament story link

Acts 7:44–50: One of the first Christian leaders of the church, Stephen, speaks about the holy tent and the temple once used by the people of Israel.

The kingdom divides

¹ Rehoboam went to Shechem where everyone was waiting to crown him king.

² Jeroboam son of Nebat heard what was happening, and he stayed in Egypt, where he had gone to hide from Solomon. ³ But the people from the northern tribes of Israel sent for him. Then together they went to Rehoboam and said, ⁴ 'Your father Solomon forced us to work very hard. But if you make our work easier, we will serve you and do whatever you ask.'

⁵ 'Give me three days to think about it,' Rehoboam replied, 'then come back for my answer.' So the people left.

⁶ Rehoboam went to some leaders who had been his father's senior officials, and he asked them, 'What should I tell these people?'

⁷ They answered, 'If you want them to serve and obey you, then you should do what they ask today. Tell them you will make their work easier.'

⁸ But Rehoboam refused their advice and went to the younger men who had grown up with him and were now his officials. ⁹ He asked, 'What do you think I should say to these people who asked me to make their work easier?'

¹⁰ His younger advisers said:

Here's what we think you should say to them: 'Compared to me, my father was weak. ¹¹ He made you work hard, but I'll make you work even harder. He punished you with whips, but I'll use whips with pieces of sharp metal!'

¹² Three days later, Jeroboam and the others came back. ¹³ Rehoboam ignored the advice of the older advisers. ¹⁴ He spoke bluntly and told them exactly what his own advisers had suggested: 'My father made you work hard, but I'll make you work even harder. He punished you with whips, but I'll use whips with pieces of sharp metal!'

¹⁵⁻¹⁶ When the people realised that Rehoboam would not listen to them, they shouted: 'We don't have to be loyal to David's family. We can do what we want. Come on, people of Israel, let's go home! Rehoboam can rule his own people.'

1 Kings 12:1–16

Commentary

Despite his wealth and wisdom, Solomon did not stay faithful to God towards the end of his life. In addition, there were already seeds of rebellion that had been sown during his reign and earlier. Many Israelites, particularly those who belonged to the northern tribes, were ready to declare independence from the king's rule in Jerusalem. It only needed one incident to split the kingdom, and Solomon's son Rehoboam provided them with exactly the excuse they needed to rebel. He handled their request for better working conditions badly, listening to the advice of his contemporaries rather than the wiser words offered by his father's officials. His attempt to play the strong man only served to alienate the ten northern tribes, who later chose Jeroboam as their new king.

From this time on, the history of God's people is divided between that of Israel in the north and that of Judah in the south. Kings from each part sometimes followed God and sometimes didn't. As time went by, a whole country's security and wealth was whittled away and they became increasingly vulnerable to attacks from the more powerful nations that surrounded them.

Questions

▶ Solomon married many times (as was the custom in those days), but some of his wives believed in other gods. Why do you think Solomon listened to his wives rather than remaining loyal to the one true God?

▶ Why didn't Rehoboam listen to the advice of his father's officials?

▶ Rehoboam's response to the rebels was to be even harsher than he had been before. What should he have done?

▶ Why hadn't Rehoboam inherited any of his father's wisdom?

Visual aid

Take a piece of old cloth and tear it into twelve pieces; place two on one side and ten on the other. This is what a prophet named Ahijah did when he spoke with a man called Jeroboam, to illustrate what would happen to Solomon's kingdom (1 Kings 11:29–32). Jeroboam later became a rival king to Rehoboam.

Activity idea

Talk about a disagreement that you have had in the family—perhaps over what TV programme to watch or where to go on a family outing or about how someone seems to have been treated unfairly. How did you resolve it? Rehoboam doesn't seem to have prayed about his problem. How might praying help you solve problems in the family?

Prayer idea

Use the strips of cloth you have torn up to help you pray. Looking ahead to any big decisions that you need to make as a family, use the ten pieces to put down as arguments for or against doing one thing or the other. Use the two pieces to make a cross to remind you also to consider what Jesus would want you to do in this situation.

Key verse

'Rehoboam ignored the advice of the older advisers' (1 Kings 12:13).

New Testament story link

1 Peter 5:3–7: Peter gives good advice about how to show respect to others when discussing things together.

Elijah stops the rain

[1] Elijah was a prophet from Tishbe in Gilead. One day he went to King Ahab and said, 'I'm a servant of the living LORD, the God of Israel. And I swear in his name that it won't rain until I say so. There won't even be any dew on the ground.'

[2] Later, the LORD said to Elijah, [3] 'Leave and go across the Jordan River so you can hide near Cherith Brook. [4] You can drink water from the brook, and eat the food I've told the ravens to bring you.'

[5] Elijah obeyed the LORD and went to live near Cherith Brook. [6] Ravens brought him bread and meat twice a day, and he drank water from the brook. [7] But after a while, it dried up because there was no rain.

[8] The LORD told Elijah, [9] 'Go to the town of Zarephath in Sidon and live there. I've told a widow in that town to give you food.'

[10] When Elijah came near the town gate of Zarephath, he saw a widow gathering sticks for a fire. 'Would you please bring me a cup of water?' he asked. [11] As she left to get it, he asked, 'Would you also please bring me a piece of bread?'

[12] The widow answered, 'In the name of the living LORD your God, I swear that I don't have any bread. All I have is a handful of flour and a little olive oil. I'm on my way home now with these few sticks to cook what I have for my son and me. After that, we will starve to death.'

[13] Elijah said, 'Everything will be fine. Do what you said. Go home and fix something for you and your son. But first, please make a small piece of bread and bring it to me. [14] The LORD God of Israel has promised that your jar of flour won't run out and your bottle of oil won't dry up before he sends rain for the crops.'

[15] The widow went home and did exactly what Elijah had told her. She and Elijah and her family had enough food for a long time. [16] The LORD kept the promise that his prophet Elijah had made, and she did not run out of flour or oil.

1 KINGS 17:1–16

Commentary

Things went from bad to worse for God's people, particularly those in the northern kingdom of Israel. King Ahab came to the throne after a series of short-lived reigns by his predecessors, all of whom had abandoned their faith in the one true God and turned to worship man-made gods. King Ahab was no different, and in particular he is remembered for marrying a non-Jew called Jezebel, who reintroduced the worship of a local god called Baal. God had warned all these kings through various prophets, but each had ignored him.

Now Ahab is confronted by Elijah, whose prediction of a long drought is the beginning of many years of tense dealings between the two men. God miraculously provides Elijah with food and drink in the desert, and also through the kindness of a widow in Jezebel's own home country, where, ironically, Elijah finds a safe haven from Ahab. The widow's hospitality is rewarded by a miracle when her oil and flour containers never hit empty for as long as Elijah stays with her. Notice the contrast between Jezebel from Sidon, who suffers from the drought, and the poor widow from Sidon, whom God looks after.

Questions

▶ How difficult do you think it was for Elijah to give God's message to the king?

▶ Why did so many kings of Israel turn away from worshipping God? God had warned them again and again, so why didn't they listen?

▶ Why is it so easy to forget God when things are going well?

▶ God looked after Elijah while he was in hiding. How have you experienced God's help and protection in tough times?

Visual aid

Fill a small jar with oil and another with flour. Imagine what it would be like if this was all you had left to feed yourself and your family.

Activity idea

Make some bread together following a simple recipe. Use flour, water and a little oil and then roll out the dough. As you do, talk about what it must be like to live on very little and not know where your next meal is coming from.

Prayer idea

Make a list together of the times you use water for washing, cooking, flushing the toilet, cleaning your teeth, drinking and so on. Many parts of the world suffer from drought. Changes in our climate are often blamed, as well as the irresponsible management of our planet's resources. Find out about a part of the world where there is drought at the moment and, using your own prayers or prayer ideas from a website or an aid magazine, pray for the people who are suffering.

Key verse

'The Lord God of Israel has promised that your jar of flour won't run out and your bottle of oil won't dry up before he sends rain for the crops' (1 Kings 17:14).

New Testament story link

Acts 11:27–30: Read about how the church in Antioch responded to news that there would be a famine affecting many people.

The contest on the mountain

26 [Baal's prophets] chose their bull, then they got it ready and prayed to Baal all morning, asking him to start the fire. They danced around the altar and shouted, 'Answer us, Baal!' But there was no answer.

27 At noon, Elijah began making fun of them. 'Pray louder!' he said. 'Baal must be a god. Perhaps he's daydreaming or using the toilet or travelling somewhere. Or perhaps he's asleep, and you have to wake him up.'

28 The prophets kept shouting louder and louder, and they cut themselves with swords and knives until they were bleeding. This was the way they worshipped, 29 and they kept it up all afternoon. But there was no answer of any kind.

30 Elijah told everyone to gather around him while he repaired the LORD's altar. 31–32 Then he used twelve stones to build an altar in honour of the LORD. Each stone stood for one of the tribes of Israel, which was the name the LORD had given to their ancestor Jacob. Elijah dug a ditch around the altar, large enough to hold almost fourteen litres. 33 He placed the wood on the altar, then they cut the bull into pieces and laid the meat on the wood.

He told the people, 'Fill four large jars with water and pour it over the meat and the wood.' After they did this, 34 he told them to do it two more times. They did exactly as he said 35 until finally, the water ran down the altar and filled the ditch.

36 When it was time for the evening sacrifice, Elijah prayed:

Our LORD, you are the God of Abraham, Isaac, and Israel. Now, prove that you are the God of this nation, and that I, your servant, have done this at your command. 37 Please answer me, so these people will know that you are the LORD God, and that you will turn their hearts back to you.

38 The LORD immediately sent fire, and it burned up the sacrifice, the wood, and the stones. It scorched the ground everywhere around the altar and dried up every drop of water in the ditch. 39 When the crowd saw what had happened, they all bowed down and shouted, 'The LORD is God! The LORD is God!'

1 KINGS 18:26–39

Commentary

After three years of hiding during the drought, it was now time for Elijah to face King Ahab again. The contest that follows is one of the most memorable stories in the Old Testament. Ahab is mocked by Elijah as someone who can't decide which god to worship, and Elijah challenges the king's so-called prophets to a public duel on Mount Carmel.

The scene is described quite comically at times as the hundreds of followers of Baal try to force their god to act, while the lonely but confident figure of Elijah orders his altar to be drenched with water, so determined is he to make it clear that this will be a genuine answer to prayer. He doesn't need to shout at God or dance about or cut himself.

Elijah's motivation was a desire, not to be proved right, but to see the nation turn back to God. Just as Moses had encountered a fire that did not burn up a bush on Mount Sinai, so here on Mount Carmel Elijah and all the people witness a fire that burns and that no amount of water can quench. This is the holy fire of God, later described as the fire of the Holy Spirit.

Questions

▶ The odds against Elijah in this contest were huge: over 850 to 1. How can God's victory for Elijah be an encouragement for you at the moment?

▶ The prophets of Baal believed that they could make their god do what they wanted him to do. Do we sometimes treat God like this?

▶ Pick out the many ways Elijah showed courage in this amazing story.

▶ How can we show that we trust in the one true God when many people around us don't?

Visual aid

Using twelve small stones, construct a model altar like the one that Elijah built on Mount Carmel. The stones stood for each of the twelve tribes, so Elijah was, in effect, putting the nation back together again, as God had always intended it to be.

Activity idea

Tell the story again to each other, adding lots of sound effects for the noisy, crazy prophets. When it comes to Elijah's part, simply recreate the sounds of stones being placed on each other, water being poured, and the whisper of a quiet prayer.

Prayer idea

True prayer doesn't have to be full of loud words. Use the simple words of the Lord's Prayer together (see page 254). It can be reduced further to nine key words: Father, Heaven, Holy, Kingdom, Will, Give, Forgive, Guide and Deliver. Say these words together slowly, allowing pictures from God to form in your mind.

Key verse

'When the crowd saw what had happened, they all bowed down and shouted, 'The Lord is God! The Lord is God!' (1 Kings 18:39).

New Testament story link

James 5:16–18: James uses the example of Elijah's prayer life as an inspiration for ours.

Earthquake, fire and whisper

⁹ᵇ While Elijah was on Mount Sinai, the LORD asked, 'Elijah, why are you here?'

¹⁰ He answered, 'LORD God All-Powerful, I've always done my best to obey you. But your people have broken their solemn promise to you. They have torn down your altars and killed all your prophets, except me. And now they are even trying to kill me!'

¹¹ 'Go out and stand on the mountain,' the LORD replied. 'I want you to see me when I pass by.'

All at once, a strong wind shook the mountain and shattered the rocks. But the LORD was not in the wind. Next, there was an earthquake, but the LORD was not in the earthquake. ¹² Then there was a fire, but the LORD was not in the fire.

Finally, there was a gentle breeze, ¹³ and when Elijah heard it, he covered his face with his coat. He went out and stood at the entrance to the cave.

The LORD asked, 'Elijah, why are you here?'

¹⁴ Elijah answered, 'LORD God All-Powerful, I've always done my best to obey you. But your people have broken their solemn promise to you. They have torn down your altars and killed all your prophets, except me. And now they are even trying to kill me!'

¹⁵ The LORD said:

Elijah, you can go back to the desert near Damascus. And when you get there, appoint Hazael to be king of Syria. ¹⁶ Then appoint Jehu son of Nimshi to be king of Israel, and Elisha son of Shaphat to take your place as my prophet. ¹⁷ Hazael will start killing the people who worship Baal. Jehu will kill those who escape from Hazael, and Elisha will kill those who escape from Jehu. ¹⁸ But seven thousand Israelites have refused to worship Baal, and they will live.

1 KINGS 19:9b–18

Commentary

How different Elijah seems in this story! Suddenly this fearless and prayerful prophet appears weak and vulnerable. He is on the run and in hiding from Queen Jezebel, full of doubt and fear and struggling to pray. Despite the amazing victory on Mount Carmel, all he feels is despair that evil still triumphs in Israel. Even this godly man can be fragile at times. God isn't into creating superheroes. Christians get frightened too and sometimes feel like running away, just as Elijah did. But God hadn't abandoned Elijah, nor does he abandon any of us. He guides, supports and waits patiently to take us on to new things.

Mount Sinai was the holy mountain, and clearly Elijah hoped to meet with God in a powerful way there, just as Moses had done in the past. However, God's voice wasn't in the drama and noise—not even in the fire, as it had been on Mount Carmel—but in the gentle whisper of a breeze. God has new plans for Elijah, and reminds him that he has never been alone. There were always many others who still believed in God. This is the comfort that Elijah and all of us need to hear.

Visual aid

Using a large piece of cardboard in the shape of a giant flame, coloured in with red, yellow and orange, make the sounds that are associated with an earthquake (use it like a wobble board) and ripple the board from top to bottom like a flame. This same board can also be used to create the effect of a very gentle breeze.

Activity idea

Imagine and re-enact Elijah's long journey to the mountain by running on the spot; pretending to trudge through the hot and dry desert; moaning and complaining; sleeping and then waking to a miraculous meal, supplied by an angel; walking for days in the heat; and finally climbing a very high mountain. Tell each other how you feel. Was this long journey perhaps a way for Elijah to work out his frustrations and disappointment before he

Questions

▶ Why do you think Elijah ran away from Jezebel? Surely the victory on Mount Carmel had proved to him that he did not need to be afraid of her?

▶ Elijah is depressed. How does God help him to move out of his depression?

▶ Elijah is also very angry that Jezebel and her prophets still have the upper hand. What makes you angry with God?

▶ What might we learn from this passage about how God speaks?

could properly hear God speaking again?

Prayer idea

In some Bibles the gentle breeze of God is translated as a 'still small voice'. In a time of prayer, make space for God to speak as you listen to some gentle sounds together—for example, quiet music on a CD, the sound of water running, sounds of nature outside, or even just the sound of your own breathing. Share together what God may have said to you.

Key verse

'Finally, there was a gentle breeze, and when Elijah heard it, he covered his face with his coat' (1 Kings 19:12–13).

New Testament story link

Luke 6:12–13: Jesus goes up a mountain to listen for the voice of God about who to choose to be his disciples.

Naboth's vineyard

¹ Naboth owned a vineyard in Jezreel near King Ahab's palace.

² One day, Ahab said, 'Naboth, your vineyard is near my palace. Give it to me so I can turn it into a vegetable garden. I'll give you a better vineyard or pay whatever you want for yours.'

³ Naboth answered, 'This vineyard has always been in my family. I won't let you have it.'

⁴ So Ahab went home, angry and depressed because of what Naboth had told him. He lay on his bed, just staring at the wall and refusing to eat a thing.

⁵ Jezebel his wife came in and asked, 'What's wrong? Why won't you eat?'

⁶ 'I asked Naboth to sell me his vineyard or to let me give him a better one,' Ahab replied. 'And he told me I couldn't have it.'

⁷ 'Aren't you the king of Israel?' Jezebel asked. 'Get out of bed and eat something! Don't worry, I'll get Naboth's vineyard for you.'

⁸⁻¹⁰ Jezebel wrote a letter to each of the leaders of the town where Naboth lived. In the letters she said:

Call everyone together and tell them to go without eating today. When they come together, give Naboth a seat at the front. Have two liars sit across from him and swear that Naboth has cursed God and the king. Then take Naboth outside and stone him to death!

She signed Ahab's name to the letters and sealed them with his seal. Then she sent them to the town leaders.

¹¹ After receiving her letters, they did exactly what she had asked. ¹² They told the people that it was a day to go without eating, and when they all came together, they seated Naboth at the front. ¹³ The two liars came in and sat across from Naboth. Then they accused him of cursing God and the king, so the people dragged Naboth outside and stoned him to death.

¹⁴ The leaders of Jezreel sent a message back to Jezebel that said, 'Naboth is dead.'

¹⁵ As soon as Jezebel got their message, she told Ahab, 'Now you can have the vineyard Naboth refused to sell. He's dead.' ¹⁶ Ahab got up and went to take over the vineyard.

1 KINGS 21:1–16

Commentary

Even though King Ahab and Queen Jezebel had been humiliated by what had happened at Mount Carmel (see page 78), they were still on the throne of Israel and showed no sign of changing their wicked ways. Naboth is murdered just so that Ahab can have a vegetable garden conveniently close to his palace.

Ahab shows no respect for Naboth's family inheritance and sulks angrily at not getting his own way, while Jezebel's carefully planned murder makes her one of the greatest villains of the Bible. Sadly, people like Naboth still suffer injustice today at the hands of those who hold money and power. This story goes on to assure us that God does see what is done and does care. He sends his prophet Elijah to challenge the king and queen and call them to account for their actions. Likewise, Christians are called to stand up for those who are treated unfairly and to insist that God's ways are different. God is always on the side of the poor and those who have no one to speak up for them.

Visual aid

Use a bunch of grapes as a focus for this story. Naboth's vineyard had been in his family for many years and this suggests that the crop would have been of a very high quality.

Activity idea

Imagine you are lawyers in court acting on behalf of Naboth. How would you go about defending him from Ahab and Jezebel, and can you find a solution to the problem to prevent it getting out of hand?

Prayer idea

We often associate certain colours with our moods and behaviours. In this story, for example, there could be green for jealousy, red for anger, blue for the feeling of depression and yellow for the cowardly behaviour of those employed by Jezebel to accuse Naboth. Using some coloured cards, pray about something that has happened to you recently and ask God to help you turn your negative feelings into more positive ones, such as green for fruitfulness, red for laughter, blue for clarity and yellow for happiness.

Questions

▶ Jezebel is clearly the real power behind the throne. How is it possible to stand up to bullies like her in everyday life?

▶ Why do you think God didn't send Elijah to intervene sooner and so perhaps save Naboth's life?

▶ This story is full of some of the worst behaviours people can show to each other. Why do we sometimes act like this?

▶ Ahab didn't seem to have any conscience about what happened to Naboth. Why do you think he could no longer tell right from wrong?

Key verse

'So Ahab went home, angry and depressed because of what Naboth had told him' (1 Kings 21:4).

New Testament story link

Matthew 5:17–20: Jesus reminds us of God's commandments, such as 'Do not murder'.

Elijah's chariot

[7] Fifty prophets followed Elijah and Elisha from Jericho, then stood at a distance and watched as the two men walked towards the river. [8] When they got there, Elijah took off his coat, then he rolled it up and struck the water with it. At once a path opened up through the river, and the two of them walked across on dry ground.

[9] After they had reached the other side, Elijah said, 'Elisha, the LORD will soon take me away. What can I do for you before that happens?'

Elisha answered, 'Please give me twice as much of your power as you give the other prophets, so I can be the one who takes your place as their leader.'

[10] 'It won't be easy,' Elijah answered. 'It can happen only if you see me as I am being taken away.'

[11] Elijah and Elisha were walking along and talking, when suddenly there appeared between them a flaming chariot pulled by fiery horses. Straight away, a strong wind took Elijah up into heaven. [12] Elisha saw this and shouted, 'Israel's cavalry and chariots have taken my master away!' After Elijah had gone, Elisha tore his clothes in sorrow.

[13] Elijah's coat had fallen off, so Elisha picked it up and walked back to the River Jordan. [14] He struck the water with the coat and wondered, 'Will the LORD perform miracles for me as he did for Elijah?' As soon as Elisha did this, a dry path opened up through the water, and he walked across.

[15] When the prophets from Jericho saw what happened, they said to each other, 'Elisha now has Elijah's power.'

They walked over to him, bowed down, [16] and said, 'There are fifty strong men here with us. Please let them go and look for your master. Maybe the Spirit of the LORD carried him off to some mountain or valley.'

'No,' Elisha replied, 'they won't find him.'

[17] They kept begging until he was embarrassed to say no. He finally agreed, and the prophets sent the men out. They looked three days for Elijah but never found him. [18] They returned to Jericho, and Elisha said, 'I told you that you wouldn't find him.'

2 KINGS 2:7–18

Commentary

Elijah is one of the most remarkable men of God in the Old Testament. Though so often in hiding, when he did turn up to speak on God's behalf, he was uncompromising and courageous. God used him to perform miracles and, most importantly, to challenge King Ahab and his wife Jezebel, who had led Israel into increasing faithlessness. Elijah regularly reminded everyone of the true God and of how God should be worshipped and served. Elisha was his young apprentice, who longed to be like his master.

When the time came for Elijah to die, Elisha wanted to stay close, because to receive a blessing from Elijah would confirm him as Elijah's true successor. There were other prophets too, but it was Elisha who stayed closest to Elijah and even saw him swept up to heaven in a chariot made of fire. He took on Elijah's job, and he also inherited his God-given powers to perform miracles—solid evidence that God was at work. Elijah's body was never found, and he is therefore one of only two people in the Old Testament who walked straight from this life into heaven. Elijah's cloak was now Elisha's as he started out on his work for God in his generation.

Questions

▶ Elisha was a devoted follower of Elijah. He wouldn't let him out of his sight. Who inspires you like this?

▶ Elisha was, in effect, a disciple of Elijah, like the disciples of Jesus. What does being a disciple mean?

▶ Why did God choose to take Elijah to heaven in this dramatic way?

▶ Elijah's miraculous crossing of the River Jordan reminded people of how God had done the same for Joshua and the Israelites centuries before. What else does it remind you of?

Visual aid

Find a piece of clothing that has been handed down in your family—maybe from a parent to a child or from an older child to a sibling. Elijah's cloak was like a badge of office that was passed on to Elisha.

Activity idea

This story has inspired one of the most famous African-American spirituals, 'Swing low, sweet chariot'. Look up the words on the internet. Perhaps you can listen to it being sung or even try singing it yourselves. It is all about the sure promise of heaven that awaits Christians, as it did Elijah. Talk together about what you think heaven is like.

Prayer idea

Elisha learned about God by watching and listening to Elijah. We do the same as we read about and talk with Jesus in prayer every day. Ask God to help you do what Jesus would do.

Key verse

'Elisha answered, "Please give me twice as much of your power as you give the other prophets, so I can be the one who takes your place as their leader"' (2 Kings 2:9).

New Testament story link

Luke 24:44–49: These are some of the last words of Jesus to his disciples before he left them. He promised them that God's power would be passed on to them.

Naaman is healed

[1b] Naaman was a brave soldier, but he had leprosy. [2] One day while the Syrian troops were raiding Israel, they captured a girl, and she became a servant of Naaman's wife. [3] Some time later the girl said, 'If your husband Naaman would go to the prophet in Samaria, he would be cured of his leprosy.'

[4] When Naaman told the king what the girl had said, [5] the king replied, 'Go ahead! I will give you a letter to take to the king of Israel.'

Naaman left and took along thirty thousand pieces of silver, six thousand pieces of gold, and ten new outfits. [6] He also carried the letter to the king of Israel. It said, 'I am sending my servant Naaman to you. Would you cure him of his leprosy?'

[7] When the king of Israel read the letter, he tore his clothes in fear and shouted, 'That Syrian king believes I can cure this man of leprosy! Does he think I'm God with power over life and death? He must be trying to pick a fight with me.'

[8] As soon as Elisha the prophet heard what had happened, he sent the Israelite king this message: 'Why are you so afraid? Send the man to me, so that he will know there is a prophet in Israel.'

[9] Naaman left with his horses and chariots and stopped at the door of Elisha's house. [10] Elisha sent someone outside to say to him, 'Go and wash seven times in the River Jordan. Then you'll be completely cured.'

[11] But Naaman stormed off, grumbling, 'Why couldn't he come out and talk to me? I thought he would be sure to stand in front of me and pray to the LORD his God, then wave his hand over my skin and cure me. [12] What about the River Abana or the River Pharpar? Those rivers in Damascus are just as good as any river in Israel. I could have washed in them and been cured.'

[13] His servants went over to him and said, 'Sir, if the prophet had told you to do something difficult, you would have done it. So why don't you do what he said? Go and wash and be cured.'

[14] Naaman walked down to the Jordan; he waded out into the water and stooped down in it seven times, just as Elisha had told him. Straight away, he was cured, and his skin became as smooth as a child's.

2 KINGS 5:1b–14

Commentary

Interestingly, it is the young servant girl who truly understands what God is like. She knows that God is with the prophet Elisha and that God can do miracles. She must have learned this when she was very small, and she had held on to her faith even as a slave in a foreign country.

Naaman and the king of Syria both imagine that God's power can be bought for the right price or that some sort of trickery must be involved. For example, Naaman takes a huge amount of money and presents with him to buy healing for his skin disease. But the king of Israel is no better. Clearly he didn't believe God could help, and instead saw the whole episode as some sort of provocation to war. Even when Naaman is instructed to wash in the River Jordan, he doesn't think much of Elisha's methods. He expects a 'magic wand' sort of God, not a healing that involves his being humbled. However, that was the only way he could be made well. God's ways are different and involve starting all over again, just like little children. It took a child to see this at the beginning, and eventually Naaman, like a child, learned it at the end.

Questions

▶ What do you think of the servant girl's courage in speaking up about faith in God to her foreign employer?

▶ Why do you think Naaman chose to listen to her?

▶ Why was Naaman so offended by Elisha's instructions?

▶ Why do you think Naaman finally agreed to wash in the river?

Visual aid

Use a bar of soap as a focus for this story. Naaman wanted to be really clean in a way that even the best soap could not provide.

Activity idea

Each of you take a different character in the story—for example, the servant girl, Naaman's wife, Naaman, the Syrian king, the Israelite king, Elisha or his servant. Now invite each character in turn to retell the story from his or her own point of view. What more can you learn about the story by exploring it in this way?

Prayer idea

For your prayer time, imagine each part of you in turn coming under the shower of God's special washing—for example, your head (washing away unhelpful thoughts); your heart (washing away selfishness); your hands (washing away any bad activities you've been involved in); your feet (washing away the memory of unhelpful places where you have been). Christians believe that because of what Jesus did, the Holy Spirit can wash us clean on the inside like this.

Key verse

'Straight away, he was cured, and his skin became as smooth as a child's' (2 Kings 5:14).

New Testament story link

Luke 4:20–29: Jesus mentions the story of Naaman in his talk in his local synagogue. Even people in his own town had wrong ideas about God.

Joash repairs the temple

[1] Joash became king of Judah in Jehu's seventh year as king of Israel, and he ruled forty years from Jerusalem. His mother Zibiah was from the town of Beersheba.

[2] Jehoiada the priest taught Joash what was right, and so for the rest of his life Joash obeyed the Lord. [3] But even Joash did not destroy the local shrines, and they were still used as places for offering sacrifices.

[4] One day, Joash said to the priests, 'Collect all the money that has been given to the Lord's temple, whether from taxes or gifts, [5] and use it to repair the temple. You priests can contribute your own money too.'

[6] But the priests never started repairing the temple. So in the twenty-third year of his rule, [7] Joash called for Jehoiada and the other priests and said, 'Why aren't you using the money to repair the temple? Don't take any more money for yourselves. It is only to be used pay for the repairs.' [8] The priests agreed that they would not collect any more money or be in charge of the temple repairs.

[9] Jehoiada found a wooden box; he cut a hole in the top of it and set it on the right side of the altar where people went into the temple. Whenever someone gave money to the temple, the priests guarding the entrance would put it into this box. [10] When the box was full of money, the king's secretary and the chief priest would count the money and put it in bags. [11] Then they would give it to the men supervising the repairs to the temple. Some of the money was used to pay the builders, the woodworkers, [12] the stonecutters, and the men who built the walls. And some was used to buy wood and stone and to pay any other costs for repairing the temple.

[13] While the repairs were being made, the money that was given to the temple was not used to make silver bowls, lamp snuffers, small sprinkling bowls, trumpets, or anything gold or silver for the temple. [14] It went only to pay for repairs. [15] The men in charge were honest, so no one had to keep track of the money.

2 Kings 12:1–15

Commentary

Joash became king of Judah when he was only seven years old. His story of survival is a remarkable one, because he had to be rescued as a baby by his aunt from his grandmother, who had seized the throne and wanted to murder all her rivals. For six years he was hidden in the temple in Jerusalem by the priest, who later had him crowned as king. No wonder the temple was a special place for Joash and that he arranged for money to be collected to repair the magnificent building that Solomon had built a century earlier. Sadly the funds were mismanaged and were used to buy new items rather than for repairs. Joash had to intervene and employ security guards to make sure that the money put in the large wooden chest was used for the right purposes.

There is always a risk that money doesn't get to the causes for which it is given. This story reminds us that God is concerned about how well we look after our own money and any money that is entrusted to us for other people's benefit.

Visual aid

Use a piggy bank as a focus. Drop in some of the loose change that

Questions

▶ If you had become king or queen, like Joash, at a young age, what would be the first things that you did for the good of the country?

▶ The temple was clearly a special place for Joash. What special place or places do you have, where you go to feel close to God?

▶ How difficult do you find it to save up for something that is not for yourself?

▶ Joash chose honest people to be in charge of the money. What does it mean to be an honest person?

you can find around the house to provide sound effects for the story.

Activity idea

Make your own special family collecting box. You could decorate an empty container from the kitchen and make a slit in the top. Decide together what special cause you will save up for in the coming weeks.

Prayer idea

Give everyone in the family a small coin. Use the coin and its design to prompt you to pray for those who govern your country, those who do not have much money, those who buy and sell in the shops nearby, those who look after local banks and businesses, and those who don't think they're very valuable. Now

look for the letters FD on the coin, which in Latin stand for 'defender of the faith'. Pray for those who speak up for Christianity in your country. Now look for the date on the coin. Use this to pray for those who were born in that year or for any other associations with the number that come to mind.

Key verse

'Jehoiada the priest taught Joash what is right, and so for the rest of his life Joash obeyed the Lord' (2 Kings 12:2).

New Testament story link

2 Timothy 3:14–17: Timothy had learned about God from a young age, just as Joash had.

Jonah runs away

¹ One day the LORD told Jonah, the son of Amittai, ² to go to the great city of Nineveh and say to the people, 'The LORD has seen your terrible sins. You are doomed!'

³ Instead, Jonah ran from the LORD. He went to the seaport of Joppa and bought a ticket on a ship that was going to Spain. Then he got on the ship and sailed away to escape.

⁴ But the LORD made a strong wind blow, and such a bad storm came up that the ship was about to be broken to pieces. ⁵ The sailors were frightened, and they all started praying to their gods. They even threw the ship's cargo overboard to make the ship lighter.

All this time, Jonah was down below deck, sound asleep. ⁶ The ship's captain went to him and said, 'How can you sleep at a time like this? Get up and pray to your God! Maybe he will have pity on us and keep us from drowning.'

⁷ Finally, the sailors got together and said, 'Let's ask our gods to show us who caused all this trouble.' It turned out to be Jonah.

⁸ They started asking him, 'Are you the one who brought all this trouble on us? What business are you in? Where do you come from? What is your country? Who are your people?'

⁹ Jonah answered, 'I'm a Hebrew, and I worship the LORD God of heaven, who made the sea and the dry land.'

¹⁰ When the sailors heard this, they were frightened, because Jonah had already told them he was running from the LORD. Then they said, 'Do you know what you have done?'

¹¹ The storm kept getting worse, until finally the sailors asked him, 'What should we do with you to make the sea calm down?'

¹² Jonah told them, 'Throw me into the sea, and it will calm down. I'm the cause of this terrible storm.'

¹³ The sailors tried their best to row to the shore. But they could not do it, and the storm kept getting worse every minute. ¹⁴ So they prayed to the LORD, 'Please don't let us drown for taking this man's life. Don't hold us guilty for killing an innocent man. All of this happened because you wanted it to.' ¹⁵ Then they threw Jonah overboard, and the sea calmed down...

¹⁷ The LORD sent a big fish to swallow Jonah, and Jonah was inside the fish for three days and three nights.

JONAH 1:1–15, 17

Commentary

Nineveh was the capital of Assyria, the superpower of Jonah's day and Israel's arch-enemy. So when Jonah is told to go and tell the people of Nineveh that God's judgement is coming on them, it perhaps appears odd at first that he decides to run away. But Jonah realises that God wants them to change their ways, so Jonah will, in effect, be giving them a second chance. As a patriotic Israelite, Jonah simply wants them destroyed.

On board ship in the middle of the storm, it is interesting to note how reluctant the foreign sailors are to get rid of Jonah, even when he offers himself to be thrown overboard. Jonah is discovering that outsiders are not to be hated, because God loves them and, in the case of the sailors, they can show compassion too. Even deadly enemies are given the hope of a new beginning. It is really Jonah who needs to change his ways as much as, and perhaps even more than, the people of Nineveh.

Questions

▶ Why, do you imagine, did Jonah think he could run away from God?

▶ How might you react if God asked you to give a second chance to people you didn't like?

▶ Was Jonah being a hero by offering to be thrown overboard, or was he just trying to run away again?

▶ What do you think was Jonah's biggest mistake?

Visual aid

Use a model boat that you can float on some water, perhaps in the bath. Re-enact the storm through which, amazingly, Jonah managed to sleep.

Activity idea

Use any simple props to hand—chairs, a table, pieces of cardboard, fabric—and build a boat to act out what happened on board Jonah's boat. Jonah sleeps; the sailors battle the storm; the crew pray and then throw cargo overboard; they wake Jonah and question him; they try their best to rescue him; they throw him overboard. Which part of the story do you think is the most important part?

Prayer idea

The sailors pray a lot in this story, but Jonah, who is God's prophet, doesn't seem to pray at all. On a large piece of paper, draw the outline of a simple boat with sails, oars, a prow and a rudder. Use each part of the boat as a focus for your prayers: the prow (ask God to guide you where you should go every day); the rudder (ask God to steer you away from places of danger); the oars (ask God to help you work hard for him each day); and the sails (ask God to fill you with the wind of his Holy Spirit).

Key verse

'I'm the cause of this terrible storm' (Jonah 1:12).

New Testament story link

Mark 4:35–41: The disciples find themselves caught in a storm, but Jesus rescues them.

Jonah is angry

¹ Jonah was really upset and angry. ² So he prayed:

Our LORD, I knew from the very beginning that you wouldn't destroy Nineveh. That's why I left my own country and headed for Spain. You are a kind and merciful God, and you are very patient. You always show love, and you don't like to punish anyone, not even foreigners.
   ³ Now let me die! I'd be better off dead.

⁴ The LORD replied, 'What right do you have to be angry?'
⁵ Jonah then left through the east gate of the city and made a shelter to protect himself from the sun. He sat under the shelter, waiting to see what would happen to Nineveh.
⁶ The LORD made a vine grow up to shade Jonah's head and protect him from the sun. Jonah was very happy to have the vine, ⁷ but early the next morning the LORD sent a worm to chew on the vine, and the vine dried up. ⁸ During the day the LORD sent a scorching wind, and the sun beat down on Jonah's head, making him feel faint. Jonah was ready to die, and he shouted, 'I wish I were dead!'
⁹ But the LORD asked, 'Jonah, do you have the right to be angry about the vine?'
   'Yes, I do,' he answered, 'and I'm angry enough to die.'

¹⁰ But the LORD said:

You are concerned about a vine that you did not plant or take care of, a vine that grew up in one night and died the next. ¹¹ In that city of Nineveh there are more than a hundred and twenty thousand people who cannot tell right from wrong, and many cattle are also there. Don't you think I should be concerned about that big city?

JONAH 4

Commentary

What a moaner Jonah turns out to be! He seems to be the sort of person who is never happy, whatever happens. In this part of the story he is angry because his preaching has been successful. The Ninevites have turned away from doing bad things and they have said sorry to God. Most people would be overjoyed to see this happen, but Jonah still can't understand that enemies—and foreign enemies at that—can be loved by God and can come to worship him. He knows all the right words to say about God, as his prayer shows, but he clearly doesn't believe it deep in his heart. He goes off in a sulk, hoping that God will change his mind and destroy the city after all.

God is patient with Jonah. Through what happens to the plant, God tries to show him that he can't help but care for people, from whatever city or country they come. Everyone is welcome in God's kingdom, not just a favoured few.

Questions

How do you react when things don't go according to plan?

Might we sometimes, like Jonah, know all the right things to say about God but not really believe them?

Can you name some people you find it difficult to like? Now can you really believe that God loves them as much as you?

What do you think Jonah might have said to God next?

Visual aid

On a map, find a part of the area where you live. Look at the streets and homes and try to understand how much God loves every single person who lives there.

Activity idea

Make a list of the things that make you angry. Now talk about them together. Is your anger fair? Are you angry only because, like Jonah, you don't get your own way? Talk about what God thinks about your anger. How can we control our anger? Do you think God ever gets angry?

Prayer idea

Use the map of the place where you live as a focus for prayer. Put stickers or sticky notes with the names of people you know next to the streets where they live. Now pray for all those people, along with their neighbours. God loves each one of them as much as he loves you. Use the words of the key verse from the story below in your prayers.

Key verse

'You are a kind and merciful God, and you are very patient. You always show love' (Jonah 4:2).

New Testament story link

Matthew 12:38–41: Jesus says that what happened to Jonah is a sign of what will happen to him, and that what the people of Nineveh did is an example for everyone to follow.

Hezekiah gets ill

¹ About this time, Hezekiah got sick and was almost dead. Isaiah the prophet went in and told him, 'The Lord says you won't ever get well. You are going to die, so you had better start doing what needs to be done.'

² Hezekiah turned toward the wall and prayed, ³ 'Don't forget that I have been faithful to you, Lord. I have obeyed you with all my heart, and I do whatever you say is right.' After this, he cried hard.

⁴ Before Isaiah got to the middle court of the palace, ⁵ the Lord sent him back to Hezekiah with this message:

Hezekiah, you are the ruler of my people, and I am the Lord God, who was worshipped by your ancestor David. I heard you pray, and I saw you cry. I will heal you, so that three days from now you will be able to worship in my temple. ⁶ I will let you live fifteen years more, while I protect you and your city from the king of Assyria. I will defend this city as an honour to me and to my servant David.

⁷ Then Isaiah said to the king's servants, 'Bring some mashed figs and place them on the king's open sore. He will then get well.'

⁸ Hezekiah asked Isaiah, 'Can you prove that the Lord will heal me, so that I can worship in his temple in three days?'

⁹ Isaiah replied, 'The Lord will prove to you that he will keep his promise. Will the shadow made by the setting sun on the stairway go forward ten steps or back ten steps?'

¹⁰ 'It's normal for the sun to go forward,' Hezekiah answered. 'But how can it go back?'

¹¹ Isaiah prayed, and the Lord made the shadow go back ten steps on the stairway built for King Ahaz.

2 KINGS 20:1–11

Commentary

Hezekiah was one of Judah's good kings. He put God first, especially during the threats from the Assyrian troops, who at one stage were camped outside the walls of Jerusalem. The Lord answered Hezekiah's heartfelt prayer for rescue, and the mysterious death of many of the enemy soldiers forced the whole army to withdraw. But even faithful kings aren't immune from becoming ill like the rest of us, and in this story Hezekiah is near to death. Again his prayers are answered and God gives him extra time on earth—although, arguably, he didn't use that time well when he rashly invited Babylonian messengers to admire the city's wealth and weaponry.

Isaiah was God's prophet at this time and brought God's answers to the king, including the confirmation of his healing by the miracle of the sun's shadow going backwards on the stairs. God granted Hezekiah peace throughout the rest of his reign, and his readiness to turn to prayer both for his country and for himself is an example for us all today.

Visual aid

Find a first aid kit and explore what is inside, including the plasters and bandages. In Hezekiah's day, a first aid box would have contained herbal remedies like mashed figs.

Activity idea

The shadow cast by the sun on Hezekiah's stairs moved in an unusual way in this story. Put a bright light next to a wall in such a way as to cast a shadow when something is placed in between. Try creating some shadow shapes with one and then two hands. Can you make the shadows move in an unusual way? Can you create animal or human figures from the shadows? How about making shadows of some things from the story—soldiers, a crown, a bed, a palace tower, stairs or figs?

Prayer idea

Make a list of the people you know who are ill at the moment. Talk about them and any ways in which you could help them or cheer them up. Now work on a special prayer together, asking God to heal them in the best way and to give them peace. Read out this prayer together, once for each of the people you have named.

Questions

▶ Why do you think God changed his mind about the timing of Hezekiah's death?

▶ Do you think it is always right to pray that God will heal people?

▶ Isaiah is the one who brings God's answers to Hezekiah. How might you be the answer to someone else's prayer?

▶ Hezekiah was given 15 more years to live. Every day of life is a gift from God, so how can we use each day well?

Key verse

'I have been faithful to you, Lord. I have obeyed you with all my heart, and I do whatever you say is right' (2 Kings 20:3).

New Testament story link

John 9:1–12: Jesus heals a blind man after the man follows some simple instructions. This healing is also a special sign from God (see John 9:39).

Josiah discovers God's law

[1] Josiah was eight years old when he became king of Judah, and he ruled thirty-one years from Jerusalem. His mother Jedidah was the daughter of Adaiah from Bozkath. [2] Josiah always obeyed the LORD, just as his ancestor David had done.

[3] After Josiah had been king for eighteen years, he told Shaphan, one of his highest officials:

Go to the LORD's temple [4] and ask Hilkiah the high priest to collect from the guards all the money that the people have donated. [5] Tell Hilkiah to give it to the men supervising the repairs to the temple. They can use some of the money to pay [6] the workers, and with the rest of it they can buy wood and stone for the repair work. [7] They are honest, so we won't ask them to keep track of the money.

[8] While Shaphan was at the temple, Hilkiah handed him a book and said, 'Look what I found here in the temple—*The Book of God's Law.*'

Shaphan read it, [9] then went back to Josiah and reported, 'Your officials collected the money in the temple and gave it to the men supervising the repairs. [10] But there's something else, Your Majesty. The priest Hilkiah gave me this book.' Then Shaphan read it out loud.

[11] When Josiah heard what was in *The Book of God's Law*, he tore his clothes in sorrow. [12] At once he called together Hilkiah, Shaphan, Ahikam son of Shaphan, Achbor son of Micaiah, and his own servant Asaiah. He said, [13] 'The LORD must be furious with me and everyone else in Judah, because our ancestors did not obey the laws written in this book. Go find out what the LORD wants us to do.'

2 KINGS 22:1–13

Commentary

Josiah turns out to be another king who puts God first. Neither his father nor his grandfather set him a very good example, but despite this, from an early age Josiah is faithful to the Lord, just like King David centuries before. As a young man Josiah decided to arrange for repairs to the temple, in the same way as his ancestor Joash (see page 88), but he was in for a shock. The high priest came across a copy of one of the first books of the Bible, in which were written the ten commandments (this may have been the book of Deuteronomy) and when Josiah read it, he realised how many of God's laws he and his people had been breaking. Josiah could see that it was not just bricks and mortar that needed repairs, but the everyday behaviour of his generation. He took advice from a prophetess called Huldah and set up a radical programme of religious reforms, including the removal of all the idols in the land, which were poles and statues that had been put up to honour other gods. Josiah was someone who took God's words seriously and responded wholeheartedly to what he read.

Visual aid

Open up a full version of the Bible and find Deuteronomy 5:1–22. Lay it down as your focus for today's story. This is probably what Josiah read in the book that Hilkiah found.

Activity idea

Ask each member of the family to bring along their favourite, most important book, and then redistribute them so that each person has someone else's book. Now allow a few minutes for everyone to go and hide the books in different places around the home. Come back together and then, on a given signal, everyone should go and try to find his or her book.

Prayer idea

Josiah didn't just read God's words but was determined to do something about them. Read the commandments again (using the visual aid) but pause after each one to pray, 'Father God, what do you want me to do to keep this commandment?' Share the ideas that come to your minds. Aim to put the commandments into practice in the days ahead.

Questions

▸ What do you think stopped Josiah from going the same way as his father and grandfather?

▸ Do you think it would have been easy for Josiah to admit that he and his people had got things so badly wrong?

▸ In the book of Deuteronomy, Josiah would have read the ten commandments. Can you remember what they are? (See page 40.)

▸ Which commandments, do you think, had the biggest impact on Josiah?

▸ Which commandments are especially meaningful for you today?

Key verse

'Go and find out what the Lord wants us to do' (2 Kings 22:13).

New Testament story link

Matthew 5:17–20: Jesus reminds everyone that God's words are to be not just read but also obeyed.

Captivity in Babylon

³ One day the king [Nebuchadnezzar of Babylonia] ordered Ashpenaz, his highest palace official, to choose some young men from the royal family of Judah and from other leading Jewish families. ⁴ The king said, 'They must be healthy, handsome, clever, wise, educated, and fit to serve in the royal palace. Teach them how to speak and write our language ⁵ and give them the same food and wine that I am served. Train them for three years, and then they can become court officials.'

⁶ Four of the young Jews chosen were Daniel, Hananiah, Mishael, and Azariah, all from the tribe of Judah. ⁷ But the king's chief official gave them Babylonian names: Daniel became Belteshazzar, Hananiah became Shadrach, Mishael became Meshach, and Azariah became Abednego.

⁸ Daniel made up his mind to eat and drink only what God had approved for his people to eat. And he asked the king's chief official for permission not to eat the food and wine served in the royal palace. ⁹ God had made the official friendly and kind to Daniel. ¹⁰ But the man still told him, 'The king has decided what you must eat and drink. And I am afraid he will kill me, if you eat something else and end up looking worse than the other young men.'

¹¹ The king's official had put a guard in charge of Daniel and his three friends. So Daniel said to the guard, ¹² 'For the next ten days, let us have only vegetables and water at mealtimes. ¹³ When the ten days are up, compare how we look with the other young men, and decide what to do with us.' ¹⁴ The guard agreed to do what Daniel had asked.

¹⁵ Ten days later, Daniel and his friends looked healthier and better than the young men who had been served food from the royal palace. ¹⁶ After this, the guard let them eat vegetables instead of the rich food and wine.

¹⁷ God made the four young men clever and wise. They read a lot of books and became well educated. Daniel could also tell the meaning of dreams and visions.

¹⁸ At the end of the three-year period set by King Nebuchadnezzar, his chief palace official brought all the young men to him. ¹⁹ The king interviewed them and discovered that none of the others were as outstanding as Daniel, Hananiah, Mishael, and Azariah. So they were given positions in the royal court.

DANIEL 1:3–19

Commentary

God had warned his people that Israel and Judah would be overrun by foreign powers if they continued to turn their backs on God's laws and God's love. They had not listened, and Jerusalem had been captured by Nebuchadnezzar, who took the king and other leaders away to live under guard in Babylon. The temple had been stripped of its gold and precious ornaments.

It seemed to everyone that God had abandoned his people, but the story of Daniel and his three friends became a sign that God was still at work. The Babylonian king treated them more kindly than they had expected and their guard was friendly too. God made sure that their vegetarian diet left them stronger than those fed on the king's rich food. God also blessed them in their language learning and their studies, so that after three years they were appointed as the king's most trusted court officials, even though they were captured foreigners. God was still with his people, just as he had promised he always would be, turning a disaster into an opportunity.

Visual aid

Put together a bowl of washed raw vegetables, such as carrot sticks, sweetcorn, peppers and peas. Imagine living just on this food for three years!

Activity idea

Daniel and his friends were given new names and had to learn a new language. Using the internet, find out what your names mean and have them translated into another language. Then choose another language, perhaps one from the Middle East where Babylon was, and learn a phrase such as 'I want to eat vegetables!' The four friends would also have had to dress as Babylonians. Find out what traditional costume was like in those days and try to dress up in the same way, with clothes you can find around the home. (According to Daniel 3, this would have included wearing a turban.)

Questions

▶ How would the people left behind in Jerusalem have felt at this time?

▶ How was it that Daniel and his friends managed to go on believing in God even though everything looked hopeless?

▶ What signs do you see in the story that God was still looking after his people?

▶ What can help us go on trusting in God when everything seems to have gone wrong?

Prayer idea

Use Scrabble letters to spell the words disaster, loss, failure and tears. Now break up the letters and look for new words of hope that God can bring out of this mess—trust, rest, courage, and so on. As you do this, pray that God will help your family and others you know to find God's love and help when all seems lost.

Key verse

'God had made the official friendly and kind to Daniel' (Daniel 1:9).

New Testament story link

Philippians 1:12–14: Although Paul was in prison, he could see that God was at work, helping him and others to believe.

The fiery furnace

13 King Nebuchadnezzar was furious. So he sent for the three young men and said, 14 'I hear that you refuse to worship my gods and the gold statue I have set up. 15 Now I am going to give you one more chance. If you bow down and worship the statue when you hear the music, everything will be all right. But if you don't, you will at once be thrown into a flaming furnace. No god can save you from me.'

16 The three men replied, 'Your Majesty, we don't need to defend ourselves. 17 The God we worship can save us from you and your flaming furnace. 18 But even if he doesn't, we still won't worship your gods and the gold statue you have set up.'

19 Nebuchadnezzar's face twisted with anger at the three men. And he ordered the furnace to be heated seven times hotter than usual. 20 Next, he commanded some of his strongest soldiers to tie up the men and throw them into the flaming furnace. 21–23 The king wanted it done at that very moment. So the soldiers tied up Shadrach, Meshach, and Abednego and threw them into the flaming furnace with all of their clothes still on, including their turbans. The fire was so hot that flames leaped out and killed the soldiers.

24 Suddenly the king jumped up and shouted, 'Weren't only three men tied up and thrown into the fire?'

'Yes, Your Majesty,' the people answered.

25 'But I see four men walking around in the fire,' the king replied. 'None of them is tied up or harmed, and the fourth one looks like a god.'

26 Nebuchadnezzar went closer to the flaming furnace and said to the three young men, 'You servants of the Most High God, come out at once!'

They came out, 27 and the king's high officials, governors, and advisers all crowded around them. The men were not burnt, their hair wasn't scorched, and their clothes didn't even smell like smoke.

DANIEL 3:13–27

Commentary

God continued to bless Daniel and his three friends even though they were far from home, in Babylonia, an enemy nation. Daniel's gift for understanding dreams earned him a top job with the king, and the other three were also given positions of influence. However, the king saw himself as even more important than God, and built a tall gold statue as a symbol of his power. Shadrach, Meshach and Abednego were loyal to the one true God and refused to bow down to the statue when the king's orchestra played. This was exactly the sort of idol worship that had been the downfall of Judah back home, and they weren't going to repeat it, even if it cost them their lives. God honoured their choice and kept them safe in the flames. The king even saw God walking in the fire with them. At last Nebuchadnezzar understood how important God was for these three men and for Daniel. The story goes on to recount how he too became a believer in Israel's God, and perhaps this was the most amazing miracle of all.

Visual aid

Assemble as many musical instruments as you can. You could also make some from greaseproof paper and combs or upturned pots and pans. As a family, recreate the sound of the mixed orchestra that the king arranged to perform as a signal for everyone to bow down to the statue.

Activity idea

To illustrate the choice of 'bow or burn' faced by Shadrach, Meshach and Abednego, build a tall tower with wooden bricks or from Lego™ pieces and place alongside it a 'furnace' created from red, yellow and orange tissue paper set into a small box. Talk about the courage it took to have faith in God in these circumstances.

Prayer idea

Christians today, in some parts of the world, also face times of testing and can suffer terribly because they believe in God. Pray for all who are having a hard time because they are Christians, and ask God to be with them, like the fourth man in the fire with Daniel's friends. Organisations such as Christian Solidarity Worldwide or the Barnabas Fund will have ideas and information to help you pray for Christians under pressure today.

Questions

▶ The friends were prepared to trust God whether he saved them or not. What does that tell you about their faith?

▶ Why do you think Nebuchadnezzar was so angry with them?

▶ Why did God choose to walk with them in the furnace?

▶ Everyone was amazed at how God saved Daniel's friends. What miracles is God doing today?

Key verse

'We don't need to defend ourselves. The God we worship can save us from you and your flaming furnace' (Daniel 3:16–17).

New Testament story link

1 Peter 5:8–11: Peter warns his readers about those who want to try to rob them of their faith, but he also promises that God will be there to help them.

Daniel in the lions' den

¹⁰ Daniel heard about the law, but when he returned home, he went upstairs and prayed in front of the window that faced Jerusalem. In the same way that he had always done, he knelt down in prayer three times a day, giving thanks to God.

¹¹ The men who had spoken to the king watched Daniel and saw him praying to his God for help. ¹² They went back to the king and said, 'Didn't you make a law that forbids anyone to pray to any god or human except you for the next thirty days? And doesn't the law say that everyone who disobeys it will be thrown into a pit of lions?'

'Yes, that's the law I made,' the king agreed. 'And just like all written laws of the Medes and Persians, it cannot be changed.'

¹³ The men then told the king, 'That Jew named Daniel, who was brought here as a captive, refuses to obey you or the law that you ordered to be written. And he still prays to his god three times a day.' ¹⁴ The king was really upset to hear about this, and for the rest of the day he tried to think how he could save Daniel.

¹⁵ At sunset the men returned and said, 'Your Majesty, remember that no written law of the Medes and Persians can be changed, not even by the king.'

¹⁶ So Darius ordered Daniel to be brought out and thrown into a pit of lions. But he said to Daniel, 'You have been faithful to your God, and I pray that he will rescue you.'

¹⁷ A stone was rolled over the pit, and it was sealed. Then Darius and his officials stamped the seal to show that no one should let Daniel out. ¹⁸ All night long the king could not sleep. He did not eat anything, and he would not let anyone come in to entertain him.

¹⁹ At daybreak the king got up and ran to the pit. ²⁰ He was anxious and shouted, 'Daniel, you were faithful and served your God. Was he able to save you from the lions?'

²¹ Daniel answered, 'Your Majesty, I hope you live for ever! ²² My God knew that I was innocent, and he sent an angel to keep the lions from eating me.'

DANIEL 6:10–22

Commentary

During the time that Daniel was in exile from Judah, various kings came and went. However, such was Daniel's God-given skill as a government adviser that he held on to his position at court, even when the kingdom of Babylon fell and the Persian empire took over. King Darius gave Daniel authority and power as a state governor, but this made some people very jealous.

As a faithful Jew, Daniel would not honour any human being more than God, so when the other advisers got the king to agree to a month of complete loyalty to the king alone, it was bound to cause a problem for Daniel. The king was caught in a trap because, try as he might, he couldn't change the law that had been passed, and so Daniel had to be punished for his daily prayers to God. The fact that God stood by Daniel and saved him from death in a lions' den was a miracle that impressed the king so much that he told his whole country to worship the one true God.

Visual aid

Arrange to sit near a window and, if at all possible, face west. This is the direction that Daniel faced, looking towards Jerusalem from Babylon, when he talked with God each day.

Questions

▶ Daniel was top adviser to several different kings. What important qualities and gifts did he have?

▶ What gave Daniel the strength to stick to his prayer routines, even when he knew it could lead to his own death?

▶ What might help you to remember to pray every day?

▶ Daniel's rescue from the lions' den is one of the great miracles of the Bible. How might Daniel have described it to his friends afterwards?

Activity idea

Try retelling the story in a series of short phrases with sound effects. Rehearse the following together and then create your drama: cheers for the new king; whispers of jealousy from the advisers; the shouted proclamation of the law to 'bow down to the king'; Daniel's quiet prayer at the window; the angry murmurs from the advisers; the king's fears and worries; the roar of the lions; the stone rolled over the den; the king's restless night; the king's shout of hope; Daniel's words 'God has sent an angel'; the king's cheer of relief.

Prayer idea

Daniel prayed three times a day.

Pray these short prayers in the morning, at lunchtime and at bedtime respectively.

- Lord God, thank you for the gift of a new day.
- Father God, help us to trust you in everything we do today.
- Loving God, thank you for keeping me safe all day long.

Key verse

'In the same way that he had always done, he knelt down in prayer three times a day, giving thanks to God' (Daniel 6:10).

New Testament story link

Acts 16:23–31: Like Daniel, Paul and Silas end up in prison because of their faith in God, but God rescues them miraculously.

Nehemiah goes to Jerusalem

¹ During the month of Nisan in the twentieth year that Artaxerxes was king, I served him his wine, as I had done before. But this was the first time I had ever looked depressed. ² So the king said, 'Why do you look so sad? You're not sick. Something must be bothering you.'

Even though I was frightened, ³ I answered, 'Your Majesty, I hope you live for ever! I feel sad because the city where my ancestors are buried is in ruins, and its gates have been burnt down.'

⁴ The king asked, 'What do you want me to do?'

I prayed to the God who rules from heaven. ⁵ Then I told the king, 'Sir, if it's all right with you, please send me back to Judah, so that I can rebuild the city where my ancestors are buried.'

⁶ The queen was sitting beside the king when he asked me, 'How long will it take, and when will you be back?' The king agreed to let me go, and I told him when I would return.

⁷ Then I asked, 'Your Majesty, would you be willing to give me letters to the governors of the provinces west of the River Euphrates, so that I can travel safely to Judah? ⁸ I will need timber to rebuild the gates of the fortress near the temple and more timber to construct the city wall and to build a place for me to live. And so, I would appreciate a letter to Asaph, who is in charge of the royal forest.' God was good to me, and the king did everything I asked.

NEHEMIAH 2:1—8

Commentary

Nehemiah lived in an area known today as Iran, working as personal servant to the king of Persia. At this period in history, the Jewish people, who had been taken away as prisoners to live in exile some 70 years earlier, were being allowed to return to Judah, and in particular to settle back in the city of Jerusalem. Ezra had already taken one group home, but the reports of conditions in Judea were not good. The capital still lay in ruins and news about this broke Nehemiah's heart. As a God-fearing Jew he longed to do something, and in today's story he is given a rare opportunity to talk with the king about how he feels and to explain what he wants to do.

God answers Nehemiah's hasty prayer as he talks to the king, and amazingly he is given permission to return, both with a pass that guarantees safe passage and the promise of building materials. Nehemiah's courageous words at the right time were hugely blessed and led eventually to the rebuilding of the city walls and the re-establishment of a safe home for God's people, back in the promised land.

Questions

▶ How do you think Nehemiah managed to remember his fellow Jews all through his years of exile?

▶ How did Nehemiah show boldness in his conversation with the king?

▶ What in the story makes you think that Nehemiah had already begun planning ahead?

▶ What did Nehemiah have to give up in order to do this new work for God?

Visual aid

Use a fine-looking drinking glass—maybe a goblet or cut-glass wine glass—to be your focus for this story. Pour out some drink and give everyone a little sip in turn. It was Nehemiah's job to test the king's drink like this.

Activity idea

Nehemiah goes through a range of emotions in the story, all of which must have expressed themselves on his face. Try miming some of his many moods, pretending in turn to be shocked, sad, depressed, fearful, hopeful, eager and amazed.

Prayer idea

Clearly Nehemiah had learned to pray in all situations, quickly and urgently. When his chance came, he prayed for the right words to say to the king, and God helped him. Talk about those times when your prayers have been simply 'help', 'please', 'come', 'hear' or 'sorry'. Work on a five- or six-word prayer together about something facing your family.

Key verse

'God was good to me' (Nehemiah 2:8).

New Testament story link

Colossians 4:2–6: Paul advises his readers to be people of prayer and to use their opportunities to speak wisely.

Rebuilding the walls

[6] The people worked hard, and we built the walls of Jerusalem halfway up again. [7] But Sanballat, Tobiah, the Arabs, the Ammonites, and the people from the city of Ashdod saw the walls going up and the holes being repaired. So they became angry [8] and decided to stir up trouble, and to fight against the people of Jerusalem. [9] But we kept on praying to our God, and we also stationed guards day and night.

[10] Meanwhile, the people of Judah were singing a sorrowful song:

'So much rubble for us to haul!
    Worn out and weary,
will we ever finish this wall?'

[11] Our enemies were saying, 'Before those Jews know what has happened, we will sneak up and kill them and put an end to their work.'

[12] On at least ten different occasions, the Jews living near our enemies warned us against attacks from every side, [13] and so I sent people to guard the wall at its lowest places and where there were still holes in it. I placed them according to families, and they stood guard with swords and spears and with bows and arrows. [14] Then I looked things over and told the leaders, the officials, and the rest of the people, 'Don't be afraid of your enemies! The Lord is great and fearsome. So think of him and fight for your relatives and children, your wives and homes!'

[15] Our enemies found out that we knew about their plot against us, but God kept them from doing what they had planned. So we went back to work on the wall.

[16] From then on, I let half of the young men work while the other half stood guard. They wore armour and had spears and shields, as well as bows and arrows. The leaders helped the workers [17] who were rebuilding the wall. Everyone who hauled building materials kept one hand free to carry a weapon. [18] Even the workers who were rebuilding the wall strapped on a sword. The worker who was to blow the signal trumpet stayed with me.

[19] I told the people and their officials and leaders, 'Our work is so spread out, that we are a long way from one another. [20] If you hear the sound of the trumpet, come quickly and gather around me. Our God will help us fight.'

NEHEMIAH 4:6–20

Commentary

Nehemiah had taken on a big job! The walls of Jerusalem were in a terrible state, and all his organisational skills were needed to gather workmen to begin the repairs. As if that wasn't challenging enough, there was also the daily mockery coming from the leaders who lived in the districts nearby. But Nehemiah was not discouraged. What is remarkable is the way in which everyone got involved in the work. Nehemiah was clearly a great team builder and encourager. His confidence in God was infectious. When the threats from neighbouring tribes grew, he arranged for some of his people to be on guard while the rest worked. God was looking after them in other ways, as on many occasions they received early warning of imminent attacks and so were prepared.

The image of the workforce with spades or trowels in one hand and swords or bows in the other is a powerful reminder that even when we pray to God for help, God also expects us to be ready to help ourselves. Nehemiah's story is an example of how to 'work together with God'.

Questions

▶ How did Nehemiah manage to cope with the threats and the insults coming from the people who lived nearby?

▶ What can we learn from the way Nehemiah 'worked together with God'?

▶ How did God answer Nehemiah's prayers for help?

▶ Nehemiah had the gift of being a good organiser and encourager. How can you be an encouragement to someone today?

▶ What do you most admire about Nehemiah and his story?

Visual aid

Collect pictures from the internet of the tools needed to build a wall. Maybe you have access to some real tools and equipment, such as a bucket, spade, trowel or spirit level.

Activity idea

Talk about what is involved in building a wall and then imagine having to carry a weapon as you worked. Using some wooden bricks or Lego™ or Duplo™ pieces, or just by drawing bricks in outline on a large piece of card, build a wall using your weaker hand only, as the other is needed to hold a weapon. It will take some patience and cooperation.

The story also says that the people sang while they worked. Can you make up a building song together, with a rhythm that will help you keep on task?

Prayer idea

Nehemiah was certainly a man of prayer. He prayed day and night. Using rectangular sticky notes to look like bricks, write on each one the name of a person, place or situation you want to pray for and then build them up as prayer bricks into a strong wall of faith in God.

Key verse

'Our God will help us fight' (Nehemiah 4:20).

New Testament story link

1 Peter 2:4–10: Peter describes Christians as stones in God's building (which is the church), each resting on the other but with Jesus as the most important stone of all.

The promise of a saviour

1 Our God has said:
'Encourage my people!
   Give them comfort.
2 Speak kindly to Jerusalem
   and announce:
Your slavery is past;
   your punishment is over.
I, the LORD, made you pay
   double for your sins.'

3 Someone is shouting:
'Clear a path in the desert!
   Make a straight road
   for the LORD our God.
4 Fill in the valleys;
flatten every hill
   and mountain.
Level the rough
   and rugged ground.
5 Then the glory of the LORD
   will appear for all to see.
The LORD has promised this!'

6 Someone told me to shout,
and I asked,
   'What should I shout?'
We humans are merely grass,
and we last no longer
   than wild flowers.

7 At the LORD's command,
flowers and grass disappear,
   and so do we.
8 Flowers and grass fade away,
but what our God has said
   will never change.

9 There is good news
   for the city of Zion.
Shout it as loud as you can
   from the highest mountain.
Don't be afraid to shout
to the towns of Judah,
   'Your God is here!'
10 Look! The powerful LORD God
is coming to rule
   with his mighty arm.
He brings with him
what he has taken in war,
   and he rewards his people.
11 The LORD cares for his nation,
just as shepherds care
   for their flocks.
He carries the lambs
   in his arms,
while gently leading
   the mother sheep.

ISAIAH 40:1–11

Commentary

God never gives up on those he calls to be his people. Even though Judah and Israel had broken his laws and turned to other so-called gods, God still loved them. Their disobedience had led to defeat in battle and the nation being taken away as prisoners and scattered across the Middle East and beyond, but God still had plans for them.

In this piece of poetry from Isaiah, the prophet assures everyone that God will come and rescue them. There will be a messenger to prepare the way and then God himself will arrive to put things right again. God's coming will be good news and whatever has been taken away from them will be given back. God will be like a shepherd caring for his sheep.

This last image of God meant such a lot to the farming community of Israel. It is a picture of a gentle loving rescue, and this is exactly the way Jesus describes himself (as the good shepherd) in the New Testament. The lost sheep of Israel will be found again and the vulnerable lambs of Judah will be safe. The scene is set for the arrival of Jesus, God's rescue plan for the whole world.

Questions

- What signs of hope are there for Israel in this passage?
- Which part of this promise of good news do you think would be most encouraging for those far from home?
- What words of hope has God spoken to you?
- How can God be both a powerful ruler and a gentle shepherd?
- Which part of these verses can you link with what you know about Jesus?

Visual aid

Make a loudspeaker from rolled-up card so that 'good news' can be shouted out loud.

Activity idea

Pour some sand into a shallow tray to be the desert described in this poem. Make a route that is at first twisty, with hills and valleys going up and down. Then reshape it all, to create a route through the desert that is flat and straight like the one that God will come along.

Prayer idea

There are at least three images in this passage that help us pray:

- flowers that blossom and fade
- a powerful and victorious ruler coming with a reward
- a shepherd carrying baby lambs

These remind us that God's words are for ever, God's power can put things right, and God's love can rescue us. Choose an image and use it as the basis of a prayer for yourself, your family and your friends.

Key verse

'The glory of the Lord will appear for all to see. The Lord has promised this!' (Isaiah 40:5).

New Testament story link

Mark 1:1–4: Mark uses Isaiah's prophetic poem to introduce us to John the Baptist, who in turn points us towards Jesus.

Zechariah receives a promise

[11] All at once an angel from the Lord appeared to Zechariah at the right side of the altar. [12] Zechariah was confused and afraid when he saw the angel. [13] But the angel told him:

Don't be afraid, Zechariah! God has heard your prayers. Your wife Elizabeth will have a son, and you must name him John. [14] His birth will make you very happy, and many people will be glad. [15] Your son will be a great servant of the Lord. He must never drink wine or beer, and the power of the Holy Spirit will be with him from the time he is born.

[16] John will lead many people in Israel to turn back to the Lord their God. [17] He will go ahead of the Lord with the same power and spirit that Elijah had. And because of John, parents will be more thoughtful of their children. And people who now disobey God will begin to think as they ought to. That is how John will get people ready for the Lord.

[18] Zechariah said to the angel, 'How will I know this is going to happen? My wife and I are both very old.'

[19] The angel answered, 'I am Gabriel, God's servant, and I was sent to tell you this good news. [20] You have not believed what I have said. So you will not be able to say a thing until all this happens. But everything will take place when it is supposed to.'

LUKE 1:11–20

Commentary

The dramatic story of how God stepped into the world in the person of Jesus Christ begins here in the innermost part of the temple, with an elderly priest called Zechariah. He shouldn't really have been surprised that an angel appeared to him. It was part of what he believed in and taught to others, but sometimes we can end up going through the routine of prayer and no longer expecting God to answer us, and certainly Zechariah didn't really seem to believe the tremendous message given to him. He and his wife were elderly and the idea of having a son seemed beyond belief, never mind the fact that this son would have a special job to do to bring people back to God and prepare the way for someone even more important.

The angel's visit literally leaves him speechless until the child is born. Zechariah couldn't believe what he was being told, despite his own faith in God, but God still used him to father John—later known as 'the Baptist'—who would point the way to Jesus as God's way of speaking to the whole world.

Questions

▶ Do we just go through the motions of prayer sometimes, so that we aren't really ready to hear God speaking to us?

▶ What was Zechariah's son going to do, according to what the angel said?

▶ Why did Zechariah doubt the angel? Is it always wrong to have doubts?

▶ What do you think the angel looked like?

Visual aid

It was behind the curtain in the Holy of Holies that Zechariah had the surprise of his life. If you can draw the curtains near to where you are reading this, take turns to hide a surprise item behind them. Can the others guess what is hidden each time?

Activity idea

Zechariah wasn't able to speak after this encounter until John was born. He would have had to use sign language. Use the internet to learn some proper sign language for key words in the story, such as temple, curtain, worship, God, surprise, baby, family and parents. You could also play a game of charades, using a form of sign language to try to describe something that happened to you recently.

Prayer idea

God interrupted Zechariah's prayer with a visit from an angel. How ready are we to let our prayer be broken into by God? Pray a familiar prayer together, such as the Lord's Prayer, pausing for a while after each line to give space for God to 'intervene'. Be ready to hear his voice in your head or perhaps 'see' a special picture with your imagination.

Key verse

'John will get people ready for the Lord' (Luke 1:17).

Old Testament story link

Judges 13:1–20: An angel appears to a husband and wife and promises them the gift of a special son.

An angel visits Mary

26 One month later God sent the angel Gabriel to the town of Nazareth in Galilee 27 with a message for a virgin named Mary. She was engaged to Joseph from the family of King David. 28 The angel greeted Mary and said, 'You are truly blessed! The Lord is with you.'

29 Mary was confused by the angel's words and wondered what they meant. 30 Then the angel told Mary, 'Don't be afraid! God is pleased with you, 31 and you will have a son. His name will be Jesus. 32 He will be great and will be called the Son of God Most High. The Lord God will make him king, as his ancestor David was. 33 He will rule the people of Israel for ever, and his kingdom will never end.'

34 Mary asked the angel, 'How can this happen? I am not married!'

35 The angel answered, 'The Holy Spirit will come down to you, and God's power will come over you. So your child will be called the holy Son of God. 36 Your relative Elizabeth is also going to have a son, even though she is old. No one thought she could ever have a baby, but in three months she will have a son. 37 Nothing is impossible for God!'

38 Mary said, 'I am the Lord's servant! Let it happen as you have said.' And the angel left her.

Luke 1:26–38

Commentary

What a surprising way for God to step into the world! Everyone longed for God to appear and put things right, but no one expected that it would involve a very ordinary young woman from an insignificant village in the poor north of a powerless country in the Middle East. God, who is called 'the most high' by the angel, chooses to send Jesus as a vulnerable, tiny baby to be brought up by a peasant family. No wonder Mary is overwhelmed. Even the angel seems awed by what God is about to do as he addresses Mary as 'truly blessed'.

Unlike Zechariah six months before, Mary doesn't doubt the angel; she is simply intrigued to know how she could have a son without a father. The answer is that this will be a miraculous birth in which God's Holy Spirit is at work. Mary's 'yes' is all that God needs, and it is on this that the rescue of the whole world depends. Heaven must have held its breath, waiting to hear what Mary would say to the angel; but this is how God always works, waiting for us to open our hearts to his plans for us and others. This is what can change everything.

Questions

▶ Do you think the angel was as surprised as Mary by God's choice of her?

▶ Why do you think the angel had to say to Mary, 'Don't be afraid'?

▶ What would this baby do, according to Gabriel's words?

▶ How was Mary reassured by Gabriel?

▶ Mary's 'yes' to God was so important. How might we say 'yes' to God today?

Visual aid

Find a photo from the internet or cut out a picture from an aid magazine of a family living in a small one-room house in a very poor part of the world. Use it to remind you of the sort of place where Mary would have lived.

Activity idea

Talk about some famous film and TV stories where superheroes or international organisations 'save the world', and wonder together about how many other ways God might have chosen to put the world right. What does this teach us about what God is like?

Prayer idea

God's solution to the mess that human beings have made of our world wasn't a clever business plan, a superstrong army or a smart piece of technology, but a God-shaped baby called Jesus. Cut out some headlines from a newspaper about the ways in which our world is not the best it can be, and then place a picture of a baby (or perhaps a small baby doll) in the middle as you pray about those things. Let the baby be a focus to remind you of God's surprising way of responding to the problems around us.

Key verse

'Nothing is impossible for God' (Luke 1:37).

Old Testament story link

Isaiah 9:6–7: Isaiah predicts the coming of a special baby to save the world.

Mary visits Elizabeth

[39] A short time later Mary hurried to a town in the hill country of Judea. [40] She went into Zechariah's home, where she greeted Elizabeth. [41] When Elizabeth heard Mary's greeting, her baby moved within her.

The Holy Spirit came upon Elizabeth. [42] Then in a loud voice she said to Mary:

God has blessed you more than any other woman! He has also blessed the child you will have. [43] Why should the mother of my Lord come to me? [44] As soon as I heard your greeting, my baby became happy and moved within me. [45] The Lord has blessed you because you believed that he will keep his promise.

[46] Mary said:

With all my heart
   I praise the Lord,
[47] and I am glad
   because of God my Saviour.
[48] He cares for me,
   his humble servant.
From now on,
all people will say
   God has blessed me.
[49] God All-Powerful has done
great things for me,
   and his name is holy.

[50] He always shows mercy
to everyone
   who worships him.
[51] The Lord has used
   his powerful arm
to scatter those
   who are proud.
[52] He drags strong rulers
   from their thrones
and puts humble people
   in places of power.
[53] God gives the hungry
   good things to eat,
and sends the rich away
   with nothing.
[54] He helps his servant Israel
and is always merciful
   to his people.
[55] The Lord made this promise
   to our ancestors,
to Abraham and his family
   for ever!

[56] Mary stayed with Elizabeth about three months. Then she went back home.

LUKE 1:39–56

Commentary

Mary's three-month stay with her cousin Elizabeth would have been a good time to stay away from prying eyes in Nazareth, where people might have started asking awkward questions about her pregnancy. It gave her a chance to hear for herself Elizabeth's story; and perhaps it also gave time for Joseph, at home, to get his head around all that had happened.

The moment when the two cousins meet is a very special one indeed. Baby John 'leaps' for joy inside Elizabeth, and Elizabeth speaks powerful words of blessing over Mary, while Mary herself bursts into song, expressing her amazement and humility about the fact that God has chosen to honour the poor and powerless like her in his plans to save the world. The two women must have been such a support to each other during this time, not just sharing the ups and downs of pregnancy but also encouraging each other in prayer and worship because God was doing such great things in their lives and, through them, for the world.

Visual aid

The meeting of Elizabeth and Mary is known as 'the visitation' and

Questions

▷ Although not yet born, it seems that the baby inside Elizabeth knew that Jesus was near. What does this tell us about the specialness of human life even before birth?

▷ Elizabeth says several times that Mary is blessed. What does it mean to be blessed?

▷ What does Mary say about herself in her song, and what does she say about God?

▷ Elizabeth and Mary were not just relations but also special friends. How can you be a special friend to someone?

there are many famous pieces of artwork based on this story. Find one from the internet and use it as a focus for the reading today.

Activity idea

We know what Elizabeth and Mary said to each other when they first met, but I wonder what other conversations happened over the next months. How did they spend their time? Create an imaginary diary of their time together—where they went, what they bought, what they prayed about and who they met.

Prayer idea

Mary's song is also known as 'the Magnificat' (taken from the first word used in the Latin translation). It covers praise to God, thanks to

God for his goodness, prayers to God for those who suffer because of powerful and oppressive governments, prayers for those who are facing hunger, and prayers for those who need special help at the moment. Use this as a pattern for prayer.

Key verse

'With all my heart, I praise the Lord' (Luke 1:46).

Old Testament story link

1 Samuel 2:1–10: This is what Hannah sang after she had received the gift of a child.

The birth of Jesus

[1] About that time Emperor Augustus gave orders for the names of all the people to be listed in record books. [2] These first records were made when Quirinius was governor of Syria.

[3] Everyone had to go to their own home town to be listed. [4] So Joseph had to leave Nazareth in Galilee and go to Bethlehem in Judea. Long ago Bethlehem had been King David's home town, and Joseph went there because he was from David's family.

[5] Mary was engaged to Joseph and travelled with him to Bethlehem. She was soon going to have a baby, [6] and while they were there, [7] she gave birth to her firstborn son. She dressed him in baby clothes and laid him on a bed of hay, because there was no room for them in the inn.

[8] That night in the fields near Bethlehem some shepherds were guarding their sheep. [9] All at once an angel came down to them from the Lord, and the brightness of the Lord's glory flashed around them. The shepherds were frightened. [10] But the angel said, 'Don't be afraid! I have good news for you, which will make everyone happy. [11] This very day in King David's home town a Saviour was born for you. He is Christ the Lord. [12] You will know who he is, because you will find him dressed in baby clothes and lying on a bed of hay.'

[13] Suddenly many other angels came down from heaven and joined in praising God. They said:

[14] 'Praise God in heaven!
Peace on earth to everyone
    who pleases God.'

[15] After the angels had left and gone back to heaven, the shepherds said to each other, 'Let's go to Bethlehem and see what the Lord has told us about.' [16] They hurried off and found Mary and Joseph, and they saw the baby lying on a bed of hay.

Luke 2:1–16

Commentary

Luke gives us a detailed account of exactly when Jesus was born. The references to the emperor, the census and the governor are important because Luke wants us to know that this really happened and that it is not some made-up story. He is telling his readers that Jesus' coming into the world is something you can find in the history books and was something that has changed the world for ever. This is what the angels mean when they surprise the poor shepherds on the hillside with their singing. Their song speaks of peace with God which is now possible for anyone, whether they are carpenters, shepherds or emperors. But all this has to start with a baby lying on a bed of hay. The long journey south to Jerusalem must have been tough for Mary, but the fact that the baby was born in Bethlehem is an important clue to who Jesus really is. He will be a king, like David long ago, but also a different sort of king because his reign will not end with his death—but that part of the story is still to come!

Visual aid

Find your nativity set, or a picture of the stable, among the Christmas decorations and wrapping paper that you have stored away. Use this as a focus for the story.

Activity idea

Everyone is travelling in this story. Mary and Joseph and many others are on their way to somewhere else because of the emperor's command, and the shepherds are running off the hillside—even leaving their sheep behind, it seems. Pretend to be these different groups as they travel, and imagine their conversations with one another. What new insights and ideas about the story can you uncover? End by choosing your favourite Christmas carol and singing it together.

Prayer idea

The angels' song expresses the joy in heaven that Jesus has been born. Think of all the good things that have happened to your family recently and, as you name them, say together, 'Glory to God in highest'. Now think of all the places on earth where sad things are happening and, as you name them, pray together, 'May there be peace in…' and 'May people do what pleases God.'

Questions

▶ Can you imagine the conversations between Mary and Joseph when they received the news that they had to go to Bethlehem?

▶ Why do you think there was no room for Mary and Joseph when they arrived in Bethlehem?

▶ The job of being a shepherd wasn't particularly popular in those days. Why do you think God chose shepherds to be the first to hear the good news?

▶ What do you think the shepherds talked about after they had found the baby in Bethlehem?

▶ Which part of this Christmas story do you like best?

Key verse

'This very day in King David's home town, a Saviour was born for you. He is Christ the Lord' (Luke 2:11).

Old Testament story link

Micah 5:2–5: This is Micah's prophecy of what would happen in Bethlehem one day.

Simeon praises the Lord

22 The time came for Mary and Joseph to do what the Law of Moses says a mother is supposed to do after her baby is born.

They took Jesus to the temple in Jerusalem and presented him to the Lord, 23 just as the Law of the Lord says, 'Each firstborn baby boy belongs to the Lord.' 24 The Law of the Lord also says that parents have to offer a sacrifice, giving at least a pair of doves or two young pigeons. So that is what Mary and Joseph did.

25 At this time a man named Simeon was living in Jerusalem. Simeon was a good man. He loved God and was waiting for God to save the people of Israel. God's Spirit came to him 26 and told him that he would not die until he had seen Christ the Lord.

27 When Mary and Joseph brought Jesus to the temple to do what the Law of Moses says should be done for a new baby, the Spirit told Simeon to go into the temple. 28 Simeon took the baby Jesus in his arms and praised God,

29 'Lord, I am your servant,
     and now I can die in peace,
because you have kept
     your promise to me.
30 With my own eyes I have seen
what you have done
     to save your people,
31 and foreign nations
     will also see this.
32 Your mighty power is a light
     for all nations,
and it will bring honour
     to your people Israel.'

33 Jesus' parents were surprised at what Simeon had said. 34 Then he blessed them and told Mary, 'This child of yours will cause many people in Israel to fall and others to stand. The child will be like a warning sign. Many people will reject him, 35 and you, Mary, will suffer as though you had been stabbed by a dagger. But all this will show what people are really thinking.'

Luke 2:22–35

Commentary

All life is a gift from God, and every child is a sign of God's generous love to the world. To help people remember this, the Jewish laws said that the firstborn child in a family 'belonged to God' and that there needed to be a special ceremony to celebrate the birth. Jesus was Mary's firstborn son and, because Bethlehem wasn't far from the temple in Jerusalem, they went there for the service; however, it didn't turn out quite as they expected. An elderly man called Simeon turned up and began singing praises to God about how special Jesus would be. Simeon was a man of prayer and, like many in Israel, was waiting for God to come and rescue his country, just as the promises in the Old Testament said would happen one day. Simeon had the faith to recognise that this rescue had arrived in the shape of a baby and he rejoiced to have seen him. He sang about what Jesus would do, but also spoke some sad words to Mary, because the way Jesus would one day rescue the world would break her heart. Can you work out why?

Questions

▶ This story takes place about six weeks after Christmas, at the beginning of February on our calendar. What new things about Jesus do we learn from what Simeon said?

▶ What sort of man was Simeon?

▶ Mary and Joseph always knew that Jesus was special and that he was from God, so why were they surprised by what Simeon told them?

▶ Mary and Joseph brought doves to say 'thank you' to God for the gift of a new baby. What could you give to God to say 'thank you' for something?

Visual aid

Use a walking stick as a way to introduce old man Simeon, who had been waiting patiently all his life to meet Jesus.

Activity idea

Simeon sang a song of praise to God as he held the baby Jesus—his very own, belated Christmas carol. He talks about Jesus being a light for the whole world. Cut out a picture of the earth and then pierce it all over with tiny pinpricks. Hold it carefully in front of a candle or a small light in a dark corner of the room and see how the whole world is lit up.

Prayer idea

Take it in turns to compose a short prayer of thanks for every person in your family. Thank God for each person's personality, gifts, funny ways, support and love. Make sure that everyone has a chance to offer a thank-you prayer in this way, for someone else rather than themselves.

Key verse

'Your mighty power is a light for all nations' (Luke 2:32).

Old Testament story link

Isaiah 11:1–9: This is Isaiah's song about the child who will come as the true king to rescue everyone one day.

Herod and the wise men

1 When Jesus was born in the village of Bethlehem in Judea, Herod was king. During this time some wise men from the east came to Jerusalem 2 and said, 'Where is the child born to be king of the Jews? We saw his star in the east and have come to worship him.'

3 When King Herod heard about this, he was worried, and so was everyone else in Jerusalem. 4 Herod brought together the chief priests and the teachers of the Law of Moses and asked them, 'Where will the Messiah be born?'

5 They told him, 'He will be born in Bethlehem, just as the prophet wrote,

6 "Bethlehem in the land
    of Judea,
you are very important among
    the towns of Judea.
From your town
    will come a leader,
who will be like a shepherd
    for my people Israel."'

7 Herod secretly called in the wise men and asked them when they had first seen the star. 8 He told them, 'Go to Bethlehem and search carefully for the child. As soon as you find him, let me know. I want to go and worship him too.'

9 The wise men listened to what the king said and then left. And the star they had seen in the east went on ahead of them until it stopped over the place where the child was. 10 They were thrilled and excited to see the star.

11 When the men went into the house and saw the child with Mary, his mother, they knelt down and worshipped him. They took out their gifts of gold, frankincense, and myrrh and gave them to him. 12 Later they were warned in a dream not to return to Herod, and they went back home by another road.

MATTHEW 2:1–12

Commentary

This story could have taken place any time up to two years after the birth of Jesus. Mary and Joseph were living in a house in Bethlehem and their eastern visitors had clearly been following the star for quite some time. They were astrologers—people who studied and found special meanings in the patterns and the brightness of the stars—and the new star that guided them was, in their understanding, the signpost to a new king. Understandably, they looked for this royal baby in a palace, but Jesus was going to be a different sort of king. Bethlehem was the birthplace of King David long ago and it was there that Herod's advisers sent the wise men.

Their arrival is a reminder that this child was going to be a gift for the whole world, and the special presents have become symbolic of the work Jesus came to do as the bringer of the kingdom of God (gold), the way to the true worship of God (frankincense) and the means by which people would find God's healing from all that was wrong inside (myrrh). These wise men from the east were among the first people to seek Jesus and, as an old saying goes, wise people still seek him.

Visual aid

Light a fragrant candle and enjoy its aroma. This is like the frankincense that was given. Perhaps you can find a gold ring and some perfume to represent the other two gifts, as well.

Activity idea

From a book or the internet, find a picture of the night sky in your part of the world. Pick out the brightest stars and the faintest ones; can you see any patterns in the stars? Identify the Pole Star and some other well-known constellations. Imagine the excitement there would be if a brand new star appeared suddenly. If possible, go out and look at the night sky.

Planets look like stars in the sky but they don't twinkle. Can you find any?

Questions

▶ Why do you think Herod was so worried when he heard what the wise men were asking about?

▶ What clues in the story can you find that Herod didn't actually want to go and worship the child?

▶ Frankincense was used in worship, and the sweet-smelling perfume of myrrh helped to overcome the smell of disease and death. Why do you think the wise men gave these particular gifts?

▶ Do you think Mary and Joseph used these gifts, or did they keep them safe as a reminder of the visit?

Prayer idea

Use the three gifts as a prompt for you to worship Jesus together. Gold is for honouring him as king in our lives; frankincense is for recognising Jesus as the one who shows us God; myrrh is for healing all our ills and pains. Combine these ideas in a simple prayer: 'King Jesus, bring us closer to God each day. Heal us and forgive us for all the things we have done that have hurt you and others.'

Key verse

'They knelt down and worshipped him' (Matthew 2:11).

Old Testament story link

Isaiah 60:4–6: Long ago, Isaiah wrote about visitors from far away who would come with gold and spices to worship God.

The escape to Egypt

13 After the wise men had gone, an angel from the Lord appeared to Joseph in a dream and said, 'Get up! Hurry and take the child and his mother to Egypt! Stay there until I tell you to return, because Herod is looking for the child and wants to kill him.'

14 That night, Joseph got up and took his wife and the child to Egypt, 15 where they stayed until Herod died. So the Lord's promise came true, just as the prophet had said, 'I called my son out of Egypt.'

16 When Herod found out that the wise men from the east had tricked him, he was very angry. He gave orders for his men to kill all the boys who lived in or near Bethlehem and were two years old and younger. This was based on what he had learned from the wise men.

17 So the Lord's promise came true, just as the prophet Jeremiah had said,

18 'In Ramah a voice was heard
    crying and weeping loudly.
Rachel was mourning
    for her children,
and she refused
to be comforted,
    because they were dead.'

19 After King Herod died, an angel from the Lord appeared in a dream to Joseph while he was still in Egypt. 20 The angel said, 'Get up and take the child and his mother back to Israel. The people who wanted to kill him are now dead.'

21 Joseph got up and left with them for Israel. 22 But when he heard that Herod's son Archelaus was now ruler of Judea, he was afraid to go there. Then in a dream he was told to go to Galilee, 23 and they went to live there in the town of Nazareth. So the Lord's promise came true, just as the prophet had said, 'He will be called a Nazarene.'

MATTHEW 2:13–23

Commentary

Jesus didn't have the best of starts in life. There was no room in the inn; his first cot was an animal feeding box; his parents were far from friends and the wider family; and now Jesus becomes a refugee in a foreign country. Even during his first years on earth, Jesus experienced the risks and discomforts that many families experience every single day. God in Jesus was not protected from the dangers of this world, and therefore he can understand the bad times that we all go through.

Herod's power-mad jealousy leads him to order one of the most terrible crimes in history, as innocent children are killed and their parents left in tears. Jesus should have been with them, and indeed he will be killed one day, but his time has not yet come. The story is written in such a way as to remind us again and again that God has a plan, promised long ago; all this is slowly but surely being worked out as the holy family are kept safe and, after several years, are guided back to Nazareth where their story began.

Visual aid

Find a map of the Middle East and trace Mary and Joseph's escape route from Bethlehem to Egypt and then back to Nazareth.

Questions

▶ God uses dreams several times in the story as a way to speak to Joseph. Long ago, another Joseph had dreams that came true. Can you recall this story and what happened? (See page 26.)

▶ Can you remember any special dreams you have had?

▶ How does Matthew, the writer, make it clear in this story that God is in control?

▶ Why did God choose to speak in dreams to Joseph, and not to Mary?

Activity idea

Imagine that Joseph kept a diary of his escape with the family from Bethlehem to Egypt and then home again. Make up some possible diary entries for the journey. Where did they stay? Who did they meet? How did they feel? Did they use the wise men's gifts or not? What problems did they face? What was their scariest moment? What was their most difficult decision? What were their greatest worries? How did they keep trusting God?

Prayer idea

Many people today are forced to leave their homeland because of war or natural disaster, to become refugees in another country. Find out about one such refugee group and pray for them. Ask that they might know God's help in the middle of their troubles. Jesus has experienced what it is like to be a refugee and is ready to support them.

Key verse

'And they went to live there in the town of Nazareth. So the Lord's promise came true' (Matthew 2:23).

Old Testament story link

Exodus 2:1–9: Moses was another child who faced death at the beginning of his life, but escaped miraculously and went on to become a great leader.

Lost in Jerusalem

41 Every year Jesus' parents went to Jerusalem for Passover. 42 And when Jesus was twelve years old, they all went there as usual for the celebration. 43 After Passover his parents left, but they did not know that Jesus had stayed on in the city. 44 They thought he was travelling with some other people, and they went a whole day before they started looking for him. 45 When they could not find him with their relatives and friends, they went back to Jerusalem and started looking for him there.

46 Three days later they found Jesus sitting in the temple, listening to the teachers and asking them questions. 47 Everyone who heard him was surprised at how much he knew and at the answers he gave.

48 When his parents found him, they were amazed. His mother said, 'Son, why have you done this to us? Your father and I have been very worried, and we have been searching for you!'

49 Jesus answered, 'Why did you have to look for me? Didn't you know that I would be in my Father's house?' 50 But they did not understand what he meant.

51 Jesus went back to Nazareth with his parents and obeyed them. His mother kept on thinking about all that had happened.

52 Jesus became wise, and he grew strong. God was pleased with him and so were the people.

Luke 2:41–52

Commentary

It is every parent's nightmare to have their child go missing. No wonder Mary was so upset and quite possibly angry when they eventually found Jesus in the temple. Three days and two sleepless nights are a lot to bear! On the other hand, Jesus was twelve by now, and becoming a young adult within the culture of his day. He was finding his independence, so this story can resonate with families where similar tensions can bubble up into rows and rebelliousness, questions and quarrels.

On another level, Mary and Joseph are being reminded that this child is not theirs to keep. He belongs to another more important Father and, one day, will be part of a much greater worldwide family. Mary only began to realise this as she returned home to Nazareth and thought back through all that had happened. One day Jesus will be back in Jerusalem for another Passover and it will seem then that Mary loses him for ever. But after another three-day wait, a much greater miracle takes place, of which this story is an early signpost.

Visual aid

Label a box 'Lost property' and talk about things that each of you have lost over the years. Were any of them ever found? If so, where? Now imagine what it must be like to lose a person.

Activity idea

Play a game of hide and seek, but with words only. For example, each person decides on something he or she is looking for and then asks the others in turn, 'Have you seen…?' They answer, 'Of course I haven't. This is a …… shop and you wouldn't find it here.' The point is that whatever you have lost is actually in the obvious place—a shoe in a shoe shop and not in the supermarket; a hat in a clothes shop and not in a zoo; a dog in a kennel and not in a fish and chip shop, and so on. Link this to the fact that Mary and Joseph looked in all the wrong places. Jesus, who is God's Son, would obviously be found in God's house.

Questions

How was it possible that Mary and Joseph didn't miss Jesus for a whole day on the way home?

Why were the teachers in the temple surprised by what Jesus said and did?

What do you make of Jesus' reply to his mother? Was he being rude and unkind?

What do you think Jesus and the teachers talked about?

Prayer idea

His parents found Jesus listening and also asking questions. Make a list of the questions you want to ask God in prayer—for example, 'Will there be pets in heaven?' or 'Who made you, God?' After a pause, pray these prayers out loud and then allow some space to listen.

Key verse

'His mother kept on thinking about all that had happened' (Luke 2:51).

Old Testament story link

1 Samuel 10:9–16: Saul has been chosen as the new king, but he has gone missing. When he is found, there is something different about him.

John the Baptist's message

2b At that time God spoke to Zechariah's son John, who was living in the desert. 3 So John went along the Jordan Valley, telling the people, 'Turn back to God and be baptised! Then your sins will be forgiven.' 4 Isaiah the prophet wrote about John when he said,

'In the desert
    someone is shouting,
"Get the road ready
    for the Lord!
Make a straight path
    for him.
5 Fill up every valley
and level every mountain
    and hill.
Straighten the crooked paths
and smooth out
    the rough roads.
6 Then everyone will see
    the saving power of God."'

7 Crowds of people came out to be baptised, but John said to them, 'You bunch of snakes! Who warned you to run from the coming judgment? 8 Do something to show that you really have given up your sins. Don't start saying that you belong to Abraham's family. God can turn these stones into children for Abraham. 9 An axe is ready to cut the trees down at their roots. Any tree that doesn't produce good fruit will be cut down and thrown into a fire.'

10 The crowds asked John, 'What should we do?'

11 John told them, 'If you have two coats, give one to someone who doesn't have any. If you have food, share it with someone else.'

12 When tax collectors came to be baptised, they asked John, 'Teacher, what should we do?'

13 John told them, 'Don't make people pay more than they owe.'

14 Some soldiers asked him, 'And what about us? What do we have to do?'

John told them, 'Don't force people to pay money to make you leave them alone. Be satisfied with your pay.'

15 Everyone became excited and wondered, 'Could John be the Messiah?'

16 John said, 'I am just baptising with water. But someone more powerful is going to come, and I am not good enough even to untie his sandals. He will baptise you with the Holy Spirit and with fire. 17 His threshing fork is in his hand, and he is ready to separate the wheat from the husks. He will store the wheat in his barn and burn the husks with a fire that never goes out.'

LUKE 3:2b–17

Commentary

Once John got the go-ahead to start his work for God, there was clearly no stopping him! He wasn't someone you could easily ignore. He had always known that he was the one chosen to prepare the way for his second cousin, Jesus. God's kingdom was arriving and people needed to get ready, to turn away from doing wrong things and to start living honest and generous lives, as God intended.

John reserved his harshest words for those who thought that just being Jewish was enough to make them acceptable to God. For John, it wasn't a case of who you are but what you are doing that proves you really want to change. His preaching drew the crowds and provoked questions, to which he gave forthright and practical answers. People even wondered if John was the special rescuer from God whom they had been expecting, but John makes it clear that he is only the warm-up act. Jesus is the one who will bring the fire of the Holy Spirit that can burn people clean on the inside. Better to welcome this fire than let it catch you unprepared.

Visual aid

Fill a bowl with water and arrange

Questions

▶ This story uses a quotation from the Old Testament to describe John's work. How do John's actions match up to this description?

▶ Why do you think so many people came to listen to John?

▶ In your own words, what does it mean to be baptised?

▶ How did John describe what Jesus would be like? What do you think this description means?

to wash clean some items that are dirty or dusty. This is a picture of what happens on the inside when people choose to be baptised and become friends of God.

Activity idea

On a large piece of paper, draw a huge tree with lots of branches. Add some fruit shapes, hanging from the branches but big enough to write on. John wanted everyone to produce good fruit as a sign that they now wanted to love God. Decide on some words to describe the sort of fruit John was looking for and add them to your tree—words such as 'sharing', 'fairness', 'generosity', and so on.

Prayer idea

As a sign of how God forgives us, cover individual bits of white paper with lots of blots and squiggles to represent the bad things that we have done or that have been done to us. Adapting words from the story, say together, 'I turn back to God who promises to forgive my sins' (v. 3) and then take away the papers and, if possible, burn them. Now give everyone a brand new, clean white piece of paper. God's forgiveness is the gift of starting all over again with a clean sheet.

Key verse

'[Jesus] will baptise you with the Holy Spirit and with fire' (Luke 3:16).

Old Testament story link

Malachi 3:1–4: The prophet Malachi describes what it will be like in the future when John comes to prepare the way for Jesus.

Baptism and temptation

13 Jesus left Galilee and went to the River Jordan to be baptised by John. 14 But John kept objecting and said, 'I ought to be baptised by you. Why have you come to me?'

15 Jesus answered, 'For now this is how it should be, because we must do all that God wants us to do.' Then John agreed.

16 So Jesus was baptised. And as soon as he came out of the water, the sky opened, and he saw the Spirit of God coming down on him like a dove. 17 Then a voice from heaven said, 'This is my own dear Son, and I am pleased with him.'

4 The Holy Spirit led Jesus into the desert, so that the devil could test him. 2 After Jesus had gone without eating for forty days and nights, he was very hungry. 3 Then the devil came to him and said, 'If you are God's Son, tell these stones to turn into bread.'

4 Jesus answered, 'The Scriptures say:

"No one can live only on food.
People need every word
    that God has spoken."'

5 Next, the devil took Jesus to the holy city and had him stand on the highest part of the temple. 6 The devil said, 'If you are God's Son, jump off. The Scriptures say:

"God will give his angels
    orders about you.
They will catch you
    in their arms,
and you won't hurt
    your feet on the stones."'

7 Jesus answered, 'The Scriptures also say, "Don't try to test the Lord your God!"'

8 Finally, the devil took Jesus up on a very high mountain and showed him all the kingdoms on earth and their power. 9 The devil said to him, 'I will give all this to you, if you will bow down and worship me.'

10 Jesus answered, 'Go away Satan! The Scriptures say:

"Worship the Lord your God
    and serve only him."'

11 Then the devil left Jesus, and angels came to help him.

MATTHEW 3:13—4:11

Commentary

This is the moment when Jesus begins his work for God as a man, aged about 30. His second cousin John has told everyone he is coming, and it is John who introduces him to the world. John knew that Jesus didn't need to come back to God and be baptised like the others. Jesus was already one with God, but he was baptised on behalf of all people, just as one day he would die on behalf of everyone. At this moment Jesus hears God's voice affirming who he is, and sees God's Spirit coming down upon him. This is a pattern for what happens when anyone is baptised—the moment they know they are truly loved by God and can be filled with his power to live differently.

However, this affirmation is immediately challenged by the devil in the desert, who deliberately questions what God has said about Jesus. He also tries to make Jesus use promises from the Bible for his own good. Jesus says 'no' to all these temptations, and because of this he can help each of us do the same.

Visual aid

To represent the three temptations, collect a small pile of stones, build a tower from bricks and find a toy globe. Use them as the focus for conversations about this part of the story.

Activity idea

Talk about your understanding of baptism. Perhaps you can talk about a baptism or baptisms in your own family. On large pieces of card cut into the shape of a drop of water, make a poster for each other, personalising God's words for each one of you: 'God says, (Name), you are my own dear child and I am pleased with you.' Display the posters as a reminder of God's love for you.

Prayer idea

Use your visual aids for the three temptations for your prayers, focusing on people who are hungry, those who are facing big decisions, and those caught up in fighting and war in different parts of the world. Ask God to show you and others how to avoid the temptations to do things that are just a quick fix, could lead to pride or involve compromising with evil.

Questions

▶ Why was John so reluctant to baptise Jesus?

▶ Why was it important for Jesus to hear God's voice and see God's Spirit?

▶ The devil offered Jesus another way to save the world—feeding the hungry by doing magic, performing a spectacular miracle and joining forces with him to conquer the world. How did Jesus deal with each of these dangerous suggestions?

▶ What sort of things tempt you away from loving God?

▶ Why did Jesus choose to go without food for so long?

Key verse

'Then a voice from heaven said, "This is my own dear Son, and I am pleased with him"' (Matthew 3:17).

Old Testament story link

Deuteronomy 6:1–9: Jesus knew his scriptures very well, and this advice from Moses was something that would have been a guide for his life.

Jesus chooses his first disciples

[1] Jesus was standing on the shore of Lake Gennesaret, teaching the people as they crowded around him to hear God's message. [2] Near the shore he saw two boats left there by some fishermen who had gone to wash their nets. [3] Jesus got into the boat that belonged to Simon and asked him to row it out a little way from the shore. Then Jesus sat down in the boat to teach the crowd.

[4] When Jesus had finished speaking, he told Simon, 'Row the boat out into the deep water and let your nets down to catch some fish.'

[5] 'Master,' Simon answered, 'we have worked hard all night long and have not caught a thing. But if you tell me to, I will let the nets down.' [6] They did it and caught so many fish that their nets began ripping apart. [7] Then they signalled for their partners in the other boat to come and help them. The men came, and together they filled the two boats so full that they both began to sink.

[8] When Simon Peter saw this happen, he knelt down in front of Jesus and said, 'Lord, don't come near me! I am a sinner.' [9] Peter and everyone with him were completely surprised at all the fish they had caught. [10] His partners James and John, the sons of Zebedee, were surprised too.

Jesus told Simon, 'Don't be afraid! From now on you will bring in people instead of fish.' [11] The men pulled their boats up on the shore. Then they left everything and went with Jesus.

Luke 5:1–11

Commentary

It seems that Jesus was good at noticing things. He noticed the four fishermen mending their nets, even though he was busy telling stories about God to the crowd. He noticed that they were not with the crowd and perhaps not even listening much to him. He noticed that they hadn't caught any fish, and finally he noticed their two fishing boats nearby, beached on the shore. All this gave him an idea. One boat out on the water would make an ideal stage to speak from. He could be easily seen and wouldn't be crushed by the crowd.

So one of the fishermen, Simon Peter, agrees to row Jesus out and be a steady hand on the tiller so that Jesus can stand and talk to the people. Jesus then suggests that they go fishing. Peter knows that the fish just aren't biting that day. The fishermen have tried since before dawn without success. However, out of respect for this holy man, he agrees to one more go. To his surprise, the resulting catch is too much for him to cope with, and his partners, James and John, have to come to the rescue. Now Jesus is speaking to Peter in a language he can really understand. If Jesus can arrange such an incredible catch, then he is certainly someone worth honouring, listening to and following. Peter's life, and the lives of his three friends, will never be the same again.

Visual aid

A small model boat and some netting will help you retell the story together.

Activity idea

Use a reference book or the internet to research how many different types of fish are caught off the shore of your country. If you can cut out or print off some images, you might like to create your own aquarium collage of the variety of fish God has created. You could look up Psalm 104:24–25 for a good picture caption.

Questions

▶ Have you ever been fishing or seen fishing boats on the shore by the sea? Describe the sights and smells.

▶ What sort of mood do you think Peter and his friends were in after their unsuccessful night on the lake?

▶ Why do you think Peter was prepared to lend Jesus his boat?

▶ What was it about Jesus that persuaded Peter to give fishing one more go that day?

▶ Why did Peter feel bad when he saw what happened?

Prayer idea

A good catch of fish was vital for Peter and his friends, and God promises to answer our prayers for the things he knows are vital for us. Find some of the fishing net-like bags that contain washing powder tablets. Cut out some fish shapes from coloured card and, on each one, write or draw a prayer to God. Put the cards in the net. Later this week, go back and take out the fish. Talk about how God has answered your family prayers and which things you still need to go on praying about.

Key verse

'Simon answered, "… But if you tell me to, I will let the nets down"' (Luke 5:5).

Old Testament story link

Genesis 12:1–5: Abram is called to follow God and begin a new chapter in his life's story.

The wedding at Cana

¹ Three days later Mary, the mother of Jesus, was at a wedding feast in the village of Cana in Galilee. ² Jesus and his disciples had also been invited and were there.

³ When the wine was all gone, Mary said to Jesus, 'They don't have any more wine.'

⁴ Jesus replied, 'Mother, my time hasn't yet come! You must not tell me what to do.'

⁵ Mary then said to the servants, 'Do whatever Jesus tells you to do.'

⁶ At the feast there were six stone water jars that were used by the people for washing themselves in the way that their religion said they must. Each jar held about a hundred litres. ⁷ Jesus told the servants to fill them to the top with water. Then after the jars had been filled, ⁸ he said, 'Now take some water and give it to the man in charge of the feast.'

The servants did as Jesus told them, ⁹ and the man in charge drank some of the water that had now turned into wine. He did not know where the wine had come from, but the servants did. He called the bridegroom over ¹⁰ and said, 'The best wine is always served first. Then after the guests have had plenty, the other wine is served. But you have kept the best until last!'

¹¹ This was Jesus' first miracle, and he did it in the village of Cana in Galilee. There Jesus showed his glory, and his disciples put their faith in him. ¹² After this, he went with his mother, his brothers, and his disciples to the town of Capernaum, where they stayed for a few days.

JOHN 2:1–12

Commentary

A village wedding, in Jesus' time, was a big occasion and the celebrations could easily go on for a week. No wonder the wine ran out! This would have been a huge embarrassment for the hosts, who may well have been friends or relatives of Mary's family. To make matters worse, it was clearly quite a society wedding, with servants on hand and even someone especially appointed in charge of the food and drink.

The miracle that takes place comes about because of Mary's total faith in her son. Jesus seems reluctant to respond to Mary at first, but out of love he does, secretly rescuing the festivities from disaster. This is his first miracle and points forward to an even greater one that will come at the first Easter, when 'his time' arrives. Then, because of who he is and what he does, the everyday water of this life can be turned into the rich wine of the best we can all become.

Just as it happened at Cana, there will be more than enough new life for all, with plenty left over.

Visual aid

Fill up a wine glass with water and place alongside it an identical glass filled with wine or non-alcoholic grape juice. Just imagine turning over 3,000 glasses of water into wine!

Activity idea

Imagine you're in charge of the food and drink at a special wedding. Lay a table together with as many fancy extras as possible—cutlery, colourful serviettes, glasses, a menu of your favourite food, balloons, party poppers, confetti on the tablecloth and favours in a bowl. Everything should be perfect; but then add a jug of water to the display. This is all there will be to drink. Talk about how people would be disappointed and even angry. After a while, make it all good again by 'discovering' some tasty juice to drink after all. Enjoy that drink together.

Questions

▶ Have you ever been to a wedding or seen one on television? What happens and why is it such a special day? Now imagine how people would feel if the food and drink were to run out at the reception!

▶ The servants must have thought that Jesus' instructions were crazy. Why did they obey him anyway?

▶ What effect did the miracle have on Mary, her family and Jesus' disciples?

▶ Do you think that this miracle might have some special meaning for us today?

Prayer idea

Nothing is too ordinary for us to bring to God in prayer. On some paper cut out in the shape of jars, and using blue ink, write prayers about anything and everything. Pin the prayers up somewhere. Come back to them later in the week and see how God has answered each prayer. When he does, colour each jar in red and thank God for the way he can change things for us.

Key verse

'Mary then said to the servants, "Do whatever Jesus tells you to do"' (John 2:5).

Old Testament story link

Exodus 15:22–27: Moses turns bitter water sweet for the people of Israel and they are led on to a place with more than enough to drink.

The paralysed man

[1] Jesus went back to Capernaum, and a few days later people heard that he was at home. [2] Then so many of them came to the house that there wasn't even standing room left in front of the door.

Jesus was still teaching [3] when four people came up, carrying a crippled man on a mat. [4] But because of the crowd, they could not get him to Jesus. So they made a hole in the roof above him and let the man down in front of everyone.

[5] When Jesus saw how much faith they had, he said to the crippled man, 'My friend, your sins are forgiven.'

[6] Some of the teachers of the Law of Moses were sitting there. They started wondering, [7] 'Why would he say such a thing? He must think he is God! Only God can forgive sins.'

[8] Straight away, Jesus knew what they were thinking, and he said, 'Why are you thinking such things? [9] Is it easier for me to tell this crippled man that his sins are forgiven or to tell him to get up and pick up his mat and go on home? [10] I will show you that the Son of Man has the right to forgive sins here on earth.' So Jesus said to the man, [11] 'Get up! Pick up your mat and go on home.'

[12] The man got straight up. He picked up his mat and went out while everyone watched in amazement. They praised God and said, 'We have never seen anything like this!'

MARK 2:1–12

Commentary

Wherever Jesus was, crowds gathered. He was such a great storyteller, and had such a compassionate way about him, that people wanted to be near him. And there were miracles too! Reports of healings soon spread and the four men with their sick friend had to check it out for themselves. They were certainly determined. Nothing was going to make them give up on helping their friend, even when it meant hard work, possible social embarrassment and even criminal damage. It was their faith and compassion that got them through to Jesus, and he recognised this. But there was an unexpected twist to the story that must have taken them by surprise as much as it did the crowds in the house. Jesus didn't heal the sick man straight away, but instead forgave his sins. Jesus wanted to give healing on the inside first. This enraged the teachers of the law, who knew that only God could do such a thing. The outer healing that came was indeed a great miracle, and it only went to prove that what the teachers were muttering about was true. Jesus is God and he can forgive sins. No wonder everyone was amazed.

Questions

▸ Have you ever been caught up in the middle of a crowd? What was it like?

▸ Why do you think the friends didn't give up when they saw how hard it was to get close to Jesus?

▸ Can you imagine what the people inside the house said to each other when they saw the roof above them being opened up?

▸ What is the most important part of this story, do you think?

Visual aid

Find an old cardboard box. Turn it upside down and then draw on windows and a door to make it into a house with a flat roof. Now cut a hole in the roof just as the friends did.

Activity idea

In many ways the real miracle of this story is the friendship between the four men who took their friend to Jesus on a mat. Have a go at picking up the youngest member of the family on a piece of carpet like a stretcher. Carrying someone like this is hard work! And how does the one on the mat feel?

Prayer idea

The friends didn't give up, despite aching muscles, rope burns, blisters and all the cuts and bruises they must have sustained as they tore open the roof. Write the names of people you know on sticky notes and stick them on to a rectangular piece of fabric. Now take a corner each and lift it up to God in prayer with words such as 'Lord Jesus, help us not to give up lifting these people to you, asking for your healing both on the outside and the inside.'

Key verse

'[Jesus] said to the crippled man, "My friend, your sins are forgiven"' (Mark 2:5).

Old Testament story link

Isaiah 61:1–3: Isaiah describes what it will be like when God's promised rescuer comes.

Choosing the twelve apostles

¹² About that time Jesus went off to a mountain to pray, and he spent the whole night there. ¹³ The next morning he called his disciples together and chose twelve of them to be his apostles. ¹⁴ One was Simon, and Jesus named him Peter. Another was Andrew, Peter's brother. There were also James, John, Philip, Bartholomew, ¹⁵ Matthew, Thomas, and James the son of Alphaeus. The rest of the apostles were Simon, known as the Eager One, ¹⁶ Jude, who was the son of James, and Judas Iscariot, who later betrayed Jesus.

¹⁷ Jesus and his apostles went down from the mountain and came to some flat, level ground. Many other disciples were there to meet him. Large crowds of people from all over Judea, Jerusalem, and the coastal cities of Tyre and Sidon were there too. ¹⁸ These people had come to listen to Jesus and to be healed of their diseases. All who were troubled by evil spirits were also healed. ¹⁹ Everyone was trying to touch Jesus, because power was going out from him and healing them all.

LUKE 6:12–19

Commentary

It was the custom in New Testament times for people to choose a particular rabbi or teacher as their spiritual mentor if they wanted to make progress in matters of faith and religion. What is remarkable in the case of Rabbi Jesus is that it is he who does the choosing. The other surprise in this story is that the ones he does pick are far from promising candidates for the job. The twelve are a mixed bunch of tradesmen from very ordinary backgrounds, alongside some who hold quite opposing views about the politics of their day. For example, Matthew had collaborated with the Romans as a tax collector while Simon was eager to have them thrown out of the country by force.

These are not the usual sort of people a rabbi would gather round him, but Jesus is guided by God to choose them because he can see what they might become. They are now the inner group among his disciples and he calls them 'apostles', which means that they have the special job of representing him when he is not around, and acting on his behalf. The encouraging thing for all of us is that Jesus calls ordinary people like these men to become his apostles, and if he can do this, there is no barrier to anyone becoming his follower.

Visual aid

Many sports teams are made up of around twelve people. Collect some team photos from the internet or a book and use them as a talking point about the sort of team Jesus put together.

Activity idea

Play a game of putting together teams of family, friends, relations, celebrities or famous people from history for different tasks, such as joining an expedition to explore a new part of the world, saving the planet from environmental disaster, putting on a big family event, or building a multipurpose entertainment centre. Justify your choices each time. It isn't easy making the right choices. No wonder Jesus spent so much time in prayer before putting together his special team.

Questions

▸ Which of the disciples were brothers and also fishermen? Who else do you recognise among the names in the list?

▸ Why do you think Jesus included Judas among the twelve apostles? Don't you think he knew that Judas would betray him one day?

▸ Why did Jesus have to spend so much time praying before he chose these men?

▸ Why do you think Jesus chose these twelve men from among so many possible candidates?

Prayer idea

Use the list of the twelve named apostles to guide your prayers for different aspects of your discipleship. For example:

- Simon Peter: thank God that he sees what we can be, not just what we are now.
- Andrew: ask for help to tell those we love about God.
- Thomas: ask for help not to doubt God.
- Philip: pray for help to ask important questions.
- Judas: pray for help not to let God down.

Key verse

'Everyone was trying to touch Jesus, because power was going out from him and healing them all' (Luke 6:19).

Old Testament story link

Exodus 18:13–27: Jethro suggests to his son-in-law, Moses, that he should choose others to help him with the work of leading God's people.

The soldier's request

¹ After Jesus had finished teaching the people, he went to Capernaum. ² In that town an army officer's servant was sick and about to die. The officer liked this servant very much. ³ And when he heard about Jesus, he sent some Jewish leaders to ask him to come and heal the servant.

⁴ The leaders went to Jesus and begged him to do something. They said, 'This man deserves your help! ⁵ He loves our nation and even built us a meeting place.' ⁶ So Jesus went with them.

When Jesus wasn't far from the house, the officer sent some friends to tell him, 'Lord, don't go to any trouble for me! I am not good enough for you to come into my house. ⁷ And I am certainly not worthy to come to you. Just say the word, and my servant will get well. ⁸ I have officers who give orders to me, and I have soldiers who take orders from me. I can say to one of them, "Go!" and he goes. I can say to another, "Come!" and he comes. I can say to my servant, "Do this!" and he will do it.'

⁹ When Jesus heard this, he was so surprised that he turned and said to the crowd following him, 'In all of Israel I've never found anyone with this much faith!'

¹⁰ The officer's friends returned and found the servant well.

LUKE 7:1–10

Commentary

At this time the Jews looked down on most foreigners and felt that they didn't deserve God's promises and blessings. This Roman officer was part of the occupying power that had taken over the country, and would normally have been feared, hated and avoided. However, the officer had impressed the local leaders with his generosity and care for his men, and so they felt that he deserved help. It must have taken courage for them to choose sides like this. Jesus, of course, didn't see it as a case of this side or that, but simply responded to someone in need.

Perhaps the officer realised it might be awkward for Jesus and the others to enter his house, so he sent a message asking Jesus to command healing from a distance, just as he commanded his men. Most people felt they needed to be near Jesus or even to touch him to be healed, but this man had a bigger faith than that, and his faith impressed Jesus.

This officer wasn't the only outsider to catch Jesus' attention during his ministry. He often found true faith not among those of his own nationality but in the hearts of those who were on the edge or even despised foreigners. It challenges us also to be on the lookout for faith in unexpected people and places.

Visual aid

Find a picture of a first-century Roman army officer in a book or on the internet.

Activity idea

Give the Roman soldier a name and choose names for other imagined members of his family and his servants, including the one who was ill. Now, as a family, become this Roman family and talk together in character about what happened from your different points of view. Who was the one who heard about Jesus and suggested going to him? Who among you doubts that Jeus will turn up? What do the servants think about the people in charge of them? What does the servant who was ill think should happen? What

Questions

▶ Why did the Jewish leaders feel that this army officer deserved Jesus' help?

▶ Do we sometimes decide that some people are more deserving of our help than others?

▶ Why was Jesus so impressed by the officer's faith?

▶ How do we show that we have faith in God?

exactly went on, that day, while Jesus was on his way?

Prayer idea

When we pray, we put our trust in Jesus, whom we cannot see, for the people in need whom we can see. Use some typical army commands to frame your prayers for others today:

- Attention: fix your heart and mind on God.
- Present arms: make a short and simple prayer to God.
- Quick march: get on with doing the best you can and be ready to become part of the answer to the prayer you have made.

Key verse

'The officer's friends returned and found the servant well' (Luke 7:10).

Old Testament story link

2 Kings 6:8–23: Elisha is under attack, but his faith in God helps his servant to see that God's invisible army is with them and they will be safe.

The parable of the sower

1 When a large crowd from several towns had gathered around Jesus, he told them this story:

5 A farmer went out to scatter seed in a field. While the farmer was doing it, some of the seeds fell along the road and were stepped on or eaten by birds. 6 Other seeds fell on rocky ground and started growing. But the plants did not have enough water and soon dried up. 7 Some other seeds fell where thorn bushes grew up and choked the plants. 8 The rest of the seeds fell on good ground where they grew and produced a hundred times as many seeds.

When Jesus had finished speaking, he said, 'If you have ears, pay attention!'

9 Jesus' disciples asked him what the story meant. 10 So he answered:

I have explained the secrets about God's kingdom to you, but for others I can only use stories. These people look, but they don't see, and they hear, but they don't understand.

11 This is what the story means: The seed is God's message, 12 and the seeds that fell along the road are the people who hear the message. But the devil comes and snatches the message out of their hearts, so that they will not believe and be saved. 13 The seeds that fell on rocky ground are the people who gladly hear the message and accept it. But they don't have deep roots, and they believe only for a little while. As soon as life gets hard, they give up.

14 The seeds that fell among the thorn bushes are also people who hear the message. But they are so eager for riches and pleasures that they never produce anything. 15 Those seeds that fell on good ground are the people who listen to the message and keep it in good and honest hearts. They last and produce a harvest.

LUKE 8:4–15

Commentary

Jesus' preferred storytelling style seems to have been the parable—a story based on everyday life that carried deeper meanings. As he explained to his disciples, he used parables to share secrets about God's kingdom, but it took real commitment from his hearers to understand them, and most people didn't bother to try.

The mysterious world of seeds and how and where they grow was a popular choice for his parables. On one level, this story simply describes what most of his listeners saw happening in the fields around them every day, which is what makes it so accessible and memorable, but what happened to the seeds in a range of soils opens up thoughts about how God's message is received or not received by all sorts of people. It seems, however, that most people, including his disciples, didn't understand the deeper meaning (at least, the first time they heard it) and certainly parables need to be heard more than once. It's all down to whether we really have 'ears to hear'; but for those who do, there is always more to discover.

Visual aid

Take a look at different sorts of seeds, both of vegetables and of other kinds of plants. Try to relate the seeds in front of you to the pictures on the packets.

Activity idea

You will need to plan this activity to last over several weeks. Choose a variety of different sorts of seeds, from cress to sunflowers, nasturtiums to sweet peas, and plant them in shallow trays in damp cotton wool or maybe under a thin layer of soil in a window box. Note how slowly the seeds grow. Do the different sorts of seeds grow differently? And if so, why?

Prayer idea

Hold seeds in the palm of your hand and link your prayers to different aspects of the life of a seed. For example, each seed has all its future life wrapped up inside it, just like you and me; each seed needs water and sunshine, just as we need to be fed with Bible stories, prayer, Christian friendship and love; each seed has the power to go on and produce more seeds, just as we can go on to do good and share God's love with others throughout our lives.

Questions

▶ What's your favourite story? Why is it special to you?

▶ Jesus used ordinary life as the subject matter for his stories. Can you find parables about God in the things you experience each day?

▶ Why couldn't the disciples understand the story?

▶ Do you think that the meaning Jesus gives is the only way to understand this story? He himself says that the seed is both God's message and also someone who listens.

Key verse

'When Jesus had finished speaking, he said, "If you have ears, pay attention!"' (Luke 8:8).

Old Testament story link

Judges 9:7–15: Gideon's only surviving son, Jotham, tells a parable to the leaders at Shechem.

The woman at the well

³ Jesus left Judea and started for Galilee again. ⁴ This time he had to go through Samaria, ⁵ and on his way he came to the town of Sychar. It was near the field that Jacob had long ago given to his son Joseph. ⁶⁻⁸ The well that Jacob had dug was still there, and Jesus sat down beside it because he was tired from travelling. It was midday, and after Jesus' disciples had gone into town to buy some food, a Samaritan woman came to draw water from the well.

Jesus asked her, 'Would you please give me a drink of water?'

⁹ 'You are a Jew,' she replied, 'and I am a Samaritan woman. How can you ask me for a drink of water when Jews and Samaritans won't have anything to do with each other?'

¹⁰ Jesus answered, 'You don't know what God wants to give you, and you don't know who is asking you for a drink. If you did, you would ask me for the water that gives life.'

¹¹ 'Sir,' the woman said, 'you don't even have a bucket, and the well is deep. Where are you going to get this life-giving water? ¹² Our ancestor Jacob dug this well for us, and his family and animals got water from it. Are you greater than Jacob?'

¹³ Jesus answered, 'Everyone who drinks this water will get thirsty again. ¹⁴ But no one who drinks the water I give will ever be thirsty again. The water I give is like a flowing fountain that gives eternal life.'

JOHN 4:3–14

Commentary

Jesus travelled mainly around Galilee, in the north of the country, but he went south to Jerusalem at least once a year—for the annual Passover festival—just as his family had done when he was a child. After one of these trips, he went home through the district known as Samaria, which had been settled by Jews who had intermarried with foreigners long ago. Because of this they weren't regarded as pure Jews and were despised by the other Jews. This explains the woman's surprise that Jesus wanted to speak to her. It was also unusual for a man to speak to a woman in public like this.

Jesus, it seems, was always breaking the rules and reaching out to people whom no one else cared about. He was genuinely thirsty, of course, but the conversation soon turns into a discussion about a different sort of water that Jesus can give, which does not involve digging a well or having a bucket. He's talking about the water of eternal life, which can quench people's spiritual thirst for meaning and purpose. The woman goes on to believe in Jesus as the Saviour of the world and ends up telling everyone in her village about the man she met beside the well.

Visual aid

Try to find one of those tiny sponges or towels that expand rapidly when put into water. See what a difference water can make to something so small and dry, and link it to the story.

Activity idea

Construct your own well: take a long cardboard tube and make two small holes in one end, opposite each other. Thread a smooth round stick through the holes. Attach some string to a small container. Tie the other end of the string to the stick and wind it round. Now, by turning the stick, lower the container down the cardboard tube. You could try doing this over some water in a sink or bath and see if you can succeed in lifting up some water to the 'surface'.

Questions

▷ Why was the woman so shocked that Jesus bothered to talk to her?

▷ In what ways is water like the gift of eternal life?

▷ Jesus was prepared to go where he might not be welcome. What sort of places are like this for you?

▷ This story shows us how to talk about faith in everyday conversation. Has something like this ever happened for you?

Prayer idea

Pour some water into a bowl and use it to help you pray.

- Listen to the sound of the water as it pours: God's Spirit is waiting to be poured out on all those who turn to him.
- Feel the wetness of the water on your skin: God wants his love to clean us and refresh us every day.
- Immerse your hands in the water: God wants his love to surround us and transform us, just as our hands look and feel different under water.
- Drink some water: God wants to fill us up so that we can cope with all that lies before us every day.

Key verse

'Jesus answered, "… The water I give is like a flowing fountain that gives eternal life"' (John 4:14).

Old Testament story link

Isaiah 32:15–20: Isaiah describes the powerful difference that water can make in the desert and likens it to the gift of God's Spirit in our lives.

John the Baptist is executed

[1] About this time Herod the ruler heard the news about Jesus [2] and told his officials, 'This is John the Baptist! He has come back from death, and that's why he has the power to work these miracles.'

[3-4] Herod had earlier arrested John and had him chained and put in prison. He did this because John had told him, 'It isn't right for you to take Herodias, the wife of your brother Philip.' [5] Herod wanted to kill John. But the people thought John was a prophet, and Herod was afraid of what they might do.

[6] When Herod's birthday came, the daughter of Herodias danced for the guests. She pleased Herod [7] so much that he swore to give her whatever she wanted. [8] But the girl's mother told her to say, 'Here on a dish I want the head of John the Baptist!'

[9] The king was sorry for what he had said. But he did not want to break the promise he had made in front of his guests. So he ordered a guard [10] to go to the prison and cut off John's head. [11] It was taken on a dish to the girl, and she gave it to her mother. [12] John's followers took his body and buried it. Then they told Jesus what had happened.

MATTHEW 14:1–12

Commentary

This Herod was the son of the one who had ordered all the baby boys in Bethlehem to be killed, soon after the birth of Jesus. John's forthright preaching, especially about the way Herod had broken his marriage vows, had landed him in prison. Herod's new wife had never forgiven him for what he had said, and when her daughter's dancing earned her any wish she wanted from the king, John's fate was sealed. Herod didn't dare go back on his promise. His position as a local king appointed by the Romans was fragile and he couldn't afford to look weak.

Herod had never wanted to have John the Baptist beheaded, however, and so the thought that Jesus might be John, come back to haunt him, was his greatest fear. Much later, as part of the Easter story, Herod did meet Jesus face to face, but he was only interested in seeing a miracle and not in changing his ways. Herod's way of being king contrasts with the true kingship of Jesus, who brings love, not fear, and life, not death, for all who become part of his kingdom.

Visual aid

Make a crown, cut from card rolled into a circle to fit your head. What motto would you write on the crown that sums up King Herod?

Questions

▶ According to the story, what sort of man was King Herod?

▶ John wasn't afraid to tell the king he had broken the law. But wouldn't it have been wiser if he had been less outspoken and avoided prison?

▶ Herod made a rash promise to his wife's daughter, and then didn't have the courage to say 'no'. How careful are we about the things we say and the promises we make?

▶ Compare the ways of King Jesus with those of King Herod. What can we learn?

Activity idea

Play a game of trying to outdo each other with ridiculous promises in exchange for things that you want. For example, someone might say, 'What will you promise me if I double your pocket money?' or 'What will you promise me if I take you to Disneyland?' The others should try to come up with more and more impossible promises, such as, 'I will clean my room twice a day for a year' or 'I will walk the dog every day for the rest of my life', and so on.

Prayer idea

Make some crowns like the one suggested in the visual aid, but this time to represent Jesus the king. Perhaps they could be in a different colour. On each one, write a promise that Jesus makes—a promise that he will never break, such as 'I will always be with you'; 'I will never turn you away'; 'I will come to you'; 'I will give you the Holy Spirit'. Use these as prompts for thank-you prayers to God.

Key verse

'John's followers took his body and buried it. Then they told Jesus what had happened' (Matthew 14:12).

Old Testament story link

Jeremiah 37:11–21: The prophet Jeremiah ends up in prison, even though he has done nothing wrong.

Healing Jairus' daughter

40 Everyone had been waiting for Jesus, and when he came back, a crowd was there to welcome him. 41 Just then the man in charge of the Jewish meeting place came and knelt down in front of Jesus. His name was Jairus, and he begged Jesus to come to his home 42 because his twelve-year-old child was dying. She was his only daughter.

While Jesus was on his way, people were crowding all around him. 43 In the crowd was a woman who had been bleeding for twelve years. She had spent everything she had on doctors, but none of them could make her well.

44 As soon as she came up behind Jesus and barely touched his clothes, her bleeding stopped.

45 'Who touched me?' Jesus asked.

While everyone was denying it, Peter said, 'Master, people are crowding all around and pushing you from every side.'

46 But Jesus answered, 'Someone touched me, because I felt power going out from me.' 47 The woman knew that she could not hide, so she came trembling and knelt down in front of Jesus. She told everyone why she had touched him and that she had been healed right away.

48 Jesus said to the woman, 'You are now well because of your faith. May God give you peace!'

49 While Jesus was speaking, someone came from Jairus' home and said, 'Your daughter has died! Why bother the teacher any more?'

50 When Jesus heard this, he told Jairus, 'Don't worry! Have faith, and your daughter will get well.'

51 Jesus went into the house, but he did not let anyone else go with him, except Peter, John, James, and the girl's father and mother. 52 Everyone was crying and weeping for the girl. But Jesus said, 'The child isn't dead. She is just asleep.' 53 The people laughed at him because they knew she was dead.

54 Jesus took hold of the girl's hand and said, 'Child, get up!' 55 She came back to life and got straight up. Jesus told them to give her something to eat. 56 Her parents were surprised, but Jesus ordered them not to tell anyone what had happened.

LUKE 8:40–56

Commentary

This is a snapshot of what seems to have been a normal busy day for Jesus. There were crowds waiting for him when he returned from time away, with people pushing to be near him. This explains why Peter and the others thought Jesus must be joking when he said someone had just touched him. But the sick woman had touched him with faith. She believed he could help her even without a word being spoken, and Jesus knew that his power to heal had been released.

The woman had spent twelve years suffering from her illness, which, coincidentally, was the length of time Jairus' daughter had been alive. It must have taken a lot of courage for the girl's father, as a synagogue leader, to kneel before Jesus and ask for help, but, like the sick woman, he believed that Jesus could make a difference. He had to go on believing, along with his wife, when news came that his daughter had died. Once again it was a single touch that transformed the situation as Jesus took the girl by the hand and brought her back to life.

It was a day of crowds everywhere, but Jesus never lost sight of the needs of individuals who came to him with faith.

Questions

▶ Imagine what was going on in Jairus' mind as he made his way through the crowds. What might he have said as he knelt before Jesus?

▶ Why do you think the woman who was ill didn't speak directly to Jesus?

▶ Jesus felt power leaving him. But how did he fill up with power again?

▶ The crowds laughed at Jesus, who wouldn't accept that the girl was dead. Do people think we are mad sometimes for believing that Jesus can change things?

Visual aid

Create a crowd scene with different figures from a toy box in your house. Bunch them all up close and try to move them together as a single unit. This is what it must have been like for Jesus, caught up with the crowds in the streets.

Activity idea

Play a game of 'Squeak, piggy, squeak'. Blindfold one member of the family and then sit in a circle or close together. After a moment, one person should come and sit close to the blindfolded one, touch them on the shoulders and squeak. Can the person guess who it was? Give everyone a go at being blindfolded.

Prayer idea

Touching Jesus and being touched by him is a simple description of what prayer is. For your prayers today, everyone should link hands in different ways to be in touch with each other and with God as you talk with him—for example, with palms upward on top of each other, asking for God's help; with hands placed against each other, upright, with fingers pointing up, praising God's name; with palms facing down on top of each other, saying 'sorry' to God.

Key verse

'Jesus said to the woman, "You are now well because of your faith. May God give you peace!"' (Luke 8:48).

Old Testament story link

2 Kings 4:8–37: Elisha prays to God and brings a boy back to life.

Feeding the 5000

[13] After Jesus heard about John, he crossed Lake Galilee to go to some place where he could be alone. But the crowds found out and followed him on foot from the towns. [14] When Jesus got out of the boat, he saw the large crowd. He felt sorry for them and healed everyone who was sick.

[15] That evening the disciples came to Jesus and said, 'This place is like a desert, and it is already late. Let the crowds leave, so they can go to the villages and buy some food.'

[16] Jesus replied, 'They don't have to leave. Why don't you give them something to eat?'

[17] But they said, 'We have only five small loaves of bread and two fish.' [18] Jesus asked his disciples to bring the food to him, [19] and he told the crowd to sit down on the grass. Jesus took the five loaves and the two fish. He looked up towards heaven and blessed the food. Then he broke the bread and handed it to his disciples, and they gave it to the people.

[20] After everyone had eaten all they wanted, Jesus' disciples picked up twelve large baskets of leftovers.

[21] There were about five thousand men who ate, not counting the women and children.

MATTHEW 14:13–21

Commentary

Jesus has just heard that John, his second cousin, has been executed in prison. Clearly he needs time to mourn, and this is why he sets off to the far side of Lake Galilee. But his popularity is at such a high point by now that the crowds get there ahead of him. We might have been angry about this, but Jesus is not sorry for himself; he is concerned for the people. He knows how much need there is in the world and he longs to do something about it. What should have been a quiet afternoon grieving turns into a busy time of healing and storytelling.

Finally his exhausted disciples just want everyone to go home for tea, when, to their surprise, Jesus suggests a picnic right there, even though they have barely enough to feed themselves. The little basket of bread and fish, however, is enough, as, blessed by Jesus, it turns into plenty for everyone.

This well-known miracle appears in all four Gospels and was clearly a favourite story among the very first Christians. It reminded them that Jesus would always provide for them and that no situation was too big for him to handle.

Questions

▶ It is always sad when a relative dies. How can we best support someone who is grieving like this?

▶ Jesus' reaction to the crowd is amazing. How would you have felt if this had happened to you?

▶ Can you imagine what sort of things the disciples said to Jesus to try to persuade him to send the crowd away?

▶ Do you think the crowd ever knew how great a miracle had just taken place?

Visual aid

Fill a small basket with five small bread rolls and, if possible, two small fish from a sardine can or supermarket packet. Imagine how this was used to feed almost 10,000 people!

Activity idea

Use the bread rolls from the visual aid suggestion and share them round so that everyone has a go at breaking one up into small, bite-size chunks. How many pieces do you have now, and so how many people would have just a taste?

Prayer idea

Collect all the broken pieces on a plate and pass it around as you pray, each taking a piece of bread to eat after each prayer, for those who don't have enough to eat today, those who are sad because someone has died recently, those needing healing today, and those who feel far from home today. As you eat the pieces, pray that Jesus, who once described himself as the bread of life, will give them strength, healing, inspiration and comfort.

Key verse
'[Jesus] looked up towards heaven and blessed the food' (Matthew 14:19).

Old Testament story link

2 Kings 4:40–44: Elisha prays to God and a small amount of bread goes a long way.

Walking on water

22 Straight away, Jesus made his disciples get into a boat and start back across the lake. But he stayed until he had sent the crowds away. 23 Then he went up on a mountain where he could be alone and pray. Later that evening, he was still there.

24 By this time the boat was a long way from the shore. It was going against the wind and was being tossed around by the waves. 25 A little while before morning, Jesus came walking on the water towards his disciples. 26 When they saw him, they thought he was a ghost. They were terrified and started screaming.

27 At once, Jesus said to them, 'Don't worry! I am Jesus. Don't be afraid.'

28 Peter replied, 'Lord, if it is really you, tell me to come to you on the water.'

29 'Come on!' Jesus said. Peter then got out of the boat and started walking on the water toward him.

30 But when Peter saw how strong the wind was, he was afraid and started sinking. 'Save me, Lord!' he shouted.

31 Straight away, Jesus reached out his hand. He helped Peter up and said, 'You don't have much faith. Why do you doubt?'

32 When Jesus and Peter got into the boat, the wind died down. 33 The men in the boat worshipped Jesus and said, 'You really are the Son of God!'

MATTHEW 14:22–33

Commentary

It was the end of a long day. Jesus had heard the news about John's death, spent the afternoon healing people and then performed the miracle with the bread and the fish. He hadn't had a moment to himself, so no wonder he wanted time alone with God. Having seen the crowds and his disciples safely on their way, he went up a mountain to pray. Unfortunately, the boat trip home for the disciples ran into difficulty and by early morning they still hadn't made it back.

Once again Jesus comes to people in need—this time, his friends—and takes the direct route to help them by walking across the water. This scares the living daylights out of them, of course, but when they realise who it is, Peter asks if he can walk on the water too. He is keen to be like his master in every way, and Jesus encourages him to come. When, however, he takes his eyes off Jesus and begins to doubt, he starts to sink, but Jesus is there to rescue him.

Christians believe that Jesus wants all of us to do amazing things too, with his help. Jesus encourages us, like Peter, to step out of the boat and take risks for him.

Questions

▶ Have you ever been in a boat when it was stormy? How did you feel?

▶ Jesus needed to pray after all that had happened that day. What makes you want to pray?

▶ Where is a good place for you to find peace and quiet?

▶ Why do you think Peter started to sink?

Visual aid

Fill a bowl with water and float a small boat in it. If you do not have a boat, make one from paper. Create some stormy waves and, by flapping a piece of card, add some wind effects as well.

Activity idea

Act out the story together. Create a boat with pieces of furniture in the room and huddle inside. Row against the current and be tossed around by imaginary waves. Suddenly spot Jesus walking on the water and react with terror. Call out to find out who it is. One of you, as Peter, should dare to step out of the boat. Try walking carefully on the water. Help Peter to get back in the boat when he begins to sink. Give an opportunity for everyone to say how they feel about what has just happened.

Prayer idea

Jesus needed to be alone to pray. He also chose to be up high. Together, walk around your home to find a good place to pray. Talk about what would make the place special and how it would help you to focus on God. When you find a place, kneel down and say a simple, familiar prayer such as the Lord's Prayer.

Key verse

'The men in the boat worshipped Jesus and said, "You really are the Son of God!"' (Matthew 14:33).

Old Testament story link

2 Kings 6:1–7: Something heavier than water floats to the surface during Elisha's ministry.

The transfiguration

[1] Six days later Jesus took Peter and the brothers James and John with him. They went up on a very high mountain where they could be alone. [2] There in front of the disciples, Jesus was completely changed. His face was shining like the sun, and his clothes became white as light.

[3] All at once Moses and Elijah were there talking with Jesus. [4] So Peter said to him, 'Lord, it is good for us to be here! Let us make three shelters, one for you, one for Moses, and one for Elijah.'

[5] While Peter was still speaking, the shadow of a bright cloud passed over them. From the cloud a voice said, 'This is my own dear Son, and I am pleased with him. Listen to what he says!' [6] When the disciples heard the voice, they were so afraid that they fell flat on the ground. [7] But Jesus came over and touched them. He said, 'Get up and don't be afraid!' [8] When they opened their eyes, they saw only Jesus.

[9] On their way down from the mountain, Jesus warned his disciples not to tell anyone what they had seen until after the Son of Man had been raised from death.

MATTHEW 17:1–9

Commentary

The disciples had been with Jesus for a while. They had been amazed by all the things he'd said and done, but lately Jesus had begun talking about suffering and death. It didn't make any sense to them. Everything was going so well, so why was he suddenly so gloomy about the future?

About a week later, Jesus takes three of his disciples up a mountain. He wants them to understand something more about who he is, particularly in the light of what is going to happen soon in Jerusalem. There on the mountain top, Jesus begins to look very different. It is as if the bright light of heaven is shining right through him. Beside him appear great leaders from long ago—Moses and Elijah. Peter wants this wonderful moment to last for ever, and suggests building shelters for all three of them. But it is impossible to tie God's glory down like this. Then they hear God's voice, which is as much for the three disciples as for Jesus. Whatever happens next, they know for sure that Jesus is God's Son and that they should listen to what he is saying. In their moments of fear and doubt, they need to keep their eyes fixed on Jesus.

Visual aid

Use the bright light of an unshaded 100W bulb: place the bulb between two mirrors opposite each other. See how the light is bounced endlessly back and forth between the mirrors, adding to its brightness and mystery.

Activity idea

On a piece of A4 paper, draw an outline of Jesus on the mountain. Colour it in with felt-tipped pens in bright colours. Now turn the paper over and brush the back lightly with an even coating of olive oil. Let it dry. When you hold the paper up to a window, the light will shine through in a very powerful way.

Questions

▶ Why do you think Jesus chose these particular disciples for this special experience?

▶ Why did Moses and Elijah appear with Jesus? What did it mean?

▶ This is the second time God's voice is heard in the Gospel story. Can you remember what God said about Jesus at his baptism?

▶ How do you think this experience would have helped the three disciples in days to come?

Prayer idea

God speaks and Jesus stands at the centre between Moses and Elijah, who represent the teachings of the Old Testament. Draw an outline of a cross on paper with enough space to write words on the cross. Now, together, think of as many descriptions of Jesus as you can, writing them on the cross in different colours—for example, light, friend, shepherd, king, defender, rock, Son of God, truth, and so on. Use some of the words to help you create one-line prayers to praise Jesus.

Key verse

'From the cloud a voice said, "This is my own dear Son, and I am pleased with him. Listen to what he says!"' (Matthew 17:5).

Old Testament story link

Exodus 24:12–18: Moses and Joshua go up into the bright light of God's glory on Mount Sinai.

The woman caught breaking the law

1 Jesus walked out to the Mount of Olives. 2 Then early the next morning he went to the temple. The people came to him, and he sat down and started teaching them.

3 The Pharisees and the teachers of the Law of Moses brought in a woman who had been caught in bed with a man who wasn't her husband. They made her stand in the middle of the crowd. 4 Then they said, 'Teacher, this woman was caught sleeping with a man who isn't her husband. 5 The Law of Moses teaches that a woman like this should be stoned to death! What do you say?'

6 They asked Jesus this question, because they wanted to test him and bring some charge against him. But Jesus simply bent over and started writing on the ground with his finger.

7 They kept on asking Jesus about the woman. Finally, he stood up and said, 'If any of you have never sinned, then go ahead and throw the first stone at her!'

8 Once again he bent over and began writing on the ground. 9 The people left one by one, beginning with the oldest. Finally, Jesus and the woman were there alone.

10 Jesus stood up and asked her, 'Where is everyone? Isn't there anyone left to accuse you?'

11 'No sir,' the woman answered.

Then Jesus told her, 'I am not going to accuse you either. You may go now, but don't sin any more.'

JOHN 8:1–11

Commentary

On his journey south to Jerusalem, Jesus spent time around the city, walking on the Mount of Olives or teaching in the temple. His life was not yet in danger, but the religious leaders were eager to discredit him. One subject that they knew he had often talked about was the Law of Moses, with its strict rules on behaviour, particularly about marriage. Surely anyone who broke one of the commandments deserved to die? Would Jesus agree or go soft on what God had said, making feeble allowances for people's weakness? The crowds, they reasoned, wouldn't follow someone who went against God's Law and appeared weak on criminal matters.

The leaders need a test case, and so they drag a woman to him who has gone off with another man, breaking her marriage vows. They try to goad Jesus into condemning her, but he says nothing at first;

he simply doodles in the sand. The answer he then gives is brilliant. He invites *them* to condemn her and kill her… but only if they can honestly say that their lives are completely clean. Of course, no one is perfect, just as the woman isn't. Only God is perfectly good, with the right to judge others. They all slink away and Jesus and the woman are left alone. She receives not his anger but his forgiveness, and walks free to start again.

Visual aid

God is not in the business of rubbing things in, but rubbing things out. Pour some sand into a shallow tray and have some fun drawing pictures and writing words with a stick and then rubbing them away again.

Activity idea

Remind yourselves as a family of the ten commandments (see page 40). The teachers of the law wanted to catch Jesus out, to prove that he was not a trustworthy teacher. Play a game of 'Simon says', trying to catch each other out with the wrong actions. The way to survive the game is to think carefully, just like Jesus did.

Questions

▶ What do you think Jesus doodled in the sand as he waited for tempers to die down?

▶ Why were the Pharisees and teachers of the law so against Jesus?

▶ How do you deal with situations when tempers flare and angry words are exchanged?

▶ Why do you think the oldest accusers left first?

▶ What do you think the woman did next?

Prayer idea

Use the sand tray from the visual aid suggestion. Think about the things that you have done wrong lately. For each of these, write a word or draw a picture in the sand. Pause, and then, using Jesus' words to the woman in the story (see the 'Key verse'), rub away what you have written or drawn.

Key verse

'Jesus told her, "I am not going to accuse you… You may go now, but don't sin any more"' (John 8:11).

Old Testament story link

Jeremiah 31:31–34: Jeremiah looks forward to the day when God will write his laws on people's hearts and he will forgive all their sins.

The good Samaritan

30 Jesus replied:

As a man was going down from Jerusalem to Jericho, robbers attacked him and grabbed everything he had. They beat him up and ran off, leaving him half dead.

31 A priest happened to be going down the same road. But when he saw the man, he walked by on the other side. 32 Later a temple helper came to the same place. But when he saw the man who had been beaten up, he also went by on the other side.

33 A man from Samaria then came travelling along that road. When he saw the man, he felt sorry for him 34 and went over to him. He treated his wounds with olive oil and wine and bandaged them. Then he put him on his own donkey and took him to an inn, where he took care of him. 35 The next morning he gave the innkeeper two silver coins and said, 'Please take care of the man. If you spend more than this on him, I will pay you when I return.'

36 Then Jesus asked, 'Which one of these three people was a real neighbour to the man who was beaten up by robbers?'

37 The teacher answered, 'The one who showed pity.'

Jesus said, 'Go and do the same!'

LUKE 10:30–37

Commentary

What was Jesus doing? Imagine telling a story where the hero is someone that everyone hates and the people who are meant to be kind turn out to be the villains of the piece! Not long before, Jesus and his disciples had been turned away from a Samaritan village on their way south to Jerusalem. Samaritans and Jews despised each other; they wouldn't normally even exchange a simple greeting and certainly never shook hands. Yet here in this story it is the Samaritan who stops, has compassion on the man who was beaten up and applies first-century medicine to the wounds.

Jesus told this story in response to a question from a religious expert who wanted to know what God's law meant when it said 'Love your neighbour'. Surely a 'neighbour' is anyone close to you and someone you get on with. But Jesus expands the word way beyond this narrow definition. Anybody in need is our neighbour. God wants people to love without limits, just as he does. Sadly, like the priest and the temple helper, we often limit our love to those who are like us. What is more, the injured man had to learn to be helped by a neighbour who was his enemy.

Visual aid

Find pictures of two local, rival sports teams—perhaps represented by team colours, scarves or mascots. The hatred between Samaritans and Jews was even more deadly than this!

Activity idea

Together, work on an up-to-date version of this parable. Who is travelling and where are they going? How do they get hurt? Who are the equivalents of the priest and the temple helper—that is, the people who should help? Who is the surprise enemy who stops? How does he or she help? Try to capture in your story the same dramatic shock that Jesus' original version had.

Questions

▶ If you were telling this story today, who would you choose as the enemy who turns out to be the hero?

▶ Can you imagine the thoughts going through the priest's head to justify his decision not to stop? And what was the temple helper thinking about?

▶ Why do you think the Samaritan stopped to help?

▶ In the light of this story, who is your neighbour?

Prayer idea

As a family, draw circles, starting small and getting bigger and bigger. For each circle, name people God wants you to care for, starting with those close to you in the family, then your friends, then those in your school and at work, then the wider local community, then those in your village, town or city, those in your country, and finally others in distant lands around the world. God's circles of love include you and me, as well as the whole universe.

Key verse

'Jesus said, "Go and do the same!"' (Luke 10:37).

Old Testament story link

Leviticus 19:9–18: Here are some of God's Old Testament laws about the practical ways in which we should love our neighbour.

Mary and Martha

38 The Lord and his disciples were travelling along and came to a village. When they got there, a woman named Martha welcomed him into her home. 39 She had a sister named Mary, who sat down in front of the Lord and was listening to what he said. 40 Martha was worried about all that had to be done. Finally, she went to Jesus and said, 'Lord, doesn't it bother you that my sister has left me to do all the work by myself? Tell her to come and help me!'

41 The Lord answered, 'Martha, Martha! You are worried and upset about so many things, 42 but only one thing is necessary. Mary has chosen what is best, and it will not be taken away from her.'

11 When Jesus had finished praying, one of his disciples said to him, 'Lord, teach us to pray, just as John taught his followers to pray.'

2 So Jesus told them, 'Pray in this way:

"Father, help us
    to honour your name.
Come and set up
    your kingdom.
3 Give us each day
    the food we need.
4 Forgive our sins,
as we forgive everyone
    who has done wrong to us.

And keep us
    from being tempted."'

LUKE 10:38—11:4

Commentary

Mary and Martha lived with their brother Lazarus in a village called Bethany, not far from Jerusalem. It seems that Jesus often stayed with this family whenever he travelled south for the festivals, although today's story may have been from the first time they met. On this occasion Martha was obviously keen to prepare a proper home-cooked meal for him, whereas, to her annoyance, Mary chose to sit and listen to Jesus telling stories. Of course, hospitality is about giving someone that much-needed meal, but it is equally about giving a guest your time and attention. Mary was certainly doing the latter and, although Martha's work in the kitchen has its place, sometimes it's possible to be so busy trying to get things right for your guest that you forget to spend time with them.

Perhaps that's true of prayer too, which is the focus for the second part of this passage. The simplicity of this version of the Lord's Prayer is what Jesus wanted his disciples to understand. In just five short sentences there is everything we really need to know about talking to God and understanding who God is. No wonder this is such a special prayer, used by millions of people around the world.

Questions

▶ What exactly did Martha get wrong? Are we in danger of making the same mistake?

▶ What is the 'one thing necessary' that Mary chose?

▶ Prayer doesn't need a lot of words, as Jesus makes clear. Can you sum up in just a few headline words the heart of the Lord's Prayer?

▶ Which part of this special prayer is most important for you at the moment?

Visual aid

Find the picture of 'Praying hands' by Albrecht Dürer in a book or on the internet. You might like to research the story behind this picture, which is about Albrecht and his brother.

Activity idea

Create a big poster of the Lord's Prayer to which everyone makes some contribution, colouring in the letters or adding decoration. You could also add your praying hands to this prayer by photographing each person's hands together in prayer, printing off the pictures and adding them as your signatures to the poster.

Prayer idea

Learn the Lord's Prayer together by heart, either in this version from Luke's Gospel or from Matthew's (Matthew 6:9–13), using the translation you are most comfortable with. Check that each of you understands the meaning of the words you are saying. Use it together whenever you pray.

Key verse

'Father, help us to honour your name' (Luke 11:2).

Old Testament story link

Psalm 63:1–8: This is one of King David's many special prayers to God.

The prodigal son

¹¹ Jesus also told them another story:

Once a man had two sons. ¹² The younger son said to his father, 'Give me my share of the property.' So the father divided his property between his two sons.

¹³ Not long after that, the younger son packed up everything he owned and left for a foreign country, where he wasted all his money in wild living. ¹⁴ He had spent everything, when a bad famine spread through that whole land. Soon he had nothing to eat.

¹⁵ He went to work for a man in that country, and the man sent him out to take care of his pigs. ¹⁶ He would have been glad to eat what the pigs were eating, but no one gave him a thing.

¹⁷ Finally, he came to his senses and said, 'My father's workers have plenty to eat, and here I am, starving to death! ¹⁸ I will go to my father and say to him, "Father, I have sinned against God in heaven and against you. ¹⁹ I am no longer good enough to be called your son. Treat me like one of your workers."'

²⁰ The younger son got up and started back to his father. But when he was still a long way off, his father saw him and felt sorry for him. He ran to his son and hugged and kissed him.

²¹ The son said, 'Father, I have sinned against God in heaven and against you. I am no longer good enough to be called your son.'

²² But his father said to the servants, 'Hurry and bring the best clothes and put them on him. Give him a ring for his finger and sandals for his feet. ²³ Get the best calf and prepare it, so we can eat and celebrate. ²⁴ This son of mine was dead, but has now come back to life. He was lost and has now been found.' And they began to celebrate.

LUKE 15:11–24

Commentary

This is possibly the most well-known of Jesus' parables. As so often, Jesus doesn't give any explanation of its meaning, but lets the story speak for itself. He was telling it for the religious leaders in particular to hear. They were upset that Jesus was the sort of teacher who welcomed all types of people to be his followers, including those with messy lives and unacceptable behaviour.

This is also part of a series of 'lost and found' stories, in each of which Jesus gives clues as to what God is like. In this story the father never gives up hope that his younger son will come home. He never disowns or forgets him, but waits patiently. When the son does come back, it is interesting that the father says nothing to his wayward boy. There are no words of rebuke or anger; he doesn't say 'I told you so' or even offer words of forgiveness, simply an extravagant welcome. The gifts of ring and sandals mean that he is fully accepted back into the family—just like the people with messy lives who had been welcomed back to God through the ministry of Jesus.

Visual aid

Find the following three simple

Questions

▶ What is it that finally prompts the younger son to go home?

▶ Why does the father never give up on his lost son?

▶ Jesus adds a further section to the story, which you can read in a complete Bible version, describing how upset the older son is that the younger son's return is being celebrated. Do you think the father is treating his two boys fairly?

▶ The people listening would have realised that this parable was really about them. What sort of reactions do you think it received?

visuals for the story: a bag of coins, a model pig (perhaps from a farm set) and a gold ring. Use them to help you retell the story to each other.

Activity idea

Create some party sound effects and activities to go along with a rereading of verses 22–24. Put on some dance music, share some favourite food and drink; use party poppers and streamers and include lots of laughter and cheering. Catch the excitement of the father's joy that his son is back home.

Prayer idea

On a large piece of paper, draw a map with 'home' in one corner. Now draw a wandering line from home all around the map, covering

as much area as possible without crossing your own line, and eventually coming back home. As each of you traces this line for him- or herself, pray something like this: 'Father God, help me not to wander away from you and your love. If I do, bring me back safely. Help me to remember that you are always waiting for me.'

Key verse

'But when he was still a long way off, his father saw him… ran to his son and hugged and kissed him' (Luke 15:20).

Old Testament story link

Genesis 33:1–15: Brothers Jacob and Esau meet again as friends after being enemies for many years.

A Pharisee and a tax collector

9 Jesus told a story to some people who thought they were better than others and who looked down on everyone else:

10 Two men went into the temple to pray. One was a Pharisee and the other a tax collector. 11 The Pharisee stood over by himself and prayed, 'God, I thank you that I am not greedy, dishonest, and unfaithful in marriage like other people. And I am really glad that I am not like that tax collector over there. 12 I go without eating for two days a week, and I give you one tenth of all I earn.'

13 The tax collector stood off at a distance and did not think he was good enough even to look up toward heaven. He was so sorry for what he had done that he pounded his chest and prayed, 'God, have pity on me! I am such a sinner.'

14 Then Jesus said, 'When the two men went home, it was the tax collector and not the Pharisee who was pleasing to God. If you put yourself above others, you will be put down. But if you humble yourself, you will be honoured.'

LUKE 18:9–14

Commentary

It seems almost too obvious to us that God wouldn't be impressed by the one who was so full of himself, and that the other person experienced God's love and forgiveness. However, to the people of Jesus' day, this story would have come as something of a shock. The Pharisees were devout and God-fearing. They studied God's law carefully and kept it to the letter. They were examples of holy living for everyone else to follow, and surely, if anyone was going to be welcomed by God into heaven, it was them. As the Pharisee says, he does all the right things, just as the Old Testament law commanded, and lives a blameless life. Everyone would agree with him when he says that he is better than the tax collector, who works for the enemy Romans and steals money from the people. But Jesus turns things upside down. The good Pharisee isn't God's favourite after all; it's the tax collector! Why?

It isn't about what you do but the sort of person you are. You may be very religious, but if that makes you proud, then your religion means nothing. And you may be very much a criminal, but if you're truly sorry, your prayer is heard. This story is an important one for any of us who try to do the right thing before God. That's good, but if it means that we look down on others, we won't please God.

Visual aid

Find two balloons. Blow up one to represent the Pharisee, full of the hot air of his good deeds. The other should not be blown up: it represents the tax collector, who realises that he's not worthy to be used by God.

Activity idea

Play a word game together in which you try to outdo each other by making up pretend good deeds you have done that will qualify you for a special award. For example: 'I rescued a cat from a tree'; 'That's nothing, I rescued a whole family from a burning building'; 'Well, listen to this, I've just given £10,000 to help the poor' and so on. All this

Questions

▶ What was wrong with the Pharisee's prayer?

▶ What was right about the tax collector's prayer?

▶ How should the Pharisee have prayed?

▶ Who is like the Pharisee and who is like the tax collector today?

boasting is just like the Pharisee's prayer.

Prayer idea

Take the balloon that was not blown up, from the visual aid suggestion, and, with a breath from everyone in turn, make a prayer of saying 'sorry' to God for the ways in which you have let God and other people down. Burst the balloon that was already blown up, and tie off the other so that it can float above you as a family, reminding you that God has heard your prayer saying 'sorry' and forgives you.

Key verse

'If you put yourself above others, you will be put down. But if you humble yourself, you will be honoured' (Luke 18:14).

Old Testament story link

Daniel 9:3–10: This is Daniel's humble prayer before God on behalf of the people of Israel who have done wrong.

The death of Lazarus

¹⁷ When Jesus got to Bethany, he found that Lazarus had already been in the tomb four days. ¹⁸ Bethany was less than three kilometres from Jerusalem, ¹⁹ and many people had come from the city to comfort Martha and Mary because their brother had died.

²⁰ When Martha heard that Jesus had arrived, she went out to meet him, but Mary stayed in the house. ²¹ Martha said to Jesus, 'Lord, if you had been here, my brother would not have died. ²² Yet even now I know that God will do anything you ask.'

²³ Jesus told her, 'Your brother will live again!'

²⁴ Martha answered, 'I know that he will be raised to life on the last day, when all the dead are raised.'

²⁵ Jesus then said, 'I am the one who raises the dead to life! Everyone who has faith in me will live, even if they die. ²⁶ And everyone who lives because of faith in me will never really die. Do you believe this?'

²⁷ 'Yes, Lord!' she replied. 'I believe that you are Christ, the Son of God. You are the one we hoped would come into the world.' ...

³⁸ Jesus was still terribly upset. So he went to the tomb, which was a cave with a stone rolled against the entrance. ³⁹ Then he told the people to roll the stone away. But Martha said, 'Lord, you know that Lazarus has been dead four days, and there will be a bad smell.'

⁴⁰ Jesus replied, 'Didn't I tell you that if you had faith, you would see the glory of God?'

⁴¹ After the stone had been rolled aside, Jesus looked up toward heaven and prayed, 'Father, I thank you for answering my prayer. ⁴² I know that you always answer my prayers. But I said this, so that the people here would believe that you sent me.'

⁴³ When Jesus had finished praying, he shouted, 'Lazarus, come out!' ⁴⁴ The man who had been dead came out. His hands and feet were wrapped with strips of burial cloth, and a cloth covered his face.

Jesus then told the people, 'Untie him and let him go.'

JOHN 11:17–27, 38–44

Commentary

This miracle happened not long before the events of Holy Week and Easter. It was as if Jesus was using this moment to prepare people for what was about to happen to him, when he died and rose again. On that day, when the stone was rolled away from his tomb, it would be an even more glorious resurrection than Lazarus' return from the dead. Lazarus would die again, but Jesus was going to beat death for ever, and this is what he tells Martha, who puts her trust in him as the Son of God.

Mary and Martha were very special to Jesus and their brother's death made him very sad, but he was also angry at the way death and suffering had spoiled God's world. This is why Jesus came—to end the grip that death had on everything and to set people free, just as Lazarus needed untying from the burial cloths that were wrapped around him. This story points not just to Jesus as a good man or a great teacher, nor even as a compassionate healer, but to the deeper truth that he was sent by God with power over life and death. This is at the heart of what Christians believe, and, like Martha, we are being invited to respond to his question, 'Do you believe this?'

Questions

▶ Why didn't Jesus arrive at Bethany sooner?

▶ Why do you think Martha believed that Jesus could bring her brother back from the dead?

▶ Can you imagine how the mourners in the garden reacted when Jesus told them to roll the stone away?

▶ Jesus prayed to God before the miracle happened. What can we learn from this prayer?

Visual aid

Use a box of tissues as a focus for all the sadness at the beginning of this story. Imagine how each person would have cried and what they would have said in appreciation of Lazarus at his funeral.

Activity idea

Use some rolls of toilet tissue or kitchen paper to wrap up one member of the family, just as Lazarus would have been wrapped up in the story. Be careful to make sure that he or she can still breathe easily! Then, on the command 'Come out!' see how quickly he or she can break free.

Prayer idea

From a large piece of paper, cut out the shape of the cross, and on one side write down all the words you can think of that are linked to suffering and death—for example, tears, sadness, darkness and fear. Now cross out each of these words, turn the paper over and cover the other side of the cross with resurrection words such as light, love, life, laughter, hope and joy. Thank God together for the power of Jesus to make everything new.

Key verse

'Jesus then said, "I am the one who raises the dead to life"' (John 11:25).

Old Testament story link

Ezekiel 37:1–11: Ezekiel has a vision of dry bones coming to life again by the power of God's word and God's Spirit.

A rich young man

¹⁶ A man came to Jesus and asked, 'Teacher, what good thing must I do to have eternal life?'

¹⁷ Jesus said to him, 'Why do you ask me about what is good? Only God is good. If you want to have eternal life, you must obey his commandments.'

¹⁸ 'Which ones?' the man asked.

Jesus answered, 'Do not murder. Be faithful in marriage. Do not steal. Do not tell lies about others. ¹⁹ Respect your father and mother. And love others as much as you love yourself.' ²⁰ The young man said, 'I have obeyed all of these. What else must I do?'

²¹ Jesus replied, 'If you want to be perfect, go sell everything you own! Give the money to the poor, and you will have riches in heaven. Then come and be my follower.' ²² When the young man heard this, he was sad, because he was very rich.

²³ Jesus said to his disciples, 'It's terribly hard for rich people to get into the kingdom of heaven! ²⁴ In fact, it's easier for a camel to go through the eye of a needle than for a rich person to get into God's kingdom.'

²⁵ When the disciples heard this, they were greatly surprised and asked, 'How can anyone ever be saved?'

²⁶ Jesus looked straight at them and said, 'There are some things that people cannot do, but God can do anything.'

²⁷ Peter replied, 'Remember, we have left everything to be your followers! What will we get?'

²⁸ Jesus answered:

Yes, all of you have become my followers. And so in the future world, when the Son of Man sits on his glorious throne, I promise that you will sit on twelve thrones to judge the twelve tribes of Israel. ²⁹ All who have given up home or brothers and sisters or father and mother or children or land for me will be given a hundred times as much. They will also have eternal life. ³⁰ But many who are now first will be last, and many who are last will be first.

MATTHEW 19:16–30

Commentary

Jesus' teaching and miracles attracted many who wanted to become his disciples. Sometimes they were just people going with the crowd, but there were also those who longed to live God's way and be part of God's kingdom. The young man in this story certainly seemed to be trying to do the right thing. He knew the ten commandments and tried to keep them, although Jesus' first words to him are a reminder that only God is truly good.

The young man is rich, and Jesus sees that this is where the real stumbling block may lie for him. Money can gain a hold on people's hearts and minds in a way that distracts them from putting God first. This rich young man, as far as we know, walked away unwilling to let go of his love of money. This surprised the disciples, who had assumed that having money was a sign of God's blessing. On the contrary, Jesus says it can be a huge problem and that it can be much harder for these people to get into God's kingdom—but not impossible!

Peter and the others have already given up a lot to follow Jesus, and he reassures them that they will one day be richly rewarded. Things

Questions

▶ Why do you think the young man wanted eternal life?

▶ What is behind the young man's question about which of the commandments he should obey?

▶ Do you think Jesus wants everyone to sell everything they have, or was this just a command for the rich man in the story?

▶ Why were the disciples surprised by what Jesus said about rich people?

are very different in God's kingdom, where the last end up coming first, and the first, last.

Visual aid

Fill up a piggy bank with lots of money so that it rattles noisily and temptingly. Use this as a focus for all the riches that belonged to the young man. He was being asked to part with quite a lot.

Activity idea

If you can get hold of a set, play the board game 'Go for broke!' where the only way to win is to lose all your money. Alternatively, imagine your family has won £10,000 in a competition and work out together how you can give it *all* away to good causes. Talk about how you would share it out, but also reflect on how it feels not to keep any back for yourselves.

Prayer idea

Remind yourself of the ten commandments (see page 40) and, in particular, the tenth: 'Do not want what belongs to someone else'. Hand out a small amount of money to everyone in the family and pray together that God will help you have a right attitude towards it, to spend it or save it wisely. It may help if you imagine what this money could buy for yourself and then for someone else you might give it to.

Key verse
'There are some things that people cannot do, but God can do anything' (Matthew 19:26).

Old Testament story link

Ecclesiastes 5:10–20: Here are some wise words from King Solomon about money and wealth.

Blind Bartimaeus

⁴⁶ Jesus and his disciples went to Jericho. And as they were leaving, they were followed by a large crowd. A blind beggar by the name of Bartimaeus son of Timaeus was sitting beside the road. ⁴⁷ When he heard that it was Jesus from Nazareth, he shouted, 'Jesus, Son of David, have pity on me!' ⁴⁸ Many people told the man to stop, but he shouted even louder, 'Son of David, have pity on me!'

⁴⁹ Jesus stopped and said, 'Call him over!'

They called out to the blind man and said, 'Don't be afraid! Come on! He is calling for you.' ⁵⁰ The man threw off his coat as he jumped up and ran to Jesus.

⁵¹ Jesus asked, 'What do you want me to do for you?'

The blind man answered, 'Master, I want to see!'

⁵² Jesus told him, 'You may go. Your eyes are healed because of your faith.'

Right away the man could see, and he went down the road with Jesus.

MARK 10:46–52

Commentary

As usual, Jesus is surrounded by crowds of people. This time he is on his way from Jericho to Jerusalem for the Passover festival. His attention is increasingly on the coming events of Holy Week and Easter, yet he still finds time to bother about one person in the crowd—a person no one else is interested in.

Bartimaeus (this is his surname, not his first name, because, sadly, in those days sick or disabled people were treated with little respect) was a regular beggar on this route. The crowd were probably used to ignoring him or telling him to shut up, and they do so all the more when he starts calling out for Jesus. He is an embarrassment to everyone and he is holding up the journey to Jerusalem. But Jesus hears and sees this nobody and treats him with respect. Bartimaeus knows who Jesus is and even gives him his proper royal title of

'Son of David', showing more understanding and faith in Jesus than the crowds around him. His faith is rewarded: his sight is restored and now he sees Jesus for himself. As he looks at Jesus, he is looking into the face of God, who wants everyone to see properly with new eyes the wonders of this world and all the people he has created.

Visual aid

Cover a walking stick with white tape. Those who have difficulty with their eyesight often walk with a stick like this.

Activity idea

Bartimaeus must have had some friends who helped him down to the Jericho–Jerusalem road each day to sit and beg. Play a trust game in which one of you is blindfolded and has to let the others guide him or her around a simple obstacle course. People who lose their sight have to learn how to compensate by using the other senses better, such as touch and hearing.

Questions

▶ How do you think Bartimaeus knew that Jesus was there?

▶ Why did the crowds want to silence Bartimaeus?

▶ Bartimaeus was a determined man. How determined are we to get close to Jesus in prayer?

▶ Why do you think Jesus picked out Bartimaeus' cries above all the noise of the crowd?

▶ Do you think Bartimaeus was among those who stayed with Jesus through the events that happened in Jerusalem in the days to come?

Prayer idea

In some parts of the world, Christians pray out loud all at the same time. This reminds us that, when we pray, we are not talking to impress each other but to connect with God. Bartimaeus' prayer was shouted out loud above the noise of the crowd. Why not try this type of prayer as a family today? On the count of three, everyone should pray their prayer out loud at the same time.

Key verse

'Jesus told him, "... Your eyes are healed because of your faith"' (Mark 10:52).

Old Testament story link

Isaiah 35:3–10: Isaiah looks forward to the day when God will change everything.

Zacchaeus in the tree

¹ Jesus was going through Jericho, ² where a man named Zacchaeus lived. He was in charge of collecting taxes and was very rich. ³⁻⁴ Jesus was heading his way, and Zacchaeus wanted to see what he was like. But Zacchaeus was a short man and could not see over the crowd. So he ran ahead and climbed up into a sycamore tree.

⁵ When Jesus got there, he looked up and said, 'Zacchaeus, hurry down! I want to stay with you today.' ⁶ Zacchaeus hurried down and gladly welcomed Jesus.

⁷ Everyone who saw this started grumbling, 'This man Zacchaeus is a sinner! And Jesus is going home to eat with him.'

⁸ Later that day Zacchaeus stood up and said to the Lord, 'I will give half of my property to the poor. And I will now pay back four times as much to everyone I have ever cheated.'

⁹ Jesus said to Zacchaeus, 'Today you and your family have been saved, because you are a true son of Abraham. ¹⁰ The Son of Man came to look for and to save people who are lost.'

LUKE 19:1–10

Commentary

After about three years on the move around the villages of Galilee, as well as regular journeys south for festivals, Jesus is now in Jericho, from where he will set out to Jerusalem for the last time. The story of his meeting with Zacchaeus is just like the encounters that have gone before. Jesus notices the ones whom others don't see—in this case, Zacchaeus hiding in the tree. Jesus cares about the ones whom others think aren't worthy of God's love and rescue: tax collector Zacchaeus belongs to the group who have betrayed their country by working for the Romans. And Jesus turns lives around for the better—just as rich Zacchaeus becomes a blessing to Jericho, repaying his debts many times over and providing money for the poor of the city.

Zacchaeus turns from being public enemy number one to public benefactor. Only an encounter with Jesus can produce such a miracle. We have no record of what they said to each other at the meal in Zacchaeus' home, but, whatever it was, everyone is astounded by the change that comes over this little man. What happened to Zacchaeus is a picture of what happens to all who come close to God through Jesus.

Visual aid

Collect together half a dozen leaves. Put them in a pile as a focus for the leaves that might well have been knocked off by Zacchaeus as he climbed the sycamore tree.

Activity idea

This story is full of emotions—the excitement of the crowd because Jesus was in town; their anger because Zacchaeus wanted to see him too; their curiosity and bewilderment that Jesus was bothering with Zacchaeus; and their shock about what Zacchaeus said he would do with his money. Have a go at making the facial expressions and sound effects that go with these feelings. What other feelings can you find and re-enact from the story?

Questions

▶ Why do you think Zacchaeus wanted to see Jesus?

▶ What do you think of the crowd's reaction when they heard that Jesus had invited himself to Zacchaeus' home?

▶ What do you think happened at the meal to bring about such a transformation in Zacchaeus' attitude to money?

▶ What do you think Zacchaeus and his family did next?

Prayer idea

Zacchaeus turned over a new leaf because of his meeting with Jesus. Cut out some leaf shapes from paper. On one side, write words or draw pictures to represent those things that you are sorry about. Zacchaeus might have written greed, hurting others, betrayal or pride. Now turn over the leaves and write new words or draw new pictures that express how you want to be different with God's help—for example, more generous, more caring, more faithful or more humble. Make these leaves your prayers to God.

Key verse

'The Son of Man came to look for and to save people who are lost' (Luke 19:10).
Note: 'Son of Man' was the way Jesus often described himself.

Old Testament story link

Ezekiel 36:25–31: Ezekiel looks forward to the day when God will forgive the wrong things we do and will give everyone a new heart that wants to love and serve him instead.

The parable of the king's servants

[11] The crowd was still listening to Jesus as he was getting close to Jerusalem. Many of them thought that God's kingdom would soon appear, [12] and Jesus told them this story:

A prince once went to a foreign country to be crowned king and then to return. [13] But before leaving, he called in ten servants and gave each of them some money. He told them, 'Use this to earn more money until I get back.'

[14] But the people of his country hated him, and they sent messengers to the foreign country to say, 'We don't want this man to be our king.'

[15] After the prince had been made king, he returned and called in his servants. He asked them how much they had earned with the money they had been given.

[16] The first servant came and said, 'Sir, with the money you gave me I have earned ten times as much.'

[17] 'That's fine, my good servant!' the king said. 'Since you have shown that you can be trusted with a small amount, you will be given ten cities to rule.'

[18] The second one came and said, 'Sir, with the money you gave me, I have earned five times as much.'

[19] The king said, 'You will be given five cities.'

[20] Another servant came and said, 'Sir, here is your money. I kept it safe in a handkerchief. [21] You are a hard man, and I was afraid of you. You take what isn't yours, and you harvest crops you didn't plant.'

[22] 'You worthless servant!' the king told him. 'You have condemned yourself by what you have just said. You knew that I am a hard man, taking what isn't mine and harvesting what I haven't planted. [23] Why didn't you put my money in the bank? On my return, I could have had the money together with interest.'

[24] Then he said to some other servants standing there, 'Take the money away from him and give it to the servant who earned ten times as much.'

LUKE 19:11–24

Commentary

As Jesus travelled to Jerusalem for the Passover, people expected this to be his big moment. They wanted him to reveal himself as God's special king and seize the country back from its enemies. Although Jesus had tried to warn them that it wasn't going to happen this way, their hopes were rising nonetheless. In this parable he tries to turn their attention to something more important—how they will prepare for God's coming kingdom.

Two of the servants use their money well and earn the king's 'well done', but the third does nothing with his gift. He doesn't take any risks because he knows how angry the king will be if he loses everything. But he's wrong. The king is more angry that he does nothing. It's better to take a risk and lose than to take no risks at all.

This story would have been very special for the first-century Christians to read as they waited for Jesus to return as king, because it showed them how to act in the meantime. The kingdom was going to come, but more slowly than they had at first expected, and this would call for patience and hard work. Those who show these qualities are the ones who will be rewarded.

Questions

▶ In this parable, who do you think are the prince, the king and the servants? What does the money represent?

▶ What do you think the king would have said to the third servant if he had used his money but lost it all, perhaps by giving it to charity or by building a hospital that then got burned down in a fire?

▶ Is there something wrong with the third servant's understanding of what the king is like?

▶ What gifts and talents do you have that you could use for God?

Visual aid

Wrap some coins in a handkerchief and make this the focus for what the last servant did with his money.

Activity idea

Imagine that everyone in the family has been given £5.00. Talk about how each of you might use it to do something good for others. Could you think of ways of using it to make more money or to increase its value in some other way? You might even give everyone a real pound coin and ask them to do something practical with it over the next week.

Prayer idea

On a separate piece of paper for each member of the family other than yourself, write these words: 'God says, "Well done…"' Fill in the name of the other member of the family, add the words 'because God has given you the gift of…' and write something that this person is good at. Give the papers to each person to read. Thank God together that he has given you all so many different talents and skills to use for him.

Key verse

'"That's fine, my good servant!" the king said. "… You have shown that you can be trusted"' (Luke 19:17).

Old Testament story link

Proverbs 3:1–12: King Solomon gives wise advice about how to live a life that will please God.

The tenants of a vineyard

[9] Jesus told the people this story:

A man once planted a vineyard and let it. Then he left the country for a long time. [10] When it was time to harvest the crop, he sent a servant to ask the tenants for his share of the grapes. But they beat up the servant and sent him away without anything. [11] So the owner sent another servant. The tenants also beat him up. They insulted him terribly and sent him away without a thing. [12] The owner sent a third servant. He was also beaten terribly and thrown out of the vineyard.

[13] The owner then said to himself, 'What am I going to do? I know what. I'll send my son, the one I love so much. They will surely respect him!'

[14] When the tenants saw the owner's son, they said to one another, 'Some day he will own the vineyard. Let's kill him! Then we can have it all for ourselves.' [15] So they threw him out of the vineyard and killed him.

Jesus asked, 'What do you think the owner of the vineyard will do? [16] I'll tell you what. He will come and kill those tenants and let someone else have his vineyard.'

When the people heard this, they said, 'This must never happen!'

[17] But Jesus looked straight at them and said, 'Then what do the Scriptures mean when they say, "The stone that the builders tossed aside is now the most important stone of all"? [18] Anyone who stumbles over this stone will get hurt, and anyone it falls on will be smashed to pieces.'

[19] The chief priests and the teachers of the Law of Moses knew that Jesus was talking about them when he was telling this story. They wanted to arrest him at once, but they were afraid of the people.

Luke 20:9–19

Commentary

Jesus had warned people that he was going to suffer and die, but they simply wouldn't accept it, so this time he put it in a story. Although many were intrigued by what he said, it was probably only the religious leaders who understood what he was talking about, and it infuriated them. They recognised that they were the ones looking after the 'vineyard', which was often used as a way of describing God's chosen people.

The leaders are portrayed as the bad guys, so concerned to keep the vineyard's harvest for themselves that they treat each of the messengers disgracefully and then even kill the owner's son. Jesus is talking about himself as the son and, once again, predicting his own death. But this won't be the end. He then turns to another famous saying from the Old Testament about a stone that is rejected but becomes the most important of all. It is a clue to the resurrection, of course, but one that most people would only have understood much later.

Visual aid

Use a bunch of grapes and a scruffy-looking toy brick as a focus for the story.

Questions

▶ Why do you think the chief priests and teachers disliked this parable so much?

▶ What prompted the owner of the vineyard to send his own son to go and collect his share of the harvest?

▶ Why did the people who were renting the vineyard kill the son?

▶ What do you think the vineyard owner should have done next?

Activity idea

Gather together 21 wooden bricks and build a small pyramid. Start with a base that is four by four and, on top, add a layer that is two by two. For the final top brick of the pyramid, you are going to use the scruffy brick from the visual aid suggestion. Put all the bricks together, but reject the one that looks scruffy and try to build your pyramid without it, only to realise that you need the one you rejected to complete it properly.

Prayer idea

Jesus describes himself both as the son who gets killed and as the rejected stone that gets used in the end. Using the bricks from the activity idea, put down one every time you can think of someone who is sad, lonely, needy or in pain. There may even be a situation in your own life as a family that has these feelings attached to it. Pause each time and then lift up the 'sad' brick, place the scruffy brick that represents Jesus beneath it and say together, 'Jesus understands what it's like to be rejected and can lift us up high again.'

Key verse

'The stone that the builders tossed aside is now the most important stone of all' (Luke 20:17).

Old Testament story link

Psalm 118:21–29: This is the psalm of praise that contains the line about the stone used in today's story.

The sheep and the goats

[31] When the Son of Man comes in his glory with all of his angels, he will sit on his royal throne. [32] The people of all nations will be brought before him, and he will separate them, as shepherds separate their sheep from their goats.

[33] He will place the sheep on his right and the goats on his left. [34] Then the king will say to those on his right, 'My father has blessed you! Come and receive the kingdom that was prepared for you before the world was created. [35] When I was hungry, you gave me something to eat, and when I was thirsty, you gave me something to drink. When I was a stranger, you welcomed me, [36] and when I was naked, you gave me clothes to wear. When I was sick, you took care of me, and when I was in jail, you visited me.'

[37] Then the ones who pleased the Lord will ask, 'When did we give you something to eat or drink? [38] When did we welcome you as a stranger or give you clothes to wear [39] or visit you while you were sick or in jail?'

[40] The king will answer, 'Whenever you did it for any of my people, no matter how unimportant they seemed, you did it for me.'

[41] Then the king will say to those on his left, 'Get away from me! You are under God's curse. Go into the everlasting fire prepared for the devil and his angels! [42] I was hungry, but you did not give me anything to eat, and I was thirsty, but you did not give me anything to drink. [43] I was a stranger, but you did not welcome me, and I was naked, but you did not give me any clothes to wear. I was sick and in jail, but you did not take care of me.'

[44] Then the people will ask, 'Lord, when did we fail to help you when you were hungry or thirsty or a stranger or naked or sick or in jail?'

[45] The king will say to them, 'Whenever you failed to help any of my people, no matter how unimportant they seemed, you failed to do it for me.'

[46] Then Jesus said, 'Those people will be punished for ever. But the ones who pleased God will have eternal life.'

MATTHEW 25:31–46

Commentary

This is possibly the last story Jesus told the crowds before his final meal, arrest and death on the cross. He wanted his listeners to know that soon it would be time to separate out those who had lived their lives generously and those who had closed their hearts to other people's needs. When God looks on our lives, it isn't how clever, rich or famous we are that matters in the end, but whether we have shown love to others.

Jesus uses the image of a shepherd sorting out the goats and sheep in his flock—a familiar sight in those times. The striking part of this parable is that those who showed kindness and love did so without realising it. Each little act of compassion had been noticed by God; every time they cared for others, it had also been a way of loving God himself. The second group is condemned for not noticing people's needs. How can anyone see the massive needs there are in this world and not want to do something to help? This is a challenging story, but also full of hope, as it is clear that God sees every little good thing done to others as a way of serving him. And because God is always more ready

to forgive than condemn, this is good news for everyone.

Questions

▶ What good things have the ones on the king's right hand done?

▶ What didn't they realise about the good deeds that they were doing?

▶ Why do you think those on his left didn't see the needs of others around them?

▶ What do you think causes God most pain?

▶ How can we do things that please God today?

Visual aid

To represent the ways of love talked about in the story, set out something to eat, a glass of water, a cup of tea, an item of clothing, a bandage and a visiting card.

Activity idea

Look through some aid magazines and find pictures of people who are hungry, thirsty, in need of clothes or hospitality, sick or in prison. Talk about what would be the best ways of helping each of these people if we came across them in everyday life. Pin up the pictures and add the words of the key verse below to create a poster for your home.

Prayer idea

Use the poster you have made with the magazine pictures, not only as a focus for prayer for those in need but also to ask God what he wants you to do about each situation. Leave some space in between your prayers to tune into what God may be saying to you.

Key verse

'Whenever you did it for any of my people, no matter how unimportant they seemed, you did it for me' (Matthew 25:40).

Old Testament story link

Ezekiel 34:11–31: Ezekiel compares God to a good shepherd and describes how he will care for his flocks and will sometimes need to divide them up.

Jesus arrives in Jerusalem

28 When Jesus had finished saying all this, he went on toward Jerusalem. 29 As he was getting near Bethphage and Bethany on the Mount of Olives, he sent two of his disciples on ahead. 30 He told them, 'Go into the next village, where you will find a young donkey that has never been ridden. Untie the donkey and bring it here. 31 If anyone asks why you are doing that, just say, "The Lord needs it."'

32 They went off and found everything just as Jesus had said. 33 While they were untying the donkey, its owners asked, 'Why are you doing that?'

34 They answered, 'The Lord needs it.'

35 Then they led the donkey to Jesus. They put some of their clothes on its back and helped Jesus get on. 36 And as he rode along, the people spread clothes on the road in front of him. 37 When Jesus was starting down the Mount of Olives, his large crowd of disciples were happy and praised God because of all the miracles they had seen. 38 They shouted,

'Blessed is the king who comes
     in the name of the Lord!
Peace in heaven
     and glory to God.'

39 Some Pharisees in the crowd said to Jesus, 'Teacher, make your disciples stop shouting!'

40 But Jesus answered, 'If they keep quiet, these stones will start shouting.'

LUKE **19:28–40**

Commentary

The final week of Jesus' life arrives. It is such an important week that each of the Gospels devotes several chapters to the events of the next few days. The news of Jesus' wonderful deeds, teaching and healing people, assures him of a hero's welcome into Jerusalem on the day we now call Palm Sunday.

In the style of a victory procession for a Roman general, people line the streets, waving palms and throwing their clothes on to the road to make a sort of red carpet for a new king. They shout out an extravagant welcome, believing that Jesus has come to rescue them from the Romans. Their words about peace and glory are almost an echo of what the angels sang on the night Jesus was born, but, just as the arrival of the king then as a helpless baby was unexpected, so this arrival takes everyone by surprise too. He chooses to ride a donkey, not a fine white stallion, which would have better suited a great king. Jesus is a different sort of king; even so, he recognises that this is a day of rejoicing because an amazing rescue is about to happen, one that the crowds cannot begin to imagine.

Questions

▶ What makes you think that Jesus had planned ahead for this special day?

▶ What was so special about this particular donkey?

▶ Why had such large crowds gathered to welcome Jesus?

▶ What sort of king was everyone expecting?

▶ Why were the Pharisees so upset?

Visual aid

Find a branch with large leaves to be your 'palms' for this story. You might even be able to find a real palm leaf somewhere, or perhaps a cross made from palm leaves.

Activity idea

Many Christians receive a palm cross at church on the Sunday when we remember this story. You may already have one. On the internet there are instructions for how to fold paper to make your own palm cross. Once you have something to wave, recreate the sounds of that day, cheering and shouting 'Hosanna!', which means 'Save us!'

Prayer idea

Use the palms of your hands to signpost different sorts of prayer.

- Wave the palms of your hands in praise of Jesus.
- Hold up your palms asking Jesus to be king of your life this day.
- Turn over your palms to let go of all that is bad.
- Press together the palms of your hands and ask God to help you to be ready to say 'yes'.
- Stretch out your palms to bless each other in the name of the one who comes in the name of the Lord.

Key verse

'Blessed is the king who comes in the name of the Lord!' (Luke 19:38).

Old Testament story link

Zechariah 9:9–10: Long ago, the prophet Zechariah wrote about the way in which the special king from God would arrive in Jerusalem.

Cleansing the temple

13 Not long before the Jewish festival of Passover, Jesus went to Jerusalem. 14 There he found people selling cattle, sheep, and doves in the temple. He also saw moneychangers sitting at their tables. 15 So he took some rope and made a whip. Then he chased everyone out of the temple, together with their sheep and cattle. He turned over the tables of the moneychangers and scattered their coins.

16 Jesus said to the people who had been selling doves, 'Get those doves out of here! Don't make my Father's house a market place.'

17 The disciples then remembered that the Scriptures say, 'My love for your house burns in me like a fire.'

18 The Jewish leaders asked Jesus, 'What miracle will you work to show us why you have done this?'

19 'Destroy this temple,' Jesus answered, 'and in three days I will build it again!'

20 The leaders replied, 'It took forty-six years to build this temple. What makes you think you can rebuild it in three days?'

21 But Jesus was talking about his body as a temple. 22 And when he was raised from death, his disciples remembered what he had told them. Then they believed the Scriptures and the words of Jesus.

JOHN 2:13–22

Commentary

To worship at the temple in Jerusalem for one of the great festivals was a high point for any Jewish believer. This was particularly true of the annual Passover celebrations, which commemorated the time when God rescued the nation from being slaves in Egypt. Thousands of pilgrims arrived and crowded into the outer courts, eager to buy the necessary animals—mainly sheep or doves—to use in the special ceremonies. The religious leaders set up market stalls and also, because the use of Roman coins was forbidden in the temple precincts, a place to change money into the right currency to spend. In fact, it had become a huge money-making event—that is, until Jesus appeared.

When he visited the temple as a young boy, Jesus told Mary that this was his father's house, and it is these words that echo around the building again as he drives out all those who are buying and selling. When challenged by the authorities, he replies with what seems to them to be a riddle, claiming that, should the temple be destroyed, he will rebuild it in three days. Only much later did his disciples realise what he had been saying. He was predicting his resurrection; however, the Jewish leaders took his words literally and stored them up as evidence to use against him when they put him on trial for insulting the temple and their God.

Visual aid

Turn a small table upside down and use it as a focus for today's story. Jesus was always turning ideas upside down, and now even the furniture is being overturned!

Activity idea

This is a story of great noise and confusion. Divide up the following sound effects among you as a family: the bleating of sheep, the lowing of cattle, the cooing of doves, the rattle of coins falling, the shouts of the stallholders and the angry voice of Jesus. Rehearse the sounds individually and then, on the count of three, all join together to recreate the noise in the temple on the day Jesus arrived. Make Jesus' words the last and loudest sound to be heard.

Prayer idea

For each of the different things in the story, create a prayer that asks God to help you not to make the same mistakes—for example, 'May we not be like sheep and wander from you'; 'May we not be like foolish cattle and miss hearing your voice'; 'May we be like doves, always knowing how to fly home back to you'; 'May we not be like coins spent on things that take us away from you.'

Questions

▶ Does it surprise you that Jesus acted so violently in this story?

▶ What was it exactly that made Jesus so angry?

▶ What did Jesus mean about rebuilding the temple in three days?

▶ When, if ever, is it right to be really angry like this?

Key verse

'"Destroy this temple," Jesus answered, "and in three days I will build it again"' (John 2:19).

Old Testament story link

Hosea 6:1–6: Hosea warns God's people of the dangers of falling away from him, but also predicts God's willingness to put them right again.

The plot to kill Jesus

1 The Festival of Thin Bread, also called Passover, was near. 2 The chief priests and the teachers of the Law of Moses were looking for a way to get rid of Jesus, because they were afraid of what the people might do. 3 Then Satan entered the heart of Judas Iscariot, who was one of the twelve apostles.

4 Judas went to talk with the chief priests and the officers of the temple police about how he could help them arrest Jesus. 5 They were very pleased and offered to pay Judas some money. 6 He agreed and started looking for a good chance to betray Jesus when the crowds were not around.

7 The day had come for the Festival of Thin Bread, and it was time to kill the Passover lambs. 8 So Jesus said to Peter and John, 'Go and prepare the Passover meal for us to eat.'

9 But they asked, 'Where do you want us to prepare it?'

10 Jesus told them, 'As you go into the city, you will meet a man carrying a jar of water. Follow him into the house 11 and say to the owner, "Our teacher wants to know where he can eat the Passover meal with his disciples." 12 The owner will take you upstairs and show you a large room ready for you to use. Prepare the meal there.'

13 Peter and John left. They found everything just as Jesus had told them, and they prepared the Passover meal.

LUKE 22:1–13

Commentary

The storm clouds were gathering. Jesus' behaviour in the temple had dismayed many people and convinced the religious leaders that Jesus was becoming an embarrassment to them and a risk, because his behaviour could provoke the Roman soldiers to come down heavily on the festival crowds. They were also fearful of losing their own position of influence and power. They could see no other solution than to have Jesus killed.

It is hard to understand what Judas' motives were in striking a deal with the chief priests. Clearly money was involved. Perhaps he also thought that Jesus needed to confront the leaders and do a spectacular miracle to convince them that he was the true king. There is no doubt what the other disciples thought about him: he was a traitor in the grip of the devil.

In the meantime, it was clear that the one person really in charge was Jesus, who had arranged a place for them all to celebrate the special Passover meal. All they had to do was to follow a man with a water jar, which would have been an unusual sight in those days, and therefore came as an almost comical game of 'follow the leader' in what was otherwise such a tragic week.

Questions

▶ Why were the chief priests and teachers of the Law so eager to get rid of Jesus?

▶ Why do you think Judas struck a deal with the religious leaders?

▶ What makes you think Jesus had planned ahead?

▶ Who would you invite to a special meal for an important festival like the Passover?

Visual aid

Dress someone from the family in dark glasses and a hoodie with the hood up. This story is all about holding secret meetings, plotting and being on the lookout, like spies, for a particular sign that will lead you to the right place to be.

Activity idea

Try to work out what prompted Judas to go and meet the religious leaders. Divide into two groups and put Judas on trial, one group accusing him and the other trying to defend him. Work out what each of you thinks about Judas and also consider what Jesus would have thought about him. Do you think Jesus would have understood and forgiven him?

Prayer idea

Whatever we think about Judas, he stands as a warning to each of us not to do the wrong thing. We all need help to discover the way ahead when faced by hard decisions. Use the letters of the name JUDAS to help you pray about this. For example, ask God to help you to **J**udge tricky situations properly; **U**nderstand the way to go; **D**ecide what will be good for other people, not just yourself; **A**dmit your need; and **S**eek God's will.

Key verse

'They found everything just as Jesus had told them' (Luke 22:13).

Old Testament story link

Psalm 37:1–9: Here is a psalm of David with advice about making the right choices in life.

The perfume offering

[1] It was now two days before Passover and the Festival of Thin Bread. The chief priests and the teachers of the Law of Moses were secretly planning to have Jesus arrested and put to death. [2] They were saying, 'We must not do it during the festival, because the people will riot.'

[3] Jesus was eating in Bethany at the home of Simon, who once had leprosy, when a woman came in with a very expensive bottle of sweet-smelling perfume. After breaking it open, she poured the perfume on Jesus' head. [4] This made some of the guests angry, and they complained, 'Why such a waste? [5] We could have sold this perfume for more than three hundred silver coins and given the money to the poor!' So they started saying cruel things to the woman.

[6] But Jesus said:

Leave her alone! Why are you bothering her? She has done a beautiful thing for me. [7] You will always have the poor with you. And whenever you want to, you can give to them. But you won't always have me here with you. [8] She has done all she could by pouring perfume on my body to prepare it for burial. [9] You may be sure that wherever the good news is told all over the world, people will remember what she has done. And they will tell others.

MARK 14:1–9

Commentary

It seems that Jesus didn't stay in the city overnight but returned with his disciples each evening to Bethany, where Mary, Martha and Lazarus lived. In this story they are dinner guests of a man called Simon, who has been a leper (perhaps Jesus healed him), when a woman appears with expensive perfume to pour over Jesus' head. She may be Mary or Martha from nearby, or possibly another woman called Mary, nicknamed 'Magdalene', who came from Galilee and whom Jesus had dramatically healed. The guests are outraged that so much costly perfume is being wasted. It could have been spent on those in need—the elderly or the sick.

As so often, Jesus' response is a surprise. He knows that he's going to die soon, and perhaps the woman is the only other person in that room to realise this. What she is offering him is a very special gift indeed; here is someone who cares for and understands him. It is an act of kindness that everyone should hear about, Jesus tells them all, and his words have come true: the woman's story has been told right around the world, including to you today.

Visual aid

Spray some perfume around and appreciate how its aroma fills the room you are in. This is what it must have been like in Simon's house when the woman poured the perfume. It was a reminder of her love for Jesus that stayed around for a long time to come.

Activity idea

What we choose to spend our money on can often cause arguments. Is it right, for example, for a church to spend money on new facilities rather than giving the money away to help people in need? Discuss the arguments for and against the woman's actions in the story. Was she right to spend so much on her devotion to Jesus? Were the guests justified to be so angry? Whose side was Jesus on, and why?

Questions

▶ Why did Jesus and the disciples decide to stay with friends outside Jerusalem?

▶ Why do you think Simon invited Jesus to a meal?

▶ What did Jesus mean by saying, 'You will always have the poor with you'? Does this mean we are not expected to give money to those in need?

▶ Why did the woman choose to use such expensive perfume? Wouldn't it have made more sense to use perfume that didn't cost so much?

Prayer idea

The smell of incense or perfume is used today by Christians in some church services. It is both something beautiful for God and a picture of our prayers and worship. Using a spray-perfume bottle, allow everyone to spray a small amount of the perfume every time he or she says a prayer. Pray that the good news of Jesus will spread like the fragrance of the perfume into every corner of people's lives and around the world.

Key verse

'But Jesus said, "… She has done a beautiful thing for me"' (Mark 14:6).

Old Testament story link

Exodus 30:1–10: Moses gives instructions for making a special altar where incense can be burnt to help people experience the special presence of God.

The Last Supper

¹⁴ When the time came for Jesus and the apostles to eat, ¹⁵ he said to them, 'I have very much wanted to eat this Passover meal with you before I suffer. ¹⁶ I tell you that I will not eat another Passover meal until it is finally eaten in God's kingdom.'

¹⁷ Jesus took a cup of wine in his hands and gave thanks to God. Then he told the apostles, 'Take this wine and share it with each other. ¹⁸ I tell you that I will not drink any more wine until God's kingdom comes.'

¹⁹ Jesus took some bread in his hands and gave thanks for it. He broke the bread and handed it to his apostles. Then he said, 'This is my body, which is given for you. Eat this as a way of remembering me!'

²⁰ After the meal he took another cup of wine in his hands. Then he said, 'This is my blood. It is poured out for you, and with it God makes his new agreement. ²¹ The one who will betray me is here at the table with me! ²² The Son of Man will die in the way that has been decided for him, but it will be terrible for the one who betrays him!'

²³ Then the apostles started arguing about who would ever do such a thing.

LUKE 22:14–23

Commentary

The Passover meal is still celebrated every year in Jewish homes. There are particular words that are said and certain foods eaten, which help tell the story of how God sent Moses to lead the Hebrews out of slavery under the Egyptians to freedom across the Red Sea. Each cup of wine that is drunk has special prayers linked to it, and the bread that is eaten is flat because it is made without yeast. The first Passover meal was eaten in such a rush, as they waited for the signal from Moses to leave Egypt, that there was no time to wait for the dough to rise. It was also during this meal that they remembered how the angel of death had passed over the Israelites' homes, which had been marked with lamb's blood on the doorposts. It was therefore not just an escape from slavery but from death itself.

Jesus was the host for this particular Passover meal with his friends, but, to their surprise, he took some of the traditional parts of the ceremony and gave them new meanings. He described the bread as his body and the wine as his blood. He wanted his disciples to have a way of remembering his death, now only hours away, which would rescue them just as the blood on the doorposts had saved the Israelites long ago. It was the only way Jesus could rescue the world and already, because of Judas, plans for his capture, trial and crucifixion were well under way.

Visual aid

You will need a piece of bread that has been made without yeast (for example, Matzo) and a cup of non-alcoholic wine. Jesus gave these ordinary items of food and drink special meanings at the Last Supper.

Activity idea

Find out what is eaten at a typical Jewish Passover meal. You could research this as a family from a book or on the internet. How is each item of food at the meal linked to the story of the escape from Egypt?

Questions

▶ Can you imagine what the atmosphere was like at the meal table during this Passover?

▶ Why do Christians today call this 'the Last Supper'?

▶ What good news does Jesus share at this meal before he begins talking about his blood and body?

▶ Have you ever been to a church service where this meal has been re-enacted? What happened?

Prayer idea

Eating the bread and drinking the wine are ways of remembering Jesus and what happened on Good Friday. Talk about the special reminders you could carry with you to help you remember to pray for your family, your friends, people in need and people far away. For example, you could choose ribbons of different colours, or beads that are differently shaped. Decide what you as a family will use as reminders while you are away from each other and from home.

Key verse

'Jesus... broke the bread and handed it to his apostles. Then he said, "This is my body"' (Luke 22:19).

Old Testament story link

Exodus 13:3–10: Moses gives instructions about the bread to be used at the Passover meal.

Gethsemane

36 Jesus went with his disciples to a place called Gethsemane. When they got there, he told them, 'Sit here while I go over there and pray.'

37 Jesus took along Peter and the two brothers, James and John. He was very sad and troubled, 38 and he said to them, 'I am so sad that I feel as if I am dying. Stay here and keep awake with me.'

39 Jesus walked on a little way. Then he knelt with his face to the ground and prayed, 'My Father, if it is possible, don't make me suffer by having me drink from this cup. But do what you want, and not what I want.'

40 He came back and found his disciples sleeping. So he said to Peter, 'Can't any of you stay awake with me for just one hour? 41 Stay awake and pray that you won't be tested. You want to do what is right, but you are weak.'

42 Again Jesus went to pray and said, 'My Father, if there is no other way, and I must suffer, I will still do what you want.'

43 Jesus came back and found them sleeping again. They simply could not keep their eyes open. 44 He left them and prayed the same prayer once more.

45 Finally, Jesus returned to his disciples and said, 'Are you still sleeping and resting? The time has come for the Son of Man to be handed over to sinners. 46 Get up! Let's go. The one who will betray me is already here.'

MATTHEW 26:36–46

Commentary

At Gethsemane there was a garden of olive trees, which seems to have been a favourite place for Jesus to find peace and quiet, away from the hustle and bustle of Jerusalem. It was here that he took his disciples late on the Thursday night after the Passover meal had finished. Jesus clearly needed time alone with God, but he also wanted his friends nearby as he faced the biggest decision of his life—a decision that would mean life or death for the whole world.

Christians believe that Jesus was not only God but also fully human, which means that Jesus felt fear and was open to temptation just like any of us. It would have been so simple just to turn his back on the suffering that lay ahead, which he calls 'the cup' he must drink. No wonder he wrestled with God. His friends must have heard his sighs and groans, but it was late and they were very tired. They couldn't stay awake to be with him, as he'd asked them to. It was already beginning to happen: even his own disciples were letting him down and he would have to face what was coming on his own. But this decision in this garden was the only way to repair the damage of that other decision in the garden of Eden long ago, when Adam and Eve gave in to the temptation to follow their way and not God's.

Visual aid

Gethsemane was a place where olives grew. Have a few olives to taste.

Activity idea

Have you ever been out in the garden or in the open, late at night? Choose an evening to do this together. Notice how different it feels to be outdoors in the dark, and listen to the sounds. Now that you are outside, is there anything that helps you to think about God or encourages you to pray? Imagine the tired disciples waiting in the dark and trying to stay awake for Jesus.

Prayer idea

It is from this story that Christians get the idea of kneeling for prayer, just as Jesus did. Traditionally Jews would stand with hands raised when they prayed, so why did Jesus do it differently here? For your prayers today, experiment with a new way of standing, sitting or kneeling, and perhaps also change what you do with your hands. Whatever you pray about, pray the prayer three times with spaces in between, just as Jesus did in the story.

Questions

▶ Why did Jesus choose to come to Gethsemane to pray rather than stay in the upstairs room in Jerusalem?

▶ What big decisions have you had to make, and what helped you to make them?

▶ Why was it important that Jesus would die on a cross?

▶ How could his closest disciples let him down in the way that they did?

Key verse

'My father, if there is no other way, and I must suffer, I will still do what you want' (Matthew 26:42).

Old Testament story link

Exodus 17:8–15: This is the story of how Moses went to pray on a hilltop with help from his friends, while the Israelites were fighting a battle down below.

Peter denies Jesus

57 After Jesus had been arrested, he was led off to the house of Caiaphas the high priest. The nation's leaders and the teachers of the Law of Moses were meeting there. 58 But Peter followed along at a distance and came to the courtyard of the high priest's palace. He went in and sat down with the guards to see what was going to happen...

69 While Peter was sitting out in the courtyard, a servant girl came up to him and said, 'You were with Jesus from Galilee.'

70 But in front of everyone Peter said, 'That isn't so! I don't know what you are talking about!'

71 When Peter had gone out to the gate, another servant girl saw him and said to some people there, 'This man was with Jesus from Nazareth.'

72 Again Peter denied it, and this time he swore, 'I don't even know that man!'

73 A little while later some people standing there walked over to Peter and said, 'We know that you are one of them. We can tell it because you talk like someone from Galilee.'

74 Peter began to curse and swear, 'I don't know that man!'

At once a cock crowed, 75 and Peter remembered that Jesus had said, 'Before a cock crows, you will say three times that you don't know me.' Then Peter went out and cried hard.

MATTHEW 26:57–58, 69–75

Commentary

Jesus had been arrested in the garden of Gethsemane and taken to the high priest's house for trial in the middle of the night. The religious leaders were anxious to get rid of him as soon as possible. The disciples had all run away when Jesus was captured, except for Peter, who followed the temple guards secretly and made his way to where Jesus was being held. Inside they were busy interrogating Jesus, accusing him of all sorts of things that he hadn't done. Jesus said very little, but just once he let them know that he was from God, and this caused uproar.

Peter was nearby in the courtyard and possibly heard the angry shouts, but was helpless to do anything. He must have been terrified and, as a result, he denied being one of Jesus' followers, even saying that he never knew him. Jesus had warned him that this would happen, but Peter hadn't believed it. No wonder he burst into tears and disappeared off into the darkness.

This is a remarkable piece of honest reporting. Peter went on to become a leader of the church, but he didn't mind people knowing how low he had once sunk. Perhaps he wanted them to understand how much Jesus loved him and, therefore, each one of us, that he could forgive even this betrayal.

Questions

▶ Was Peter brave or foolish to follow Jesus to the courtyard?

▶ Have you ever let someone down? How did you feel?

▶ Have you ever been let down by someone else? Were you able to forgive them?

▶ What was it that made Peter betray his best friend like this?

Visual aid

Find a picture of a cockerel and have a go at adding your own sound effects to the story. This sound must have been a permanent reminder to Peter of what happened that night.

Activity idea

Peter was put under pressure to reply quickly to the people's questions. So much must have been going on his head: should he say 'yes' to knowing Jesus or deny all knowledge of him? Between you, try to imagine the quarrel going on inside his own mind before he spoke. What arguments are there for saying one thing or the other? What were the risks involved? What was his head saying as opposed to his heart? Try to step into Peter's conscience and explore the story from this point of view.

Prayer idea

After a short time of quiet, ask God to forgive you for the ways you have let him down and then be honest with each other and forgive each other for the ways you have let each other down. Sometimes, as for Peter, tears are involved when we say 'sorry' properly like this.

Key verse

'Then Peter went out and cried hard' (Matthew 26:75).

Old Testament story link

Psalm 51:1–19: This is David's prayer, saying 'sorry' after he had let God down very badly.

The death sentence

¹⁵ During Passover the governor always freed a prisoner chosen by the people. ¹⁶ At that time a well-known terrorist named Jesus Barabbas was in jail. ¹⁷ So when the crowd came together, Pilate asked them, 'Which prisoner do you want me to set free? Do you want Jesus Barabbas or Jesus who is called the Messiah?' ¹⁸ Pilate knew that the leaders had brought Jesus to him because they were jealous.

¹⁹ While Pilate was judging the case, his wife sent him a message. It said, 'Don't have anything to do with that innocent man. I have had nightmares because of him.'

²⁰ But the chief priests and the leaders convinced the crowds to ask for Barabbas to be set free and for Jesus to be killed. ²¹ Pilate asked the crowd again, 'Which of these two men do you want me to set free?'

'Barabbas!' they replied.

²² Pilate asked them, 'What am I to do with Jesus, who is called the Messiah?'

They all yelled, 'Nail him to a cross!'

²³ Pilate answered, 'But what crime has he done?'

'Nail him to a cross!' they yelled even louder.

²⁴ Pilate saw that there was nothing he could do and that the people were starting to riot. So he took some water and washed his hands in front of them and said, 'I won't have anything to do with killing this man. You are the ones doing it!'

²⁵ Everyone answered, 'We and our own families will take the blame for his death!'

²⁶ Pilate set Barabbas free. Then he ordered his soldiers to beat Jesus with a whip and nail him to a cross.

MATTHEW 27:15–26

The tragic events of Good Friday are rapidly moving to a conclusion. The trial in the early morning resulted in a verdict of 'guilty', but, because the Romans held power in Judea, the religious leaders had to ask the Roman governor to approve Jesus' death sentence. Pontius Pilate interrogated Jesus but could find no reason to condemn him, so he thought he would appeal to the crowds, using the local custom of setting a prisoner free at Passover time. Barabbas was someone who had tried to get rid of the Romans by force, but he had been captured. He had tried to be the sort of revolutionary king the people wanted, and that many had hoped Jesus would become. So who would the crowd choose? The chief priests and leaders left nothing to chance and stirred up the people to call for Barabbas.

It's hard to believe that so many who must have heard

Jesus speak, or, at the very least, heard of the miracles he has done, now turn against him. It seems that people in a crowd often act against their better judgement. Pilate can't find any fault in Jesus, and even Pilate's wife declares that he is innocent on the basis of a dream she has had. The truth is that only through the willing death of someone who had done nothing wrong could the power of evil be broken.

Visual aid

Make a bowl of water, some soap and a towel available. Give everybody the opportunity to wash their hands. Pilate washed his hands as a way of letting the people know that, whatever happened next, it was not his responsibility—but does this really let him off the hook?

Activity idea

From the internet find a picture depicting the moment when Pilate presented Jesus to the crowd. There is a famous one by the artist Antonio Ciseri, called *Behold the Man!* Talk about the different people you can see in the picture and imagine what each one is

Questions

▶ What impression of Pilate's character do you get from the story?

▶ What do you think Barabbas thought about Jesus and what happened that day?

▶ Have you ever gone along with what everyone is saying even when you didn't agree?

▶ How does this story make you feel?

---

thinking at that moment. What do you think is going through Jesus' mind as the crowds call for his death?

Prayer idea

Barabbas is a murderer, the leaders are jealous, Pilate blames the crowd, and the crowds are swayed by the feelings of the moment; only Jesus is innocent. On a blank outline of a cross, use different dark colours to scribble inside the outline until the cross is all coloured in. Each scribble represents some of the bad things that Jesus is going to battle with on the cross, such as the hatred and hurt, betrayal and anger that are all represented in this story.

Key verse

'Pilate answered, "But what crime has he done?"' (Matthew 27:23).

Old Testament story link

Isaiah 52:13—53:10: Long ago, the prophet Isaiah wrote about someone who would suffer on behalf of others to take away what was wrong.

The road to the cross

26 As Jesus was being led away, some soldiers grabbed hold of a man from Cyrene named Simon. He was coming in from the fields, but they put the cross on him and made him carry it behind Jesus.

27 A large crowd was following Jesus, and in the crowd a lot of women were crying and weeping for him. 28 Jesus turned to the women and said:

Women of Jerusalem, don't cry for me! Cry for yourselves and for your children. 29 Some day people will say, 'Women who never had children are really fortunate!' 30 At that time everyone will say to the mountains, 'Fall on us!' They will say to the hills, 'Hide us!' 31 If this can happen when the wood is green, what do you think will happen when it is dry?

32 Two criminals were led out to be put to death with Jesus.

33 When the soldiers came to the place called 'The Skull', they nailed Jesus to a cross. They also nailed the two criminals to crosses, one on each side of Jesus.

34–35 Jesus said, 'Father, forgive these people! They don't know what they're doing.'

While the crowd stood there watching Jesus, the soldiers gambled for his clothes. The leaders insulted him by saying, 'He saved others. Now he should save himself, if he really is God's chosen Messiah!'

36 The soldiers made fun of Jesus and brought him some wine. 37 They said, 'If you are the king of the Jews, save yourself!'

LUKE 23:26–37

Commentary

To die as a criminal on a cross was a terrible punishment, designed to act as a deterrent to those who were thinking of breaking the law. It was public, cruel and humiliating. The criminals had to carry a heavy crosspiece of wood to the place where they would be executed so that everyone could see them on their journey through the streets. Jesus and two others had to carry their own crosses in this way, but it was too much for Jesus, who was weak from all the beatings he had received, and a passerby was ordered to carry the wooden beam instead. Jesus had some sad words to say to the women who were crying. He seems to be predicting the day when even more terrible things would happen to people in Jerusalem as the result of war.

The place where the crosses were set up was known as 'The Skull'. Perhaps the rocks there looked like a human skull, or maybe it was just because it was the place where so many had died. Jesus was nailed to the cross. He was laughed at by the crowds and insulted by the soldiers. It is the most horrible climax of evil that you can imagine, but right at the heart of all this darkness come Jesus' words of forgiveness. The worst that could be done to him has happened, but it has not broken him, because God's love is still alive inside him. This love will soon show itself stronger than death itself.

Visual aid

A simple cross is the focus you need for today's story. You will also need some small stones for the activity idea below.

Activity idea

Jesus once talked about 'taking up your cross' as a way of describing what it meant to follow him. In fact, anyone who literally did this was on their way to execution. Jesus was asking people to put all that was bad to death if they wanted to be his disciples. Next to the simple cross, build up a large pile of stones to represent all the bad things you can think of in this world

Questions

▶ What do you think Simon told his family about what had happened that day?

▶ What did Jesus mean by his words to the women?

▶ What, for you, is the worst part of this story?

▶ How did the leaders insult Jesus?

today—things like murder, violence, lying, abuse and hatred. When you have finished, rearrange the stones to spell the letters of the word 'forgiven'.

Prayer idea

On a large piece of paper, draw several big teardrops to represent the suffering of the world and then, as a prayer, draw a cross inside each of the teardrops. Below all of this, write the words, 'God understands because Jesus suffered on the cross.'

Key verse

'Jesus said, "Father, forgive these people!"' (Luke 23:34).

Old Testament story link

Zechariah 3:1–10: Zechariah had a vision of a man called Joshua, who had all his dirty clothes taken away. Later he writes that this is a picture of guilt being taken away in one single day.

The crucifixion

38 Above him was a sign that said, 'This is the King of the Jews.'

39 One of the criminals hanging there also insulted Jesus by saying, 'Aren't you the Messiah? Save yourself and save us!'

40 But the other criminal told the first one off, 'Don't you fear God? Aren't you getting the same punishment as this man? 41 We got what was coming to us, but he didn't do anything wrong.' 42 Then he said to Jesus, 'Remember me when you come into power!'

43 Jesus replied, 'I promise that today you will be with me in paradise.'

44 Around midday the sky turned dark and stayed that way until the middle of the afternoon. 45 The sun stopped shining, and the curtain in the temple split down the middle. 46 Jesus shouted, 'Father, I put myself in your hands!' Then he died.

47 When the Roman officer saw what had happened, he praised God and said, 'Jesus must really have been a good man!'

48 A crowd had gathered to see the terrible sight. Then after they had seen it, they felt brokenhearted and went home. 49 All of Jesus' close friends and the women who had come with him from Galilee stood at a distance and watched.

LUKE 23:38–49

Commentary

Even when he was hanging from the cross, Jesus continued to show love and bring hope to others. The criminals on either side of him were going through the same agony, but, unlike Jesus, they had committed crimes and deserved to die. One joined in with the crowd's insults. The other is clearly sorry for what he has done and simply hopes to be part of God's kingdom when he dies. Jesus promises that this criminal will be with him in paradise that day.

By now it is afternoon and the end is near. It is almost as if the whole world goes dark, but it is also the moment when Jesus defeats the powers of darkness. The curtain in the innermost part of the temple, where the high priest used to go and meet with God once a year, is torn apart, and the way to God is now open because of what Jesus has done. Only a completely innocent man could have achieved this; even the Roman soldier agrees that Jesus has done no wrong.

The crowd and Jesus' friends saw only defeat and went away broken-hearted, but in fact what had happened that day was the greatest miracle Jesus had ever done.

Questions

▶ The two criminals had quite different attitudes towards Jesus. What could explain this, do you think?

▶ The second criminal ends up being the first person to get into heaven because of what happened at the cross. Is this a surprise?

▶ Why do you think it went so dark that afternoon?

▶ The officer on guard duty had probably only just met Jesus, so what made him think that Jesus was such a good man?

▶ Can you imagine what was going on in the minds of Jesus' close friends and the women who were watching at a distance?

Visual aid

Find an old piece of fabric that will tear easily from top to bottom. Drape it over a board showing the word 'heaven', and then pull it away to reveal what is hidden behind it.

Activity idea

Talk about what it would have been like to witness all these things. Strangely, Christians call this day Good Friday. Talk about why they call it 'good'. Now take the letters of the phrase 'Jesus dies' and rearrange them to read 'Jesus' side'. Because of his death we can all come close to God.

Prayer idea

Anyone can get to heaven because of Jesus. The second criminal discovered this to be true. Offer a special prayer—either out loud or quietly—to say that you will trust Jesus just as the thief on the cross did. Heaven starts right here and now for everyone who prays this sort of prayer.

Key verse

'Jesus replied, "I promise that today you will be with me in paradise"' (Luke 23:43).

Old Testament story link

Psalm 22: Many people believe that Jesus was remembering this psalm as he hung on the cross.

The empty tomb

11 Mary Magdalene stood crying outside the tomb. She was still weeping, when she stooped down 12 and saw two angels inside. They were dressed in white and were sitting where Jesus' body had been. One was at the head and the other was at the foot. 13 The angels asked Mary, 'Why are you crying?'

She answered, 'They have taken away my Lord's body! I don't know where they have put him.'

14 As soon as Mary said this, she turned around and saw Jesus standing there. But she did not know who he was. 15 Jesus asked her, 'Why are you crying? Who are you looking for?'

She thought he was the gardener and said, 'Sir, if you have taken his body away, please tell me, so I can go and get him.'

16 Then Jesus said to her, 'Mary!'

She turned and said to him, 'Rabboni.' The Aramaic word 'Rabboni' means 'Teacher'.

17 Jesus told her, 'Don't hold on to me! I have not yet gone to the Father. But tell my disciples that I am going to the one who is my Father and my God, as well as your Father and your God.' 18 Mary Magdalene then went and told the disciples that she had seen the Lord. She also told them what he had said to her.

JOHN 20:11–18

Commentary

Jesus' dead body had been hastily taken down from the cross just before sunset on the Friday. A Jewish leader who was a secret disciple offered his own rock tomb nearby for the burial, and a stone was rolled over the entrance. The women, including Mary Magdalene, had watched all this. The next day was a special Jewish sabbath, so no one travelled anywhere.

It wasn't until early on the Sunday morning that Mary could go to the tomb to pay her last respects. To her surprise, the stone had been rolled away. She ran to fetch Peter and John, who came to see for themselves what had happened. After they left, Mary was alone in the garden in tears, trying to make sense of what had happened. This is when she saw the angels, and then heard a voice asking her why she was crying.

Clearly Jesus looked different from before. Her last

sight of him had been of a terribly disfigured body on a cross, and perhaps that is why she did not recognise him at first. Only when he said her name did she realise that this was really Jesus, back from the dead. Mary longed to hold on to him, but Jesus wanted her to learn not to cling to his earthly body any more, but to trust him as a spiritual presence, just as everyone else would do who came to believe in Jesus later.

Visual aid

Look at some pictures from the internet of people's ideas about the resurrection of Jesus. Many artists have found it hard to portray this moment. Perhaps a simple abstract painting of blinding light is the best that can be achieved.

Activity idea

Use some craft materials (possibly air-drying clay) to create a cave with an entrance over which you place a round stone. Alternatively, create a tomb and entrance from some of the furniture and blankets that you can find around the home. Inside the cave place some cloths, piled neatly like the grave clothes that Jesus left behind.

Questions

▶ How did Mary imagine she would be able to roll the stone back from the tomb?

▶ Why didn't Mary recognise Jesus at first?

▶ What did Mary fear might have happened to Jesus' body?

▶ What helped Mary to recognise that it was Jesus?

▶ Why didn't Jesus allow Mary to touch him?

Prayer idea

A traditional greeting between Christians on Easter Day is 'Christ is risen', to which the reply is 'He is risen indeed. Hallelujah.' Use this as a family at the end of each prayer you make today. Your prayers could perhaps be focused on those who are sad because someone has died, those who are frightened about the future, and those who tell others that Jesus is risen from the dead.

Key verse

'Tell my disciples that I am going to the one who is my Father and my God' (John 20:17).

Old Testament story link

Exodus 15:11–18: This is part of the song of victory that Moses and the people sang after they had escaped from Egypt through the Red Sea.

The road to Emmaus

¹³ That same day two of Jesus' disciples were going to the village of Emmaus, which was about eleven kilometres from Jerusalem. ¹⁴ As they were talking and thinking about what had happened, ¹⁵ Jesus came near and started walking along beside them. ¹⁶ But they did not know who he was.

¹⁷ Jesus asked them, 'What were you talking about as you walked along?'

The two of them stood there looking sad and gloomy. ¹⁸ Then the one named Cleopas asked Jesus, 'Are you the only person from Jerusalem who didn't know what was happening there these last few days?'

¹⁹ 'What do you mean?' Jesus asked.

They answered:

Those things that happened to Jesus from Nazareth. By what he did and said he showed that he was a powerful prophet, who pleased God and all the people. ²⁰ Then the chief priests and our leaders had him arrested and sentenced to die on a cross...

²² Some women in our group surprised us. They had gone to the tomb early in the morning, ²³ but did not find the body of Jesus. They came back, saying that they had seen a vision of angels who told them that he is alive...

²⁵ Then Jesus asked the two disciples, '... ²⁶ Didn't you know that the Messiah would have to suffer before he was given his glory?' ²⁷ Jesus then explained everything written about himself in the Scriptures...

²⁸ When the two of them came near the village where they were going, Jesus seemed to be going further. ²⁹ They begged him, 'Stay with us! It's already late, and the sun is going down.' So Jesus went into the house to stay with them.

³⁰ After Jesus sat down to eat, he took some bread. He blessed it and broke it. Then he gave it to them. ³¹ At once they knew who he was, but he disappeared. ³² They said to each other, 'When he talked with us along the road and explained the Scriptures to us, didn't it warm our hearts?' ³³ So they got up at once and returned to Jerusalem.

LUKE 24:13–20, 22–23, 25–33a (ABRIDGED)

Commentary

Jesus appeared first to Mary beside the empty tomb. Now he turns up on the road from Jerusalem to Emmaus. The two disciples are on their way home after all that has happened over the weekend. When Jesus joins them, they don't recognise him: perhaps he was wearing travelling clothes that obscured his face or it was just getting dark. They are surprised that he hasn't heard about the crucifixion and the rumours of Jesus being alive again, and even more surprised when he tells them that it was all prophesied in the Old Testament. Hadn't they realised that this was the way God's special rescuer was going to come and save everyone?

Jesus then goes on to explain the whole Bible story of God's plan to mend the world, and it is such an exciting story that the disciples beg him to stay and tell them more. Only indoors, in the light of the house, and particularly as he breaks the bread at the meal table, do they recognise Jesus. They must have kicked themselves for not knowing at once that it was him. Jesus is alive, and this is so wonderful that, even though it is dark by now, they set out straight away to run back to Jerusalem and tell the others the good news.

Questions

▶ What mood do you think the two disciples were in as they walked home to Emmaus?

▶ Why didn't they recognise Jesus at first?

▶ Why didn't Jesus reveal himself to them straight away?

▶ What was it in the end that made them recognise Jesus?

Visual aid

Take a complete Bible and put a series of bookmarks in the Old Testament section, on each of which is written 'This story points to Jesus'. Lots of Old Testament stories have clues in them about what will happen when God sends his special rescuer. Can you think of any?

Activity idea

Play a game of 'Guess who?' as a family. One person should write the names of famous people (you could include Bible characters) on sticky labels and fix one label on to each person's back, so that everyone can see everyone else's name but not their own. Ask questions that can be answered only by 'yes' or 'no' to see if you can find out who you are.

Prayer idea

The Old Testament has lots of stories and picture language to help us understand what God is like, and Jesus used many of these images to describe himself. Using these picture words, create prayers to God; for example, ask him to be a shepherd, food, father, king, lion, rock or water for you and your family.

Key verse

'Jesus then explained everything written about himself in the Scriptures' (Luke 24:27).

Old Testament story link

Deuteronomy 18:15–19: Moses predicts that God will send a special prophet one day. This could have been one of the Bible passages that Jesus talked about with the two disciples.

Doubting Thomas

19 The disciples were afraid of the Jewish leaders, and on the evening of that same Sunday they locked themselves in a room. Suddenly, Jesus appeared in the middle of the group. He greeted them 20 and showed them his hands and his side. When the disciples saw the Lord, they became very happy.

21 After Jesus had greeted them again, he said, 'I am sending you, just as the Father has sent me.' 22 Then he breathed on them and said, 'Receive the Holy Spirit. 23 If you forgive anyone's sins, they will be forgiven. But if you don't forgive their sins, they will not be forgiven.'

24 Although Thomas the Twin was one of the twelve disciples, he wasn't with the others when Jesus appeared to them. 25 So they told him, 'We have seen the Lord!'

But Thomas said, 'First, I must see the nail scars in his hands and touch them with my finger. I must put my hand where the spear went into his side. I won't believe unless I do this!'

26 A week later the disciples were together again. This time, Thomas was with them. Jesus came in while the doors were still locked and stood in the middle of the group. He greeted his disciples 27 and said to Thomas, 'Put your finger here and look at my hands! Put your hand into my side. Stop doubting and have faith!'

28 Thomas replied, 'You are my Lord and my God!'

29 Jesus said, 'Thomas, do you have faith because you have seen me? The people who have faith in me without seeing me are the ones who are really blessed!'

John 20:19–29

Commentary

It is the evening of the first Easter Day, and although the disciples have heard stories about Jesus being alive, they haven't yet seen him for themselves. They are also scared that the religious leaders will come and hunt them down. They think they might even be accused of stealing Jesus' body and spreading rumours that he is alive.

The doors are locked, but suddenly Jesus appears in the room. It seems that his new resurrection body can walk through walls, but at the same time it is a real body. He shows them the nail marks in his hands, and the place where the spear went into his side, to prove that he has really died. Jesus gives them a new job to do and, just as God breathed into Adam to give him life, Jesus breathes God's Spirit into his disciples to give them new life as his representatives on earth.

Poor Thomas misses out on

this first visit and, understandably, when he hears about it, he thinks the others are all mad, deluded in their grief and simply imagining that they have seen Jesus. But a week later, Jesus appears to Thomas as well, and he worships Jesus as God. This neatly sums up what it means to be a Christian—to acknowledge Jesus as Lord and God. Unlike Thomas, we do this based on what we have heard and read and not on the evidence of our own eyes. This is faith, and Jesus promises that we will be blessed.

Visual aid

Learn British Sign Language for the name of 'Jesus', which is simply pointing to each wrist in turn, one after the other. In other words, Jesus is recognised by the sign of the nail marks in his hands.

Activity idea

Lots of people, like Thomas, say, 'I won't believe until I see him for myself.' As a family, talk together about how you can answer someone who says this to you. Thomas did see Jesus alive, but he also saw something deeper, and that's what really convinced him.

Questions

▶ What were the disciples afraid of?

▶ Why do you think they didn't greet Jesus when he appeared?

▶ What sort of body did Jesus have at this time?

▶ What was the new work that Jesus gave his disciples to do?

▶ Why didn't Thomas need to touch the wounds as he had originally asked to do?

Prayer idea

'But Jesus is alive' are four powerful words that sit at the heart of what Christians believe. Make up a series of short prayers together, starting off each time, 'Lord, I know you are alive because…' Each time, thank God with all your heart for what you have prayed.

Key verse

'Thomas replied, "You are my Lord and my God"' (John 20:28).

Old Testament story link

Zephaniah 3:14–17: Zephaniah tells us of the day when God will bring victory for his people and refresh their lives with his love.

203

At Lake Galilee

¹ Jesus later appeared to his disciples along the shore of Lake Tiberias. ² Simon Peter, Thomas the Twin, Nathanael from Cana in Galilee, and the brothers James and John, were there, together with two other disciples. ³ Simon Peter said, 'I'm going fishing!'

The others said, 'We will go with you.' They went out in their boat. But they didn't catch a thing that night.

⁴ Early the next morning Jesus stood on the shore, but the disciples did not realise who he was. ⁵ Jesus shouted, 'Friends, have you caught anything?'

'No!' they answered.

⁶ So he told them, 'Let your net down on the right side of your boat, and you will catch some fish.'

They did, and the net was so full of fish that they could not drag it up into the boat.

⁷ Jesus' favourite disciple told Peter, 'It's the Lord!' When Simon heard that it was the Lord, he put on the clothes that he had taken off while he was working. Then he jumped into the water. ⁸ The boat was only about a hundred metres from shore. So the other disciples stayed in the boat and dragged in the net full of fish.

⁹ When the disciples got out of the boat, they saw some bread and a charcoal fire with fish on it. ¹⁰ Jesus told his disciples, 'Bring some of the fish you just caught.' ¹¹ Simon Peter got back into the boat and dragged the net to shore. In it were one hundred and fifty-three large fish, but still the net did not rip.

¹² Jesus said, 'Come and eat!' But none of the disciples dared ask who he was. They knew he was the Lord. ¹³ Jesus took the bread in his hands and gave some of it to his disciples. He did the same with the fish. ¹⁴ This was the third time that Jesus appeared to his disciples after he was raised from death.

JOHN 21:1–14

Commentary

Jesus kept appearing and disappearing again in the weeks after the first Easter Day, and each time he took the disciples by surprise. He was no longer limited to one time and one place as before, and this was preparing them for what it would be like in the future. He was available to all, as long as they opened their eyes to look.

The disciples had returned to Galilee after the Passover. They'd been told by Jesus to go there and wait. Unsure of what to do next, they returned to their occupation as fishermen. It was something they could do—or, at least, they thought it was. Unfortunately, they had an unsuccessful night of fishing and it took the advice of a stranger on the shore to direct them to where the fish were. Suddenly John (Jesus' favourite disciple) recognised the man. Perhaps he remembered a time when something very similar had happened (see page 130).

In great excitement, Peter was first ashore, and the friends gathered around the fire where Jesus had a meal ready for them. It must have stirred their memories of when he broke bread and shared fish for the 5000 at the picnic. It was also like another 'last supper', but this time it was on the victory side of Easter. Jesus was providing for them, as he always would. They were going to be 'fishers of people' just as he had told them once, and soon thousands would be coming into the net of the kingdom of God.

Visual aid

Arrange to have some pieces of fish and bread to eat alongside this story. Notice how Jesus, even with his new resurrection body, can still eat fish.

Activity idea

Try a fishing game with magnets on string and fish with magnets attached in a 'pool' on the floor. How many fish can each member of the family catch in a given time? You can buy strips of small magnets in most craft stores.

Questions

▶ What do you think the seven disciples were thinking about as they set out in the boat to fish that night?

▶ Why was it John who recognised Jesus first?

▶ Why were they all so nervous about asking Jesus who he was? Did Jesus look a little different?

▶ How did this event encourage the disciples for the future?

Prayer idea

Many people have tried to work out some special meaning in the fact that there were 153 fish. Perhaps it simply means that there were a lot—and they were big fish, too. The number could represent the huge harvest of people coming home to God when the disciples started doing the work that Jesus gave them to do. Focus your prayers on those who are busy telling people about Jesus for the first time. Pray for a big harvest of people to come to know God's love.

Key verse

'[Jesus] told them, "Let your net down on the right side of your boat, and you will catch some fish"' (John 21:6).

Old Testament story link

Psalm 67: This psalm celebrates the great blessings that God will bring right around the world.

Jesus ascends to heaven

4 While [Jesus] was still with them, he said:

Don't leave Jerusalem yet. Wait here for the Father to give you the Holy Spirit, just as I told you he has promised to do. 5 John baptised with water, but in a few days you will be baptised with the Holy Spirit.

6 While the apostles were still with Jesus, they asked him, 'Lord, are you now going to give Israel its own king again?'
7 Jesus said to them, 'You don't need to know the time of those events that only the Father controls. 8 But the Holy Spirit will come upon you and give you power. Then you will tell everyone about me in Jerusalem, in all Judea, in Samaria, and everywhere in the world.' 9 After Jesus had said this and while they were watching, he was taken up into a cloud. They could not see him, 10 but as he went up, they kept looking up into the sky.
Suddenly two men dressed in white clothes were standing there beside them. 11 They said, 'Why are you men from Galilee standing here and looking up into the sky? Jesus has been taken to heaven. But he will come back in the same way that you have seen him go.'

ACTS 1:4–11

Commentary

For 40 days after Easter, Jesus kept appearing to the disciples, both as a group and individually, sometimes up in Galilee but also in and around Jerusalem. During this time he was preparing them for the next stage in God's plan. Now it was over to the disciples, and those who would believe because of them, to bring people into the kingdom. It would start in Jerusalem and slowly spread outward to include nearby countries and eventually the whole world. But Jesus knew they would need help. He couldn't be with everyone, everywhere, all the time, even in his new body, so he told them to wait in Jerusalem for God's power to come. He would come back to them in a new, invisible form—God the Holy Spirit. They needed to be filled and surrounded with the Spirit in order to do this new work.
Interestingly, the disciples still didn't quite understand the scale of the task and were

thinking about a new king just for Israel. On the Mount of Olives above Gethsemane, where Jesus prayed just before his death, he finally left them. We call this 'the ascension', but it happened only so that Jesus could live in his disciples by his Spirit and, one day at the end of time, could return again when the job they were about to begin would be completed.

Visual aid

Use a picture of some traffic lights. The 'stop, wait, go' colours are a simple way to remember the instructions that Jesus gave his disciples before he left.

Activity idea

In today's story we hear Jesus' last important instructions to his disciples. Do you really think they were up to the job ahead of them? Talk together about this and make a list of all the arguments for and against trusting the future of the kingdom of God to this small bunch of believers.

Questions

▶ What do you think Jesus meant by being baptised in the Holy Spirit?

▶ Do you think that the disciples really understood how big a plan they were caught up in?

▶ Why did Jesus need to go back to heaven?

▶ What did the angels mean about Jesus coming back in the same way that the disciples saw him go?

Prayer idea

Jesus' strategy for growing the kingdom of God was to start where you are (in Jerusalem), go to those you know (Judea), then take the message to those people you don't know so well or even don't like (Samaria), and only afterwards set off into the whole world. On a piece of paper draw a set of concentric circles getting larger and larger. Put your family at the centre and then, in each circle further away from the centre, put the names of people who are close to you, neighbours and friends, people you are not so sure about, or people a long way away. Ask God for the power of the Holy Spirit to help you find practical ways of loving these people.

Key verse

'The Holy Spirit will come upon you and give you power' (Acts 1:8).

Old Testament story link

Zechariah 4:1–9: Zechariah receives a message from God about the power of God's Spirit and the promise to bless small beginnings.

Pentecost

¹ On the day of Pentecost all the Lord's followers were together in one place. ² Suddenly there was a noise from heaven like the sound of a mighty wind! It filled the house where they were meeting. ³ Then they saw what looked like fiery tongues moving in all directions, and a tongue came and settled on each person there. ⁴ The Holy Spirit took control of everyone, and they began speaking whatever languages the Spirit let them speak.

⁵ Many religious Jews from every country in the world were living in Jerusalem. ⁶ And when they heard this noise, a crowd gathered. But they were surprised, because they were hearing everything in their own languages. ⁷ They were excited and amazed, and said:

Don't all these who are speaking come from Galilee? ⁸ Then why do we hear them speaking our very own languages? ⁹ Some of us are from Parthia, Media, and Elam. Others are from Mesopotamia, Judea, Cappadocia, Pontus, Asia, ¹⁰ Phrygia, Pamphylia, Egypt, parts of Libya near Cyrene, Rome, ¹¹ Crete, and Arabia. Some of us were born Jews, and others of us have chosen to be Jews. Yet we all hear them using our own languages to tell the wonderful things God has done.

¹² Everyone was excited and confused. Some of them even kept asking each other, 'What does all this mean?'

¹³ Others made fun of the Lord's followers and said, 'They are drunk.'

ACTS 2:1–13

Commentary

The day of Pentecost was the moment when Jesus' promise came true. The disciples were filled with the Holy Spirit, the power from on high that he had talked about and that they would need in order to start their work of sharing God's love with the whole world. Pentecost happened 50 days after Passover, and it was a harvest festival as well as being a time when the Jews remembered the day when God gave them the ten commandments.

For these first disciples, it took on a new meaning. They were the harvest of Jesus' work, and by God's Spirit his laws were now written on their hearts. Just as when Moses met with God at the burning bush, so these first believers were now on fire with the mysterious flame of God's power. Just as Moses had climbed Sinai to be given the law and the mountain had shaken with

God's glory, so the room where the disciples met thundered with God's presence. And just as God had breathed life into his first creation, Adam, so the wind of the Spirit filled the believers, giving them a new beginning as new creations. The wind literally blew them out on to the streets as each disciple bubbled over with words about God; and miraculously the cosmopolitan population of Jerusalem could all understand what they were saying, in every language spoken there. This was the birthday of the new people of God, the Christian church.

Visual aid

The Holy Spirit fell on the disciples as wind and fire. Tie some yellow, red and orange ribbons to the protective grill in front of an ordinary domestic fan so that when it is on, they blow outward like flames.

Activity idea

The Holy Spirit enabled the disciples to speak about God in languages that could be understood by each person in the crowd. Find out how to say words like 'Praise God', 'The Lord is great'

Questions

▶ What ideas do we get from this story about what the Holy Spirit is like?

▶ Why do you think God chose to come as the Holy Spirit in such a dramatic way?

▶ What different reactions did the crowds have to what happened?

▶ How did the disciples change from the way they were only moments before?

and 'Jesus is king' in a variety of languages. On the count of three, start shouting out these phrases together to give you a flavour of what it might have sounded like at the first Pentecost.

Prayer idea

What happened at Pentecost was a signpost to what the disciples would do next. The nationalities within the crowd represent the world as people understood it then, and the disciples would be taking the story of Jesus to these different places. Open up an atlas and find Jerusalem. Can you find some of the countries mentioned? Pray for God's church at work in these different places.

Key verse

'We all hear them using our own languages to tell the wonderful things God has done' (Acts 2:11).

Old Testament story link

Joel 2:28–32: Joel predicts the day when God's Spirit will be poured out on everyone.

Peter and John heal a lame man

¹ The time of prayer was about three o'clock in the afternoon, and Peter and John were going into the temple. ² A man who had been born lame was being carried to the temple door. Each day he was placed beside this door, known as the Beautiful Gate. He sat there and begged from the people who were going in.

³ The man saw Peter and John entering the temple, and he asked them for money. ⁴ But they looked straight at him and said, 'Look up at us!'

⁵ The man stared at them and thought he was going to get something. ⁶ But Peter said, 'I don't have any silver or gold! But I will give you what I do have. In the name of Jesus Christ from Nazareth, get up and start walking.' ⁷ Peter then took him by the right hand and helped him up.

At once the man's feet and ankles became strong, ⁸ and he jumped up and started walking. He went with Peter and John into the temple, walking and jumping and praising God. ⁹ Everyone saw him walking around and praising God. ¹⁰ They knew that he was the beggar who had been lying beside the Beautiful Gate, and they were completely surprised. They could not imagine what had happened to the man.

ACTS 3:1–10

Commentary

After Pentecost everything changed for the disciples. They began telling everyone the story of Jesus and how his death and resurrection had opened up the way to God. Large numbers of people became believers. They spent time in prayer and worship and were busy doing acts of kindness that had a huge impact on Jerusalem. The disciples were gaining in confidence, too, realising that Jesus wanted them, by his Spirit, to start doing the things that they had seen him do.

On their way to the temple to pray, Peter and John noticed a lame man lying on a mat. Perhaps they remembered the time when another man had been brought to Jesus and lowered through the roof to reach him (see page 134). Courageously Peter and John followed Jesus' example and, on the authority of his name, told the man to get up and walk. He was healed in just the same way! God's Spirit in the disciples was giving them the power to carry on Jesus' work, just as Jesus had asked them to. Everyone was amazed to see the man jumping for joy, and this led to more opportunities for the disciples to tell people about Jesus and what God had done for the world through him. The good news was on the move.

Questions

▶ Peter and John went to the temple to pray. Why do you think they didn't just pray in their own homes?

▶ Why do you think his friends carried the lame man every day to the temple gate to beg?

▶ What gave Peter and John the confidence to heal this man?

▶ What do you think the crowd thought about what had happened?

Visual aid

Make a home-made stretcher using two old jackets and some broom handles. Thread the handles up the sleeves and stretch out the jackets between them. You might dare to try to carry something on it!

Activity idea

Challenge each other to act out this healing. Lie down on the ground, still and helpless. Then, when you hear Peter's words, imagine that you can feel strength coming back into your feet and ankles. Begin to twitch them and then move the other parts of your legs, and slowly the rest of your body. Get up carefully, realising the new strength you are feeling, and end up dancing as excitedly as you can.

Prayer idea

The Beautiful Gate was certainly very striking, but someone who was lame, like this man, would not have been allowed to go any further into the temple. Focus on those who are sick at home or in hospital. Ask God to come close to them and give them new hope and joy, like the man in the story.

Key verse

'In the name of Jesus Christ from Nazareth, get up and start walking' (Acts 3:6).

Old Testament story link

Numbers 21:4–9: Once, in the desert, poisonous snakes had bitten the people of Israel and they were dying. But Moses had a pole set up with a bronze snake on it. Looking at this snake brought healing.

Stephen is killed

8 God gave Stephen the power to work great miracles and wonders among the people. 9 But some Jews from Cyrene and Alexandria were members of a group who called themselves 'Free Men'. They started arguing with Stephen. Some others from Cilicia and Asia also argued with him. 10 But they were no match for Stephen, who spoke with the great wisdom that the Spirit gave him. 11 So they talked some men into saying, 'We heard Stephen say terrible things against Moses and God!'

12 They turned the people and their leaders and the teachers of the Law of Moses against Stephen. Then they all grabbed Stephen and dragged him in front of the council.

13 Some men agreed to tell lies about Stephen, and they said, 'This man keeps on saying terrible things about this holy temple and the Law of Moses. 14 We have heard him claim that Jesus from Nazareth will destroy this place and change the customs that Moses gave us.' 15 Then all the council members stared at Stephen. They saw that his face looked like the face of an angel...

7 54 When the council members heard Stephen's speech, they were angry and furious. 55 But Stephen was filled with the Holy Spirit. He looked toward heaven, where he saw our glorious God and Jesus standing at his right side. 56 Then Stephen said, 'I see heaven open and the Son of Man standing at the right side of God!'

57 The council members shouted and covered their ears. At once they all attacked Stephen 58 and dragged him out of the city. Then they started throwing stones at him. The men who had brought charges against him put their coats at the feet of a young man named Saul.

59 As Stephen was being stoned to death, he called out, 'Lord Jesus, please welcome me!' 60 He knelt down and shouted, 'Lord, don't blame them for what they have done.' Then he died.

ACTS 6:8–15; 7:54–60

Commentary

The first church in Jerusalem was growing so fast that people like Stephen were appointed to care for its members properly. His job was to make sure that everyone, particularly the widows, had enough to eat. But Stephen was also a great speaker. As one of the new disciples, he aroused jealousy in his former Greek-speaking, Jewish friends. They made up lies about him and brought him before the temple officials.

Jesus warned his disciples that they would face opposition, and Stephen ends up on trial like his master, accused of insulting the Jewish religion. He is given the grace to stay calm, explaining what God has done for everyone through the death and resurrection of Jesus. Maybe he knows that this means he will be killed, as Jesus was, but he is ready for it. He even sees Jesus standing up to welcome him into heaven, which only infuriates his accusers further. And just like Jesus, he dies with words of forgiveness on his lips.

The way Stephen died must have made a huge impression on Saul, who was watching. But more of him later!

Questions

▶ Why were Stephen's former Jewish friends jealous of him?

▶ In what way do you think Stephen had the face of an angel?

▶ Why do you think God gave Stephen a glimpse of heaven just before he died?

▶ What gave Stephen the power to forgive his enemies?

Visual aid

Find a variety of ideas from books or the internet of what angels might look like. Which pictures do you like best, and why?

Activity idea

It's not easy keeping calm when people argue with us. Share your best tips for keeping calm under pressure. Is it to do with staying silent, or speaking softly, or perhaps counting to ten in your head before you speak? What might Stephen have suggested as good advice?

Prayer idea

Stephen knew his Old Testament very well. Use this Family Bible to help you pray today by opening it up at any of the stories in the Old Testament part and using the headings to help you praise and thank God. For example:

- The story of creation: 'Praise you for making such a wonderful world.'
- God's promise: 'Thank you that you have given us so many amazing promises.'
- God speaks to Samuel: 'Thank you that you promise to speak to us when we pray.'

Key verse

'Then Stephen said, "I see heaven open and the Son of Man standing at the right side of God!"' (Acts 7:56).

Old Testament story link

2 Chronicles 24:20–22: Like Stephen, Zechariah is murdered for speaking the truth. However, notice how his last words are very different from Stephen's.

Philip and the Ethiopian

26 The Lord's angel said to Philip, 'Go south along the desert road that leads from Jerusalem to Gaza.' 27 So Philip left.

An important Ethiopian official happened to be going along that road in his chariot. He was the chief treasurer for Candace, the Queen of Ethiopia. The official had gone to Jerusalem to worship 28 and was now on his way home. He was sitting in his chariot, reading the book of the prophet Isaiah.

29 The Spirit told Philip to catch up with the chariot. 30 Philip ran up close and heard the man reading aloud from the book of Isaiah. Philip asked him, 'Do you understand what you are reading?'

31 The official answered, 'How can I understand unless someone helps me?' He then invited Philip to come up and sit beside him.

32 The man was reading the passage that said,

'He was led like a sheep
    on its way to be killed.
He was silent as a lamb
whose wool
    is being cut off,
and he did not say
    a word.
33 He was treated like a nobody
and did not receive
    a fair trial.
How can he have children,
if his life
    is snatched away?'

34 The official said to Philip, 'Tell me, was the prophet talking about himself or about someone else?' 35 So Philip began at this place in the Scriptures and explained the good news about Jesus.

36–37 As they were going along the road, they came to a place where there was some water. The official said, 'Look! Here is some water. Why can't I be baptised?' 38 He ordered the chariot to stop. Then they both went down into the water, and Philip baptised him.

39 After they had come out of the water, the Lord's Spirit took Philip away. The official never saw him again, but he was very happy as he went on his way.

40 Philip later appeared in Azotus. He went from town to town, all the way to Caesarea, telling people about Jesus.

Acts 8:26–40

Commentary

Like Stephen, Philip had been chosen to look after the fast-growing church in Jerusalem. However, after Stephen's murder, many disciples left the city, fearing what would happen next. This might have looked like a setback, but in fact it meant that the story of Jesus started to spread among the towns and villages. Philip travelled up to Samaria, but suddenly God had new work for him to do, not with a large crowd but with just one person.

The Ethiopian treasurer was clearly someone who had chosen to become Jewish even though he was not Jewish by birth. This is why he had travelled up to Jerusalem for one of the festivals there. He was also a devout man, determined to understand the Jewish scriptures better. The passage he was looking at comes from Isaiah and is about someone having to suffer like a lamb being led to the slaughter. This was Philip's God-given opportunity to tell the treasurer how Jesus had been killed and had come back to life so that everyone could be forgiven. The treasurer was baptised there and then and went on his way rejoicing. He then took the news about Jesus back to his home country.

Questions

▶ How do you think Philip felt about being taken away from his successful work in Samaria to wait around on a lonely desert road?

▶ How had God been preparing the Ethiopian treasurer to hear the good news about Jesus?

▶ Can you guess what sort of things Philip might have said to the treasurer?

▶ What can we learn from the way God used Philip to do his work?

Visual aid

The words of Isaiah that the treasurer was reading would have been written on a scroll. Attach the two ends of a roll of paper to two rolling pins and practise unrolling the paper from one end to the other so that the words of the text travel in between.

Activity idea

The treasurer's chariot was probably quite a grand vehicle. Using a chair covered with colourful fabric, some small open umbrellas or large circles of card for wheels, plenty of gold decorative extras and some lengths of leather or string to be the reins and harnesses for the horses, make your own version of the chariot. If you have lots of cardboard boxes available, you could have a go at making some junk box horses.

Prayer idea

Use four fingers and a thumb to represent some of the ways God speaks by his Holy Spirit—through words or pictures in our head; the advice of friends; the way circumstances turn out; a Bible story; a sense of inner peace about what to do. Hold each digit with the other hand, and ask God to help you hear his voice better day by day.

Key verse

'So Philip began at this place in the Scriptures and explained the good news about Jesus' (Acts 8:35).

Old Testament story link

1 Kings 18:41–46: Elijah was someone else who listened carefully to God and also once had to outrun a chariot!

The road to Damascus

¹ Saul kept on threatening to kill the Lord's followers. He even went to the high priest ² and asked for letters to the Jewish leaders in Damascus. He did this because he wanted to arrest and take to Jerusalem any man or woman who had accepted the Lord's Way. ³ When Saul had almost reached Damascus, a bright light from heaven suddenly flashed around him. ⁴ He fell to the ground and heard a voice that said, 'Saul! Saul! Why are you so cruel to me?'

⁵ 'Who are you?' Saul asked.

'I am Jesus,' the Lord answered. 'I am the one you are so cruel to. ⁶ Now get up and go into the city, where you will be told what to do.'

⁷ The men with Saul stood there speechless. They had heard the voice, but they had not seen anyone. ⁸ Saul got up from the ground, and when he opened his eyes, he could not see a thing. Someone then led him by the hand to Damascus, ⁹ and for three days he was blind and did not eat or drink.

¹⁰ A follower named Ananias lived in Damascus, and the Lord spoke to him in a vision. Ananias answered, 'Lord, here I am.'

¹¹ The Lord said to him, 'Get up and go to the house of Judas on Straight Street. When you get there, you will find a man named Saul from the city of Tarsus. Saul is praying, ¹² and he has seen a vision. He saw a man named Ananias coming to him and putting his hands on him, so that he could see again.'

ACTS 9:1–12

Commentary

After Stephen's murder, it became much harder in Jerusalem to be a follower of the way of Jesus. The Jewish authorities had threatened the disciples several times. Saul, a leading Pharisee, was particularly determined to stop their lies and dangerous teaching. He was given authority to hunt down believers wherever they could be found, including up at Damascus in Syria, but Jesus quite literally stopped him in his tracks with a blinding light. He heard Jesus speak to him and was forced to rethink everything that he believed.

Ananias knew Saul's reputation as a persecutor of Christians, so it took great courage for him to go and bring healing to Saul, but his obedience opened the door to a brand new chapter not only in Saul's life but in the story of the Christian church. Saul went on, under his Roman name Paul, to be one of the most effective and influential disciples of Jesus. Through his ministry, churches began to spring up all over the Roman Empire. Saul never forgot what happened to him on the Damascus road, and he often told his story to others to help them to believe in Jesus too.

Visual aid

Arrange for a camera flash to go off once or twice. This can often leave us blinking and having difficulty in refocusing our sight. God's flashlight blinded Saul, but it was because he needed to see everything in a new way.

Activity idea

The Christians now had to watch their backs. Anyone might be a spy for the Pharisees. Challenge each other to put the message 'Saul is on his way' into some sort of code. Maybe you could rewrite it, turning every letter into the next but one letter in the alphabet, or perhaps turn it into a message with a double meaning, such as 'The vulture is flying north'. Who can come up with the best ideas?

Questions

▶ What was it that kept people believing in Jesus even when it was so dangerous?

▶ Why was Saul so opposed to what the Christians were saying about Jesus?

▶ Why did Jesus need to appear to Saul so dramatically?

▶ What must have been going through Ananias' mind when he set off for Straight Street?

▶ What was the biggest change for Saul?

Prayer idea

By changing one letter at a time, the word 'hate' can become 'love' in five simple moves: hate—gate—gave—give—live—love. Try to use each of these separate words in five simple prayers to God. For example: 'Thank you, Lord Jesus, that you are our gate into heaven'; 'Thank you, Lord Jesus, that you gave your life for us on the cross', and so on.

Key verse

'"Who are you?" Saul asked. "I am Jesus," the Lord answered' (Acts 9:5).

Old Testament story link

Daniel 4:28–37: This is the story of how King Nebuchadnezzar came to believe in the one true God after a very strange experience.

Peter brings Dorcas back to life

³⁶ In Joppa there was a follower named Tabitha. Her Greek name was Dorcas, which means 'deer'. She was always doing good things for people and had given much to the poor. ³⁷ But she became ill and died, and her body was washed and placed in an upstairs room. ³⁸ Joppa wasn't far from Lydda, and the followers heard that Peter was there. They sent two men to say to him, 'Please come with us as quickly as you can!' ³⁹ Straight away, Peter went with them.

The men took Peter upstairs into the room. Many widows were there crying. They showed him the coats and clothes that Dorcas had made while she was still alive.

⁴⁰ After Peter had sent everyone out of the room, he knelt down and prayed. Then he turned to the body of Dorcas and said, 'Tabitha, get up!' The woman opened her eyes, and when she saw Peter, she sat up. ⁴¹ He took her by the hand and helped her to her feet.

Peter called in the widows and the other followers and showed them that Dorcas had been raised from death. ⁴² Everyone in Joppa heard what had happened, and many of them put their faith in the Lord. ⁴³ Peter stayed on for a while in Joppa in the house of a man named Simon, who made leather.

Acts 9:36–43

Commentary

Like the other disciples, Peter had left Jerusalem when the religious authorities began to clamp down. He travelled through some of the towns along Israel's coastline, where he tried to do the sort of things that Jesus used to do, trusting in the power of the Holy Spirit. People were healed, and this drew crowds with whom he could then share the story of God's love in Jesus. When he heard the news of Tabitha's death, he didn't hesitate to go and see what he could do. Maybe he remembered the time when Jesus took him, along with James and John, into the home of Jairus, whose daughter had died. Jesus had trusted God to raise her from the dead then, so now it was Peter's turn to trust that the Holy Spirit would do the same through him.

There was clearly great affection for Tabitha, also known as Dorcas, who was well known in the port of Joppa. When she was brought back to life, it must have caused quite a stir. Once again an amazing miracle opened up the opportunity to spread the message so that many people began following Jesus here too. The church in Jerusalem may have been temporarily silenced, but the gospel was bearing fruit elsewhere.

Questions

▶ What impression of Dorcas's character do we get from the story?

▶ Why did Peter think that he could help someone who was already dead?

▶ How is this story like the one in which Jairus's daughter was raised to life? (See page 146.)

▶ Why does God sometimes work through his followers to do miracles like this?

▶ Why don't more miracles like this happen?

Visual aid

Dorcas was clearly a brilliant seamstress and tailor. Lay out a selection of items of clothing, handmade if possible.

Activity idea

Bring together a variety of coloured materials, some in bright and others in duller colours. Now try telling the story using the different materials to represent the moods of the story—for example, happiness, love, shock, sadness, hope, mystery, joy, surprise and excitement.

Prayer idea

Miracles are given as signposts to Jesus and God's love. Use the separate letters of the word 'miracle' as a way of pointing to God's character, by thinking of a word that goes with each letter— for example, **m**erciful, **i**nfinite, **r**eal, **a**ctive, **c**ompassionate, **l**oving and **e**verlasting. Turn each of these words into a prayer of thanksgiving to God.

Key verse

'Straight away, Peter went with them' (Acts 9:39).

Old Testament story link

1 Kings 17:17–24: The prophet Elijah brings a boy back to life.

Peter in prison

¹ At that time King Herod caused terrible suffering for some members of the church. ² He ordered soldiers to cut off the head of James, the brother of John. ³ When Herod saw that this pleased the Jewish people, he had Peter arrested during the Festival of Thin Bread. ⁴ He put Peter in jail and ordered four squads of soldiers to guard him. Herod planned to put him on trial in public after the festival.

⁵ While Peter was being kept in jail, the church never stopped praying to God for him.

⁶ The night before Peter was to be put on trial, he was asleep and bound by two chains. A soldier was guarding him on each side, and two other soldiers were guarding the entrance to the jail. ⁷ Suddenly an angel from the Lord appeared, and light flashed around in the cell. The angel poked Peter in the side and woke him up. Then he said, 'Quick! Get up!'

The chains fell off his hands, ⁸ and the angel said, 'Get dressed and put on your sandals.' Peter did what he was told. Then the angel said, 'Now put on your coat and follow me.' ⁹ Peter left with the angel, but he thought everything was only a dream. ¹⁰ They went past the two groups of soldiers, and when they came to the iron gate to the city, it opened by itself. They went out and were going along the street, when all at once the angel disappeared.

¹¹ Peter now realised what had happened, and he said, 'I am certain that the Lord sent his angel to rescue me from Herod and from everything the Jewish leaders planned to do to me.' ¹² Then Peter went to the house of Mary the mother of John whose other name was Mark. Many of the Lord's followers had come together there and were praying.

¹³ Peter knocked on the gate, and a servant named Rhoda came to answer. ¹⁴ When she heard Peter's voice, she was too excited to open the gate. She ran back into the house and said that Peter was standing there.

¹⁵ 'You are mad!' everyone told her. But she kept saying that it was Peter. Then they said, 'It must be his angel.' ¹⁶ But Peter kept on knocking, until finally they opened the gate. They saw him and were completely amazed.

ACTS 12:1–16

Commentary

The name of Herod keeps coming up in the New Testament, and each member of this infamous family seems to have been as power-mad and unpredictable as the others. King Herod the Great murdered children in his attempt to get rid of Jesus as a baby, his son had John the Baptist killed, and now his grandson is attacking the church. He has executed James, and now Peter has been arrested and is awaiting trial.

It is Passover time—twelve years on from the first Easter—so is Peter going to be killed just like his Lord? The church believes in the power of prayer, however, and an amazing miracle occurs. An angel releases Peter from his chains, walks him past the guards and takes him through locked gates. The funny thing is that when Peter does arrive at Mary's home, the disciples can't believe the answer to their own prayers, and Rhoda leaves Peter outside while she tries to convince them it's really him.

God clearly still had work for Peter to do; it wasn't time for him to die just yet. In fact, he continued to lead the church in Jerusalem and Judea for a long while and then travelled west, ending up in Rome before Jesus called him home to heaven.

Questions

▶ How do you imagine the disciples reacted to the news of what happened to James?

▶ Why did God rescue Peter and not James?

▶ How daring are our prayers? And do we believe God will really answer?

▶ Can you imagine how Peter felt, left outside when Rhoda forgot to open the door?

Visual aid

Use a chain and a padlock to represent the chains that held Peter and the locked iron gate through which he passed with the angel.

Activity idea

Perhaps you have a set of those metal puzzles that you have to disentangle carefully, following a certain sequence. Alternatively, use a combination lock from a case or a bike lock. Give some clues to the others as to what the code might be and see how long it takes for them to break the combination. Imagine how Peter must have felt when the chains broke and the lock gave way.

Prayer idea

The church in Mary's house had seen many amazing answers to prayer, but this time it must have seemed like praying to move a mountain. Write your special prayers for today on strips of paper bent round into loops and interlocked to make a prayer chain.

Key verse

'While Peter was being kept in jail, the church never stopped praying to God for him' (Acts 12:5).

Old Testament story link

Psalm 130: The first Christians often used the Psalms to help them pray. Perhaps Rhoda, Mary and their friends used the words of this psalm when they prayed for Peter.

Paul at Philippi in Greece

¹⁶ One day on our way to the place of prayer, we were met by a slave girl. She had a spirit in her that gave her the power to tell the future. By doing this she made a lot of money for her owners. ¹⁷ The girl followed Paul and the rest of us and kept yelling, 'These men are servants of the Most High God! They are telling you how to be saved.'

¹⁸ This went on for several days. Finally, Paul got so upset that he turned and said to the spirit, 'In the name of Jesus Christ, I order you to leave this girl alone!' At once the evil spirit left her.

¹⁹ When the girl's owners realised that they had lost all chances for making more money, they grabbed Paul and Silas and dragged them into court. ²⁰ They told the officials, 'These Jews are upsetting our city! ²¹ They are telling us to do things we Romans are not allowed to do.'

²² The crowd joined in the attack on Paul and Silas. Then the officials tore the clothes off the two men and ordered them to be beaten with a whip. ²³ After they had been badly beaten, they were put in jail, and the jailer was told to guard them carefully. ²⁴ The jailer did as he was told. He put them deep inside the jail and chained their feet to heavy blocks of wood.

²⁵ About midnight Paul and Silas were praying and singing praises to God, while the other prisoners listened. ²⁶ Suddenly a strong earthquake shook the jail to its foundations. The doors opened, and the chains fell from all the prisoners.

²⁷ When the jailer woke up and saw that the doors were open, he thought that the prisoners had escaped. He pulled out his sword and was about to kill himself. ²⁸ But Paul shouted, 'Don't harm yourself! No one has escaped.'

²⁹ The jailer asked for a torch and went into the jail. He was shaking all over as he knelt down in front of Paul and Silas. ³⁰ After he had led them out of the jail, he asked, 'What must I do to be saved?'

³¹ They replied, 'Have faith in the Lord Jesus and you will be saved! This is also true for everyone who lives in your home.'

ACTS 16:16–31

Commentary

Paul had met with Jesus on his way to Damascus many years before, and it had turned his life upside down (see page 216). At the time of this story, he is in northern Greece, in a town called Philippi. Wherever he travelled, he first found out where the local Jewish people met to worship and went to tell them about Jesus. Sometimes they believed that Jesus was the Lord, but often he was forced to move on to another venue to share the good news with non-Jews. In his travels he often got into trouble for being a Christian, as he does here in Philippi.

The slave girl's owners are angry that they have lost their source of income when Paul heals her of the voices in her head, so very soon Paul and Silas find themselves before the magistrates, publicly beaten, and put in prison. But nothing can dampen their confidence and joy in Jesus. Even at midnight they are singing hymns, which must have been quite a surprise to the other prisoners! God hears them too. After the earthquake, not only are they free of their chains but even the jailer becomes a follower of Jesus.

Questions

▶ Do you know people who have become Christians in a dramatic way, like Paul did?

▶ Why did Paul always go to the Jews first with his message?

▶ Why were the slave girl's owners so angry?

▶ What do you think the other prisoners thought about Paul and Silas's reaction to being in prison?

Visual aid

Paul was a great traveller, covering thousands of miles by boat or on foot, all around the Mediterranean region. Open a map of this part of the world. Find Jerusalem and then Antioch (now known as Antakya in Syria), which is where Paul first sailed from. Paul also visited Cyprus, Turkey (look for Iconium, now called Konya, and Ephesus) and Greece (look for Athens, Corinth, Thessalonika and Philippi—now a ruin, but not far from the city of Kavala).

Activity idea

Paul and Silas sang hymns at midnight. Choose a favourite Christian song or chorus that you all know and sing it together at the tops of your voices, just as they did.

Prayer idea

Focus on those who do a lot of travelling—perhaps someone in your own family. Also pray for people going on holiday or going overseas to share God's love with those in need. 'Father God, who in Jesus travelled from heaven to earth out of love for us, help those who are on journeys today, by car, train, plane or boat, and please keep them safe.'

Key verse

'[Paul and Silas] replied, "Have faith in the Lord Jesus and you will be saved"' (Acts 16:31).

Old Testament story link

Jonah 3: Jonah was an Old Testament missionary who travelled to Nineveh, in modern-day Iraq, to tell its population to turn back to God.

An accident in Troas

3b Paul was about to sail to Syria. But some of the Jewish leaders plotted against him, so he decided to return by way of Macedonia. 4 With him were Sopater, son of Pyrrhus from Berea, and Aristarchus and Secundus from Thessalonica. Gaius from Derbe was also with him, and so were Timothy and the two Asians, Tychicus and Trophimus. 5 They went on ahead to Troas and waited for us there. 6 After the Festival of Thin Bread, we sailed from Philippi. Five days later we met them in Troas and stayed there for a week.

7 On the first day of the week we met to break bread together. Paul spoke to the people until midnight because he was leaving the next morning. 8 In the upstairs room where we were meeting, there were a lot of lamps. 9 A young man by the name of Eutychus was sitting on a window sill. While Paul was speaking, the young man got very sleepy. Finally, he went to sleep and fell three floors all the way down to the ground. When they picked him up, he was dead.

10 Paul went down and bent over Eutychus. He took him in his arms and said, 'Don't worry! He's alive.' 11 After Paul had gone back upstairs, he broke bread, and ate with us. He then spoke until dawn and left. 12 Then the followers took the young man home alive and were very happy.

ACTS 20:3b–12

Commentary

Paul had many adventures on his travels around the eastern end of the Mediterranean. He shared the story of Jesus with thousands, helped set up churches and encouraged a number of travelling companions, including Timothy and Titus, to go on and become leaders. He also suffered for his faith: there were long and difficult journeys by sea; he was beaten up, spent time in prisons, was threatened by the authorities and on more than one occasion had to defend himself in public before angry crowds. But his faith in Jesus was strong and he never gave up. Finally he knew that God wanted him to go to Rome. But he wanted to return to Jerusalem first, and, on the way, to say farewell to so many friends he had made. He must have suspected that his trip to Rome could well be his last journey.

Here at Troas, Paul met with the Christian church in a third-floor room of a building in the city. The meeting took place in the evening and poor Eutychus, who had probably been at work during the day, possibly as a slave in someone's home, was too tired to stay awake. His fall from the window proved fatal, but Paul brought him back to life by the power of the Holy Spirit.

Questions

▶ What sort of things went on at a church service, according to this story?

▶ What do you think Paul had to say to the believers that evening?

▶ What gave Paul confidence to believe that he could pray for the young man who had died?

▶ What do you think Eutychus remembered of that evening?

Visual aid

The room must have been very crowded. People were obviously sitting on the window sills and, because there was almost certainly no glass in the windows, this is why Eutychus fell. Can you arrange to sit (safely) on a window sill or near a window for today's story?

Activity idea

Clearly Paul's storytelling went on for a very long time! How long a story can you tell together? Play a game in which the first person starts telling a made-up story, but, after ten seconds, there is a bell or other signal for the next person to pick up the story. Each person can take the story in whichever direction they like, but they must not finish it.

Prayer idea

Eutychus's fall was an accident. God doesn't stop such things happening to us, but he does promise to be there for us when they happen. God can sometimes even make use of what happens as part of his good plans for us. Pray for those involved in caring for sick or injured people. Think of ambulance staff, nurses, doctors, health workers and paramedics. Pray that they will exercise skill and show compassion.

Key verse

'Paul took him in his arms and said, "Don't worry! He's alive"' (Acts 20:10).

Old Testament story link

Isaiah 43:1–7: God promises to be with us and help us, whatever we are going through.

Shipwreck on the way to Rome

⁹ By now we had already lost a lot of time, and sailing was no longer safe... ¹¹ But Julius listened to the captain of the ship and its owner, rather than to Paul.

¹² The harbour at Fair Havens wasn't a good place to spend the winter. Because of this, almost everyone agreed that we should at least try to sail along the coast of Crete as far as Phoenix. It had a harbour that opened toward the south-west and north-west, and we could spend the winter there.

¹³ When a gentle wind from the south started blowing, the men thought it was a good time to do what they had planned. So they pulled up the anchor, and we sailed along the coast of Crete. ¹⁴ But soon a strong wind called 'The North-easter' blew against us from the island. ¹⁵ The wind struck the ship, and we could not sail against it. So we let the wind carry the ship.

¹⁶ We went along the island of Cauda on the side that was protected from the wind. We had a hard time holding the lifeboat in place, ¹⁷ but finally we got it where it belonged. Then the sailors wrapped ropes around the ship to hold it together. They lowered the sail and let the ship drift along, because they were afraid it might hit the sandbanks in the gulf of Syrtis.

¹⁸ The storm was so fierce that the next day they threw some of the ship's cargo overboard. ¹⁹ Then on the third day, with their bare hands they threw overboard some of the ship's gear. ²⁰ For several days we could not see either the sun or the stars. A strong wind kept blowing, and we finally gave up all hope of being saved.

²¹ Since none of us had eaten anything for a long time, Paul stood up and told the men:

You should have listened to me! If you had stayed on in Crete, you would not have had this damage and loss. ²² But now I beg you to cheer up, because you will be safe. Only the ship will be lost.

²³ I belong to God, and I worship him. Last night he sent an angel ²⁴ to tell me, 'Paul, don't be afraid! You will stand trial before the Emperor. And because of you, God will save the lives of everyone on the ship.' ²⁵ Cheer up! I am sure that God will do exactly what he promised.

ACTS 27:9a, 11–25

Commentary

After Paul's return to Jerusalem from his many missionary journeys, he ran into trouble with the Jewish leaders. He ended up in prison for two years, but even there he made use of his time to tell the story of Jesus to two Roman governors and a local king. Finally, as a Roman citizen, he appealed to be tried before the emperor in Rome, which meant a long journey by sea; but Paul knew that this was where God wanted him to go.

It was a dangerous time of year to sail and the people on board soon began to pay the price, losing their cargo as they tried to keep the ship afloat in the storm. Clearly Paul had been praying and God assured him that they would get through, even if the boat was wrecked. That's exactly what happened. They were shipwrecked off the island of Malta with no loss of life, and many of the islanders became Christians. Paul never lost an opportunity to tell people about the kingdom of God!

Paul did eventually get to Rome, where he was put under house arrest to await trial. This didn't stop him meeting fellow Christians to encourage them, writing letters and even making plans to take the good news one day to the ends of the earth.

Questions

▶ Why didn't the Roman officer believe what Paul had told him?

▶ Sailing on the high seas in those days was always risky. What were the dangers they had to face?

▶ It was a big ship, with 276 people on board. What different jobs might they have done and how did they work together to try to save the vessel?

▶ How did God speak to Paul on board the ship?

▶ Do you think the crew believed Paul when he told them that they would be safe?

Visual aid

Create a boat from the furniture and household items around you. Imagine what it must be like to be caught in a violent storm. Perhaps some cushions or pillows can be the cargo you throw overboard.

Activity idea

Imagine that your own home is in danger of being destroyed, like Paul's ship, and that you only have time to save five items. What would you take with you? If you had to leave in an even greater hurry, what one thing would you take? God answered Paul's prayers and saved the most important things— their lives. The ship's cargo or our possessions are always going to be less valuable than human life.

Prayer idea

Paul remembers to pray in the middle of the chaos of the storm at sea. Find some newspaper headlines and ask God to rescue the people from whatever storms they are in. Perhaps the Christians in Crete, who knew that Paul was sailing nearby in the storm, were praying for him.

Key verse

'Don't be afraid… God will save the lives of everyone on the ship' (Acts 27:24).

Old Testament story link

2 Chronicles 20:1–23: Jehoshaphat faces huge threats from his enemies, but remembers to pray to God for help.

John's vision of heaven

¹ I saw a new heaven and a new earth. The first heaven and the first earth had disappeared, and so had the sea. ² Then I saw New Jerusalem, that holy city, coming down from God in heaven. It was like a bride dressed in her wedding gown and ready to meet her husband.

³ I heard a loud voice shout from the throne:

God's home is now with his people. He will live with them, and they will be his own. Yes, God will make his home among his people. ⁴ He will wipe all tears from their eyes, and there will be no more death, suffering, crying, or pain. These things of the past are gone forever.

⁵ Then the one sitting on the throne said:

I am making everything new. Write down what I have said. My words are true and can be trusted. ⁶ Everything is finished! I am Alpha and Omega, the beginning and the end. I will freely give water from the life-giving fountain to everyone who is thirsty. ⁷ All who win the victory will be given these blessings. I will be their God, and they will be my people.

REVELATION 21:1–7

Commentary

The story of the Bible ends with a shout of celebration. All that has been spoiled and broken is made new again. It's just as God had planned it to be at the very beginning, when he created a perfect world for people and himself to enjoy. The paradise of the garden of Eden has become the perfection of the new Jerusalem on earth.

All the images in this story are positive. The arrival of the new creation will be like a wedding, like a peaceful home, like a place swept clean of all suffering, like a fountain with life-giving water. When John had this vision, it was near the end of his own life. He knew that this was what God had waiting for him and for all who put their trust in Jesus' death and resurrection. In the meantime, Christians were to work towards this victory over evil in God's strength. The one who sits on the throne describes himself as being the first and last letters of the Greek alphabet: God was there at the start and will be there at the end. In an earlier part of John's vision, Jesus describes himself this way too. In other words, Jesus is God and God is Jesus, and all those whose lives are made new because of him will be part of this amazing new heaven and earth one day.

Questions

▶ From this story, which aspects of heaven do you like the most?

▶ How would you describe heaven to someone?

▶ Which part of this vision do you find most comforting?

▶ In what ways might people be thirsty, and what is this water that God promises to give them to drink?

Visual aid

Lay out letters of the alphabet on a table, perhaps from a Scrabble™ set. In our language, God says that he is the A and the Z. What might some of the letters in between stand for, if, perhaps, they are words describing heaven?

Activity idea

Roll out a large piece of paper and use paints, crayons, felt and other craft materials to create an image of heaven. It could be done with words or different colours, with pictures or abstract creations. Make your own 'Heaven is…' poster together.

Prayer idea

John wrote these words to Christians who were facing very difficult circumstances. Pick up on some of the images in the story to create your own prayers of thanks to God for the promise of heaven and for what it will be like. Round off your prayers together by using the opening words of the Lord's Prayer: 'Our Father in heaven, your name is holy. May your kingdom come and your will be done on earth, just as it is in heaven.'

Key verse

'The one sitting on the throne said, "I am making everything new"' (Revelation 21:5).

Old Testament story link

Isaiah 65:17–23: Here is a another picture of the new creation, this time from the prophet Isaiah.

Guidance and support

Praise the God and Father of our Lord Jesus Christ for the spiritual blessings that Christ has brought us from heaven. Before the world was created, God had Christ choose us to live with him and to be his holy and innocent and loving people. God was kind and decided that Christ would choose us to be God's own

Faith begins at home

Being a parent or carer is said to be one of the hardest jobs an adult will ever do. Whether you agree or not, the reality seems to be that it is a role that requires time, attention and a great deal of learning along the way.

Various studies and research have suggested that the parent/carer has the primary influence upon a child overall. They also suggest that he or she holds the primary responsibility for encouraging and supporting the development of faith. This is a significant responsibility alongside all the other roles. It can be a challenge for parents who have grown up with a knowledge and understanding of the Christian faith, and maybe even more so for those who have not grown up with this knowledge.

Whatever a parent/carer's level of knowledge, there are some important points to recognise at the start.

- It is never too late to start exploring, discussing and living out faith in the home.
- There is no set or right way to live out faith in the home. Flexibility is a key aspect. What works for one family will not be right for another. It is important to find out what is most suitable for you and your family.
- The adults do not have to know all the answers. It is more about being on a journey together as a family. You may all be at different stages but can enjoy the opportunities to explore and discuss the journey as you learn more about faith together.
- It is not about measuring levels of faith and does not involve success and failure. Faith is an ongoing learning experience throughout life.
- It does not necessarily require you to add pressure to your already busy lives by spending numerous additional hours every week. It is possible to build faith into your existing everyday activities.
- All families are different. The term 'family' in this book refers to all backgrounds, sizes and shapes of families.
- The way in which faith is lived out in the home may vary depending on the ages, interests and learning styles of your family. The same is true when it comes to reading and exploring the Bible together.

The following sections will explore this more fully, offering some practical ideas and signposting resources available, but some suggestions to get started include:

» Reading the Bible in a traditional style, followed by discussions about a passage or story.
» Starting with an activity that introduces a Bible story. This might include food, craft, construction, challenges or quizzes.
» Watching a film together. Many films and TV programmes have content that can open up an issue or trigger a faith-related discussion.

Whatever your preference, a key aspect is enjoyment. It may take a while, but it is worth making the time to find out what works best for your family, taking into consideration age, time and budget and being willing to be flexible and adapt as the seasons of family life change.

Establishing a time and place

First of all, it is worth noting that, as with living out faith in the home generally, there is no golden rule regarding a time and place for families to read or explore the Bible together. What works for one family will be different for another, so again flexibility is the key.

Families with younger children have suggested that they find it helpful to include it as part of their existing family routine. For many, it seems that just before bedtime works well. The familiar routine of food, bath, story and bed may lend itself to including a Bible story, either in addition to a non-biblical story or alternated on different days. Others have suggested that the start of the day is a good time, spending about 15 minutes after breakfast, perhaps on two or three days a week. This obviously may be easier to do at weekends with school-age children.

However, there is a need to be adaptable. If a child is tired or things have run later than planned, as is inevitable at times, then bedtime may not be the most suitable opportunity on that particular day and may in fact lead to a negative response. In these situations, be prepared to let it go and pick it up another day.

The same applies to setting aside time in the morning. If people are running late, it may not be helpful to add to that pressure. Instead you could postpone your time together and agree to pray for one another on your way to work or school.

For some families, having a regular time set aside offers a discipline that they find helpful. For others it may be unrealistic or seem too repetitive, or could induce a feeling of guilt if it is missed or forgotten or simply slips from the routine. In these cases, varying the time may be more effective, again depending on what each family finds works best.

Families with older children may have to be more proactive about creating time and opportunities to read and explore the Bible together. As life gets busier with school, extracurricular activities and emerging social lives, a parent may have less control over time and how it is used. Fitting your exploration of faith into a daily or regular routine may become much more difficult. However, it is important that there are specific times set to prevent it from slipping quietly into the background, unnoticed, as other aspects of life fill the gap.

That is not to say that such family times become a burden, and, indeed, there are ways in which faith can be integrated into busy schedules, but it is important to keep it in mind as the shape of family life changes. Specific ideas as to how you might do this are included in the section on supporting your child's faith (see page 244).

Once you have set the time aside, how you might go about using it may vary. The next guidance section will cover this in more detail, but the important element at the outset is that time is set aside to engage with the Bible as a family in a way that is positive.

Reading the Bible together

Reading the Bible individually may be familiar to some adults and children, but for others it may be something they have not regularly done before. The encouraging thing is that it is never too late to start. For many families, the challenge is how to read the Bible together. How, when and which Bible to read are all common questions, as well as how to keep everyone interested, particularly if there is a wide range of ages in the family. This is something that requires a flexible approach and a willingness to adapt and change the pattern to meet different life stages and phases.

Which Bible?

Perhaps the first question is which Bible to read together.

There is a wide variety of Bible versions available for adults as well as for teenagers and children. Those written for young children may offer a selection of Bible stories. The stories may or may not be in chronological order, which is worth knowing when you are trying to understand the timing of events.

Picture books are particularly popular with younger children, as are lift-the-flap and sticker books. They not only hold the child's interest but will help those whose learning style is visual. Children may learn a story more easily by seeing the pictures.

As a child gets older, some of the children's Bibles with increased text as well as pictures may become appropriate. Looking further ahead still, some may prefer to move on to a children's version of an adult translation, such as the NIV children's version, which offers a more adult-style text.

You may wish to look for a Bible with a particular style. It may include a specific type of graphics, such as cartoon-type pictures, or pictures of battles if you have children who would enjoy that. There are also some editions in particular artistic styles, such as the

Manga Bible. The important point is that the language and style need to be understandable to the reader. If children (or adults) don't understand what is being read, they may quickly become uninterested and distracted by other things around them.

If you have younger children, it may be that you use a children's Bible for your family time together and your own choice for your individual reading time. Some just beginning their journey into the Bible have mentioned that they find the children's/teenage Bible more helpful as they start out.

So, having decided which Bible to use, another question might be how to read and explore the Bible together.

Reading and discussing Bible passages

Families may be familiar with selecting and reading a passage and then taking time for discussion. Some have developed this approach by reading the passage and allowing each person to share what they feel are the key points or message. It isn't a test, but gives each person the chance to express their opinion. It can help children to focus if they are listening for the key points.

For those who prefer some guidance, there are Bible reading notes for families that contain some Bible verses as well as an explanation and sometimes a few follow-up questions. The 'Further resources' section at the end of the book highlights a number of the resources currently available (see page 256).

Another suggestion might be to look at different versions of the same story in different Bibles—maybe a children's Bible, the Good News Bible and The Message, or any selection that you might choose. Take note when different words are used: do you feel that this alters the story in any way and, if so, how? This may also be a useful exercise if you have children

of different ages: each person can read their age-appropriate version and it can be an interesting way of engaging with the text. You don't need to have all of the versions in the house, as there are websites that offer a wide variety of online versions of the Bible.

Using activities to introduce a Bible story or theme

Some families may find it more helpful to begin the time with an activity that is fun and interactive as a way of generating a discussion. That activity might be food, construction, craft or quiz based. For example, one idea could be to build a wall around an imaginary city using wooden building blocks before reading the story about the wall of Jericho.

Another idea might be to place an object on a table that relates to the story or passage you are looking at, such as a flower, stone or light.

If time and creativity allow, you may want to hide some items around the house that are related to the story, such as a torch, candle or light bulb to bring a focus on a reading about Jesus as the light of the world.

Personalising Bible readings

If individuals have favourite stories or verses, write them down on pieces of paper and store them in a special box. Let someone choose one from the box to determine what you will look at together. What is it that makes this story a favourite? Are there certain situations that these passages help to explain or deal with? Take time to consider how you might live out what you have read.

Whatever you prefer, take time to enjoy it: it's a time to 'wander and wonder' together.

Handling difficult questions

We have probably all heard or experienced at first hand a young child asking one of those difficult questions—often in public at what seems an inappropriate moment! As children develop, they will come across people and situations that can result in confusion, disappointment, sadness or anger, and can raise questions for them.

Many adults may have found themselves in the situation of not knowing how to answer. The key here is not to know all the answers but to offer a safe environment in which children of all ages can question, explore and challenge without the fear of being judged or ridiculed.

The question from a child aged three years will be very different from that of a young person at 16, but both are equally valid and important. When difficult questions arise, it is helpful when possible to respond with age-appropriate answers while being realistic about the issues. Helping the child to see other people's perspectives without undermining the issue is an important life skill.

However, there may be times when we simply don't know the answers or there aren't any answers we can give. Faith is about a journey of learning throughout life, and, whether we have grown up with a knowledge of the Christian faith or have just started out, we continue to learn. The key element is that adults and children can journey together, taking time to discuss, express opinions and explore some possible answers together.

When questions arise about a person's behaviour, it may be difficult to respond without seeming to be judgemental. There may be times when someone says they are a Christian but it is difficult to see how their behaviour matches with that claim. A possible way to address this issue might be to emphasise the fact that God gives humans freedom of choice—the opportunity to choose how we live. However, we may not always choose wisely and therefore there may be consequences. This point can also be helpful as family members consider their own behaviour and responses to situations.

For issues such as illness, death and bereavement, it may be appropriate that you openly share your own lack of understanding and how you feel, while talking about the need to trust that God knows best, even if we can't understand. This is not an easy subject, but it is important that children see vulnerability and honesty in adults. Walking together through difficult times can strengthen both relationships and faith. This is covered in more detail in the section on supporting your child's faith (see page 244).

Some people may find it helpful to discuss difficult issues while doing something else, as it can be easier not to have eye contact. Such discussions could happen while in the car, walking or gardening, for example. Teenagers in particular may be more open to talking in these environments.

Others might find it helpful to do some kind of craft. Although we sometimes assume that boys would prefer not to do craft, they may well enjoy cutting out two identical pictures of a car, train, football goal or whatever their interest may be. On one they can write down the difficulties they are facing or how they feel. They can then stick the second picture on the top so that no one else can see what they have written, and it becomes something shared between them and God. Obviously girls can do the same, using pictures representing their own interests.

It may also be a beneficial learning experience for children to know when adults are going through difficult times. If this is appropriate, it can help them to develop awareness and sensitivity and also, importantly, reassures them that there is nothing wrong with them if they have questions or doubts at any time.

How do we handle difficult questions about the Bible?

It is quite possible that you will come across some difficult questions as you read and learn more about the Bible. There are some aspects of scripture that are difficult to understand and some events and situations described in it that were far from perfect, which may well raise questions for children and adults. The temptation might be to avoid or skip over these difficulties. However, it is possible to explore them appropriately, depending on the ages of your children. Where necessary, it may be helpful to seek answers, information or guidance from trusted people and sources such as church leaders, books or the internet. Further information can be found in the 'Further resources' section (see page 256).

Praying as a family

It seems so much easier to talk with each other than to talk together with God, doesn't it? As a result, prayer often gets pushed to the edge of our time together as a family. So how can we help our children develop committed and meaningful prayer lives? How do we go about not simply teaching our children about prayer but helping them to become genuine pray-ers?

A good place to start tackling this question is to ask ourselves what helps us to pray. Of course, answers will be as wide-ranging as our varying tastes and characters, but the point is that this variety will also be true for children. Some children will be helped by popping balloons that say 'thank you', 'sorry' and 'please', but equally, many will be helped by silence or something beautiful to look at. In other words, there is not just one way to help children into family prayer.

So where do we start if we wish to introduce our children to the habit of prayer? Here are three guiding principles.

- The first and most powerful influence on our children's prayer life will be our own. How we pray and the words we use will be their model. However, your own praying should not be an exercise in saying something clever or reinforcing the truth of the Bible story, but rather a genuine response to God. It doesn't need to be complicated, as both the writer of Ecclesiastes (5:2) and Jesus (Matthew 6:5) remind us; we simply need to speak words from the heart. Let's model what we long to pass on.
- It is helpful to create an agreed and regular pattern for praying together. Praying in lots of creative ways can be fun, but when it comes to fostering good habits of prayer for children, a regular pattern is vital. We know that children flourish best where there are clear routines. Within these, they find the freedom to experiment and express themselves in prayer, because there they feel unthreatened and secure. Perhaps this may mean always sitting in a certain way and passing around a special object that gives permission for each member of the family in

turn to pray; perhaps it means always using simple gestures for thanks and praise and 'Amen', which act as a repeated accompaniment to any prayers that are said. There are many methods you can adopt.

- A key ingredient in leading children into a habit of prayer is to have a simple focus. Having a physical focus will remind everyone that you are deliberately choosing to come into the presence of God. It may be a lighted candle or a cross, or perhaps a piece of craft that has come out of your Bible time together. It could be a special picture or a globe that reminds you that you are talking with the Creator of heaven and earth. Choose your focus carefully, for it will often become something that, at other times and places, will help your children into the presence of God. Why not decide together as a family what your focus will be and then make it a regular feature of your time of prayer?

Prayer is a very intimate and personal experience. It is therefore not surprising that adults often find praying as a family a little uncomfortable. However, children may not find it strange to pray together. Perhaps this is part of their special closeness to the kingdom of which Jesus speaks (Matthew 18:1–5). When it comes to the experience of prayer as a natural response to the presence of God, children very often lead the way. The good habits that feed this sort of prayer will stay with them on into their adult journey of faith.

Creating shared memories

Do you have childhood memories attached to a place, person or event? Were there places you often visited or things you always did together as a family or as a group of friends?

For many of us, certain sights, sounds, smells or even tastes can bring back childhood memories. Creating shared memories together as a family can be an important aspect of both relationship- and faith-building. The activities themselves may not be faith-related, but may be more about getting to know, understand and accept one another. This in itself forms an important foundation for establishing and maintaining positive relationships. It is important that children of all ages feel that they and their opinions are valued. However, the benefits extend further. Not only do these things help us to exist as a family, but they also offer a foundation on which faith may grow.

Some families have shared how they set aside a 'family time'—when the family spends time together that is not interrupted by phones or invitations to other events. It could be watching a film, or simply a regular mealtime made special by taking it in turns to choose the meal, or a takeaway if the budget allows. It is the principle of developing a familiar routine rather than the specific activity that is important.

One family with a four-year-old and a nine-year-old on a limited income sets aside Friday evening to watch a film and enjoy shop-bought fish and chips or pizza. Another family with young children sets aside time to bake together or a day to take a trip out, often to a familiar place.

Some families enjoy creating a 'wall of memories' —a pinboard of photographs of special people and places and times they have spent together. It could include tickets to an event or travel tickets—anything that reminds you of the time you have spent together.

The same principle can be used within a faith situation. These same families set aside time, either at the start of the day or at bedtime, to pray or read the Bible together, which becomes as natural a part of life as the film and meal or day trip. The same pinboard can include notes about answers to prayer or times of encouragement that may have come through other people or situations. These are both examples of how faith can be integrated into daily life.

The opportunity to create these memories and connect faith can vary from times at home to those spent out and about, such as visiting extended family, or a trip to the zoo, beach or park. Trips out may be a good time to talk about God's creation. Which is your favourite animal or fish? Which do you think took God longest to create? Which part of the creation story do you like best? These are simple discussions that help to integrate the Bible with our everyday lives.

An alternative idea is to have a 'thank you' box. Some families write down something they want to give thanks for from the week that has passed or from a holiday time together. They then put them in the box to draw out as a focus for prayer.

Watching TV programmes and films together can be a way of opening up conversations about faith. A wide variety of family films lend themselves to this approach. Many have relevance to our own daily experiences, dealing with issues about relationships, good and evil, justice and fairness and other subjects that are significant for adults and children. Teenagers may find this a more appealing way to discuss faith issues, and it may be an easier path into exploring faith for those families who are starting to engage with faith when their children are older.

You may find that you enter into your own discussions naturally. For those who would prefer more guidance, there is a website listed in the 'Further resources' section (see page 256) that gives information about specific films.

All of these occasions can be not only enjoyable but also useful in the sense that there is a regular time in place for occasions when problems or issues need to be discussed. Whatever form it takes, the principle of having time and opportunity to create those special memories is the key element.

Supporting your child's faith

Every child is different, even within the same family, and therefore each needs to be supported differently in their faith journey as in the rest of their lives. Some children are great talkers and like to explore, debate and challenge by way of talking things through with others. Some prefer to think, ponder and reflect on things before drawing any conclusions. Either process is perfectly acceptable and children need to feel reassured in that knowledge.

The important role of the parent/carer is to ensure that children know they can discuss anything without fear of judgement or comparison with others. There may be times when the discussions are difficult, but it is important that a child feels heard and their opinion is valued, even if it differs from the views of their parents.

Timing is also important. As we have said before, when children are younger you may be better able to establish a set pattern or have time to talk with them on a regular basis. As children grow older it may become more a case of working around their schedule rather than yours. You may need to think and work creatively at this stage. Families with older children or teenagers may find that car journeys are a valuable time. Rather than seeing these journeys as simply a 'taxi service', use the time to talk with your child. It might be helpful not to talk only about faith; try asking their opinion and advice on various subjects—which phones, computers or tablets they feel are best, for example—that connect with their world. This shows them that their opinion is valued and sets a foundation for talking about faith-related issues.

That said, you may find that the time when they ask those all-important questions or want to discuss issues may be late at night or just as you come home from work, or generally not at the most convenient time. It is important to be flexible, however—to recognise the importance of this moment. Often, at these times, something has come to a head for the young person. It may be something they have been struggling with for a while or an incident at school, and the timing of your response is important. These occasions can provide a natural opportunity to talk about and apply the Bible and the Christian faith to what is being discussed.

Supporting faith through difficult times

Supporting your child's faith through difficult times is all-important. These difficulties might include relationship issues at school, illness, death and bereavement of friends or family, family breakdown and divorce. It is valuable to recognise where faith and words from scripture can help—for example, looking to Psalm 3, where David shares honestly about his struggles, and seeing the value of prayer at these times.

Being able to support children when they are doubting their faith is something we may not have thought about. All too often, we may assume that children simply accept what they are told, don't question or doubt faith, and somehow are more resilient to difficulties. For many, however, this may not be true. The cause may be any of those listed above, but it can also happen without a specific cause.

How might we help them to accept, understand or maybe see things differently? Some resources and practical suggestions to address these situations can be found in the 'Further resources' section (see page 256).

As every child is different, the ways in which they express their faith may also vary greatly. Some children and young people are keen to be involved in church life, join in the action songs and always be the first to volunteer in all-age services. Others may be reluctant to go at all or to join in while they are there, and may prefer to stand motionless through the liveliest action song. This is not necessarily a reflection on their faith; it may simply reflect their personality.

Another important way of supporting a child or young person's faith is for them to see faith lived out in you. That doesn't mean you have to know all of the answers to everything. In fact, admitting you don't know at times and exploring ideas together can be more beneficial to both. It means that they need to see what faith looks like when it is lived out in daily life. How does it affect the decisions we make? How does it work during the tough times? Where appropriate, it can be helpful for children to know about issues and concerns and be invited to be involved in praying for them—which takes us back to where we started and the importance of finding and experiencing God in our everyday lives.

Overview of the Bible

There are various ways to look at the content of the Bible. Here is one way of looking at what is in the Bible as a family.

In the beginning, God made the heavens and the earth. He began by saying, 'Let there be light,' and there was light. Next he made the water and that was good. Then God made the land and he saw that that was good. Afterwards came the sun, moon and stars to give light for the day and the night. This too was good. Then he filled the waters with fish of all kinds and the air with birds and he said that that was good. Finally he made the creatures and he also made people—you and me—and put them in charge of his world, to look after it. When God saw everything that he had made, he said that it was very good. When he had finished creating the world, God rested.

God made everything good but soon the world began to go bad. People chose not to care for God's world or even for each other. God was sad and decided to start all over again by sending a flood.

Only Noah's family truly believed in God so they were kept safe in a boat called an ark. On board were representatives of all the animals that God had made, so that God could fill his cleaned-up world again with life after the flood.

When the flood was over, Noah and his family and the animals came out. They remembered to thank God for all that he had done. Then God gave them a sign that he would never stop loving his world and its people in future. He gave them a rainbow.

God kept his promise. He never stopped loving people. He wanted to help them trust him, whatever happened. Once, he spoke to a man called Abraham and told him and his wife Sarah to set out on a dangerous journey across the desert to a new place to live, called Canaan. Abraham could not see God but he believed that God was always close. God looked after them on their long journey. He gave them a safe place to live. He also promised them that he would give them a son and that from this son would come a family and a great nation. In that nation, one day, a very special person would be born, who would bring God's love to the whole world. God's family would be world-big and contain as many people as there are stars in the sky or grains of sand in the desert. God kept his promise.

God's people didn't find it easy to trust God. They often made mistakes and often deliberately chose to go their own way, ending up in trouble. Many years after Abraham, they found themselves as slaves in Egypt. Their situation seemed hopeless but God did not forget them. He sent Moses to bring them to freedom. The Pharaoh in Egypt let them go only when a terrible thing happened. All the eldest boy children of the Egyptians, including the Pharaoh's own child, died. God's people, however, were kept safe. They had put lambs' blood around the doors of their houses, so the angel of death had passed over them and they were saved. Moses led them across the Red Sea to freedom.

God's people had been in such a rush to leave, however, that there had been no time to bake proper bread for the journey. Their bread had no yeast or leaven in it, so it was flat. They called it unleavened bread. Whenever they ate this bread, they remembered how God had brought them from slavery to freedom.

God guided Moses and he led them through the desert to a new home. God gave them miraculous food to eat and water to drink; but even then, some of them began to doubt God's love. It was so easy to forget the best way to live. So God called Moses up a mountain and gave him the law, which included the ten commandments. These ten rules would help people to know how to come close to God. They told the people how to love God and to love other people.

After a journey of 40 years, the people were finally ready to come to God's promised land. This was the place where they would be safe. In order to get into this land, they had one more thing to do. They needed to cross the River Jordan. It seemed impossible but Joshua, who had taken over from Moses as leader, trusted God to show them how. The priests went

out into the water first, carrying the great golden chest that contained the ten commandments, and they stood in the middle of the river. As soon as the priests were there, the River Jordan began to dry up so that the people could cross safely. After many years of walking through the desert, they could walk into God's special home for them. Their feet were dusty from their desert journey but as they crossed the wet riverbed they were cleaned, ready for a new beginning.

God kept on looking after his people in the new land, but there were so many temptations for the people to forget him and go their own way. There were great leaders and kings, such as David and Solomon, but even they didn't always choose God's way. They built special places to worship God—even a golden temple in Jerusalem—but they began to forget that God was everywhere, not just in a building.

God sent special people to remind them of his love and warn them of the dangers of turning away from his love. These were called prophets, but not everyone listened to their messages. Finally God decided that the only way to show his love to them was to come and live with them himself. God decided to wrap himself up very small, and he quietly entered his own world as a tiny baby.

God had planned this all along as the way that he was going to show people what he was really like and how he could keep them safe for ever. God was inside a human body, and we call him Jesus.

Jesus shone bright with God's light. When he was about 30 years old, he went to the River Jordan, where his cousin John was baptising people. He asked John to baptise him. John was surprised. He knew how special Jesus was. Jesus should baptise *him*! However, Jesus insisted and so he went down into the water and came out again. People nearby said they heard God's voice; others saw a dove coming close to

Guidance and support

Jesus. Jesus was showing everyone the way to start a new life with God. The washing of baptism became a picture of how people enter into the safe place of trusting God for ever.

Jesus began teaching people about God and his ways. Crowds gathered to listen. Once, he was speaking to a great crowd of men, women and children on a mountainside in Galilee. He told them about what things are like when God is king. He described the sort of lives God's people should lead. He said that people would be happy if they knew that they needed God; happy if they were sad about being far from him; happy if they always put others first. They would be happy if they longed for what was good and right, and happy if they were kind and said 'no' to all that was bad; happy if they were people who made peace. Everyone else might think they were crazy and laugh at them, but this was the only way to be happy and make God happy too.

Jesus said and did amazing things. Everyone knew that he was special and that he was showing them what God was like. However, very few really knew who he was. He called himself by many names. Once he said he was the light; on other occasions he called himself the good shepherd and the way, and once he described himself as the door. But Jesus knew that the only way for him to rescue people from the badness that keeps spoiling our lives was to go to Jerusalem and to die on a cross. Everyone now who comes to God through this door can be safe and rescued from all that is bad. The cross gave people the power to choose to do what is right.

After three days, Jesus was seen alive again in a new Easter way. He could now always be there for his people, to lead them into what was good and true. Although people could not see him, he was there in a new invisible way and people followed him. He wanted everyone to be filled with light as he was filled with light, and to take God's love out into the world so that more and more people would become part of God's new beginning. God's promise to Abraham was coming true. God's family was growing and growing and was becoming as many as the stars in the sky or the grains of sand in the desert.

Jesus wanted everyone to remember him so that they would not forget how to come close to God wherever they were. He had given them a way to do this—not a rainbow this time, but a simple meal to share together. It had first been part of the meal he had eaten with his friends the night before he died. There had been bread to eat and wine to drink. Every time Christians eat and drink in this way, they remember Jesus. They remember how he died and then came back to life to be with everyone everywhere for ever.

The story ends with a new beginning. The first creation will be over and, because of Jesus, all that is bad and that spoils God's world will be washed away. Everyone will be able to choose to be safe in Jesus. The Bible promises that God will make a new heaven and a new earth, full of light. This is the light of God and of Jesus his Son. All that was broken will be mended and all that was painful will be healed. This is how the Bible ends, but really it is just the first page of a new book that will go on for ever.

"Praise the God and Father of our Lord Jesus Christ for the spiritual blessings that Christ has brought us from heaven. Before the world was created, God had Christ choose us to live with him and to be his holy and innocent and loving people. ⁵God was kind and decided that Christ would choose us to be God's own

Best-loved Bible passages

Best-loved Bible passages

The good shepherd

¹ You, LORD, are my shepherd.
I will never be in need.
² You let me rest in fields of green grass.
You lead me to streams
of peaceful water,
³ and you refresh my life.

You are true to your name,
and you lead me
along the right paths.
⁴ I may walk through valleys
as dark as death,
but I won't be afraid.
You are with me,
and your shepherd's rod
makes me feel safe.

⁵ You treat me to a feast,
while my enemies watch.
You honour me as your guest,
and you fill my cup until it overflows.

⁶ Your kindness and love
will always be with me
each day of my life,
and I will live for ever
in your house, LORD.

PSALM 23

A prayer for forgiveness

¹ You are kind, God!
Please have pity on me.
You are always merciful!
Please wipe away my sins.
² Wash me clean from all
of my sin and guilt.
³ I know about my sins,
and I cannot forget my terrible guilt.
⁴ You are really the one
I have sinned against;
I have disobeyed you
and have done wrong.
So it is right and fair for you
to correct and punish me.

⁵ I have sinned and done wrong
since the day I was born.
⁶ But you want complete honesty,
so teach me true wisdom.
⁷ Wash me with hyssop
until I am clean and whiter than snow.
⁸ Let me be happy and joyful!
You crushed my bones,
now let them celebrate.
⁹ Turn your eyes from my sin
and cover my guilt.
¹⁰ Create pure thoughts in me
and make me faithful again.

¹¹ Don't chase me away from you
or take your Holy Spirit away from me.

¹² Make me as happy as you did
when you saved me;
make me want to obey!
¹³ I will teach sinners your Law,
and they will return to you.
¹⁴ Keep me from any deadly sin.
Only you can save me!
Then I will shout and sing
about your power to save.

¹⁵ Help me to speak,
and I will praise you, Lord.
¹⁶ Offerings and sacrifices
are not what you want.
¹⁷ The way to please you
is to feel sorrow deep in our hearts.
This is the kind of sacrifice
you won't refuse.

¹⁸ Please be willing, Lord,
to help the city of Zion
and to rebuild its walls.
¹⁹ Then you will be pleased
with the proper sacrifices,
and we will offer bulls
on your altar once again.

PSALM 51

The joy of worship

1 LORD God All-Powerful,
    your temple is so lovely!
2 Deep in my heart I long for your
temple,
    and with all that I am
    I sing joyful songs to you.

3 LORD God All-Powerful,
    my King and my God,
sparrows find a home near your
altars;
    swallows build nests there
    to raise their young.

4 You bless everyone
    who lives in your house,
    and they sing your praises.
5 You bless all who depend
    on you for their strength
    and all who deeply desire
    to visit your temple.
6 When they reach Dry Valley,
    springs start flowing,
    and the autumn rain fills it
    with pools of water.
7 Your people grow stronger,
    and you, the God of gods,
    will be seen in Zion.

8 LORD God All-Powerful,
    the God of Jacob,
    please answer my prayer!

9 You are the shield
    that protects your people,
    and I am your chosen one.
    Won't you smile on me?

10 One day in your temple is better
    than a thousand anywhere else.
I would rather serve in your house,
    than live in the homes of the
wicked.

11 Our LORD and our God,
    you are like the sun
    and also like a shield.
You treat us with kindness
    and with honour,
    never denying any good thing
    to those who live right.

12 LORD God All-Powerful,
    you bless everyone who trusts
you.

PSALM 84

Everything has its time

1 Everything on earth has its own
time
    and its own season.
2 There is a time for birth and
death,
    planting and reaping,

3 for killing and healing,
destroying and building,
4 for crying and laughing,
    weeping and dancing,
5 for throwing stones
    and gathering stones,
    embracing and parting.
6 There is a time for finding and
losing,
    keeping and giving,
7 for tearing and sewing,
    listening and speaking.
8 There is also a time for love and
hate,
    for war and peace.

ECCLESIASTES 3:1–8

What God's servant did for us

1 Has anyone believed us
or seen the mighty power
    of the LORD in action?
2 Like a young plant or a root
    that sprouts in dry ground,
the servant grew up
    obeying the LORD.
He wasn't some handsome king.
Nothing about the way he looked
    made him attractive to us.
3 He was hated and rejected;
his life was filled with sorrow

Best-loved Bible passages

and terrible suffering.
No one wanted to look at him.
We despised him and said,
   'He is a nobody!'

⁴ He suffered and endured
   great pain for us,
but we thought his suffering
   was punishment from God.
⁵ He was wounded and crushed
   because of our sins;
by taking our punishment,
   he made us completely well.
⁶ All of us were like sheep
   that had wandered off.
We had each gone our own way,
but the LORD gave him
   the punishment we deserved.

⁷ He was painfully abused,
   but he did not complain.
He was silent like a lamb
   being led to the butcher,
as quiet as a sheep
   having its wool cut off.

⁸ He was condemned to death
   without a fair trial.
Who could have imagined
   what would happen to him?
His life was taken away
because of the sinful things
   my people had done.

⁹ He wasn't dishonest or violent,
but he was buried in a tomb
   of cruel and rich people.

¹⁰ The LORD decided his servant
   would suffer as a sacrifice
to take away the sin
   and guilt of others.
Now the servant will live
   to see his own descendants.
He did everything
   the LORD had planned.

¹¹ By suffering, the servant
will learn the true meaning
   of obeying the LORD.
Although he is innocent,
he will take the punishment
   for the sins of others,
so that many of them
   will no longer be guilty.
¹² The LORD will reward him
with honour and power
   for sacrificing his life.
Others thought he was a sinner,
but he suffered for our sins
   and asked God to forgive us.

ISAIAH 53

The Word of life

¹ In the beginning was the one
   who is called the Word.
The Word was with God
   and was truly God.
² From the very beginning
   the Word was with God.

³ And with this Word,
   God created all things.
Nothing was made
   without the Word.
Everything that was created
   ⁴ received its life from him,
and his life gave light
   to everyone.
⁵ The light keeps shining
   in the dark,
and darkness has never
   put it out.
⁶ God sent a man named John,
   ⁷ who came to tell
   about the light
and to lead all people
   to have faith.
⁸ John wasn't that light.
He came only to tell
   about the light.

⁹ The true light that shines
on everyone
   was coming into the world.
¹⁰ The Word was in the world,

but no one knew him,
though God had made the world
     with his Word.
[11] He came into his own world,
but his own nation
     did not welcome him.
[12] Yet some people accepted him
     and put their faith in him.
So he gave them the right
     to be the children of God.
[13] They were not God's children
by nature or because
     of any human desires.
God himself was the one
     who made them his children.

[14] The Word became
a human being
     and lived here with us.
We saw his true glory,
the glory of the only Son
     of the Father.
From him all the kindness
and all the truth of God
     have come down to us.

JOHN 1:1–14

Mary's song of praise

[46] Mary said:

With all my heart
     I praise the Lord,
[47] and I am glad
     because of God my Saviour.
[48] He cares for me,
     his humble servant.
From now on,
all people will say
     God has blessed me.
[49] God All-Powerful has done
great things for me,
     and his name is holy.
[50] He always shows mercy
to everyone
     who worships him.
[51] The Lord has used
     his powerful arm
to scatter those
     who are proud.
[52] He drags strong rulers
     from their thrones
and puts humble people
     in places of power.
[53] God gives the hungry
     good things to eat,
and sends the rich away
     with nothing.
[54] He helps his servant Israel
and is always merciful
     to his people.

[55] The Lord made this promise
     to our ancestors,
to Abraham and his family
     for ever!

LUKE 1:46–55

The Beatitudes

[1b] Jesus' disciples gathered around
him, [2] and he taught them:

[3] God blesses those people
     who depend only on him.
They belong to the kingdom
     of heaven!
[4] God blesses those people
who grieve.
     They will find comfort!
[5] God blesses those people
     who are humble.
The earth will belong
     to them!
[6] God blesses those people
who want to obey him
     more than to eat or drink.
They will be given
     what they want!
[7] God blesses those people
     who are merciful.
They will be treated
     with mercy!
[8] God blesses those people

253

Best-loved Bible passages

whose hearts are pure.
  They will see him!
⁹ God blesses those people
  who make peace.
They will be called
  his children!
¹⁰ God blesses those people
who are treated badly
  for doing right.
They belong to the kingdom
  of heaven.

¹¹ God will bless you when people insult you, ill-treat you, and tell all kinds of evil lies about you because of me. ¹² Be happy and excited! You will have a great reward in heaven. People did these same things to the prophets who lived long ago.

MATTHEW 5:1b–12

The Lord's Prayer

⁹ You should pray like this:

Our Father in heaven,
help us to honour
  your name.
¹⁰ Come and set up
  your kingdom,
so that everyone on earth

will obey you,
as you are obeyed
  in heaven.
¹¹ Give us our food for today.
¹² Forgive us for doing wrong,
  as we forgive others.
¹³ Keep us from being tempted
  and protect us from evil.

MATTHEW 6:9–13

Love

¹ What if I could speak
all languages of humans
  and of angels?
If I did not love others,
  I would be nothing more
than a noisy gong
  or a clanging cymbal.
² What if I could prophesy
and understand all secrets
  and all knowledge?
And what if I had faith
  that moved mountains?
I would be nothing,
  unless I loved others.
³ What if I gave away all
  that I owned
and let myself
  be burnt alive?
I would gain nothing,

unless I loved others.
⁴ Love is kind and patient,
never jealous, boastful,
  proud, or ⁵ rude.
Love isn't selfish
  or quick-tempered.
It doesn't keep a record
  of wrongs that others do.
⁶ Love rejoices in the truth,
  but not in evil.
⁷ Love is always supportive,
loyal, hopeful,
  and trusting.
⁸ Love never fails!

Everyone who prophesies
  will stop,
and unknown languages
will no longer
  be spoken.
All that we know
  will be forgotten.
⁹ We don't know everything,
and our prophecies
  are not complete.
¹⁰ But what is perfect
  will some day appear,
and what isn't perfect
  will then disappear.

¹¹ When we were children,
we thought and reasoned
  as children do.

But when we grew up,
    we stopped our childish ways.
[12] Now all we can see of God
is like a cloudy picture
    in a mirror.
Later we will see him
    face to face.
We don't know everything,
    but then we will,
just as God completely
    understands us.
[13] For now there are faith,
    hope, and love.
But of these three,
    the greatest is love.

1 CORINTHIANS 13

True humility

[1] Christ encourages you, and his love comforts you. God's Spirit unites you, and you are concerned for others. [2] Now make me completely happy! Live in harmony by showing love for each other. Be united in what you think, as if you were only one person. [3] Don't be jealous or proud, but be humble and consider others more important than yourselves. [4] Care about them as much as you care about yourselves [5] and think the same way that Christ Jesus thought:

[6] Christ was truly God.
But he did not try to remain
    equal with God.
[7] Instead he gave up everything
    and became a slave,
when he became
    like one of us.

[8] Christ was humble.
He obeyed God and even died
    on a cross.
[9] Then God gave Christ
    the highest place
and honoured his name
    above all others.

[10] So at the name of Jesus
    everyone will bow down,
those in heaven, on earth,
    and under the earth.
[11] And to the glory
    of God the Father
everyone will openly agree,
    'Jesus Christ is Lord!'

PHILIPPIANS 2:1–11

Further resources

Publishers of Bibles, books and resources for children and families

Barnabas for Children (a ministry of BRF): www.barnabasforchildren.org.uk; www.brfonline.org.uk
Bible Society: www.biblesociety.org.uk
Authentic Media: www.authenticmedia.co.uk
CWR: www.cwr.org.uk
The Good Book Company: www.thegoodbook.co.uk
Kevin Mayhew: www.kevinmayhew.com
Lion Hudson: www.lionhudson.com

Websites to support families to live out faith in the home

Faith in Homes: Ideas to help families live out faith in the home. Useful websites and resources available from the UK and overseas; family events across the UK: www.faithinhomes.org.uk
Table Talk for families: Conversation cards to stimulate discussion: www.table-talk.org
The Daily Doughnut: Bite-sized Bible study for all the family: www.thedailydoughnut.com
GodVenture: Simple, creative ways for families to pray and explore the Bible together: www.godventure.co.uk
Non-Stop Story Shop: Fun, interactive and informative Bible stories from Bob Hartman: http://nonstopstoryshop.goodsie.com/more-stories
What's in the Bible: An animated series of DVDs of Bible stories with downloadable activities for children and families: http://whatsinthebible.com/activities

Websites to support general parenting

Commonsense media: Information for parents/carers related to the content of recently released films, computer games and books: www.commonsensemedia.org/reviews
Damaris: Guidance and conversation starters based on recent films: www.damaris.org
Care for the Family: A national charity that aims to promote strong family life and to help those facing family difficulties: www.careforthefamily.org.uk

Practical help for facing difficult times

Using the Psalms to help: see www.faithinhomes.org.uk/7177
Working through doubt: see www.faithinhomes.org.uk/children-doubting-faith-can-it-happen/
When God seems far away/seeing things differently: see www.faithinhomes.org.uk/7192
Death and bereavement: see www.thegoodbookstall.org.uk/section/59/children-bereavement/
Divorce: *The Essential Guide to Children and Separation: Surviving divorce and family break-up* by Jennifer Croly (Lion Hudson, 2013)
Helping Children Cope with Divorce by Rosemary Wells, 3rd edn (Sheldon Press, 2003)
Two Homes for Tyler: A story about understanding divorce by Pamela Kennedy (GP Kids, 2008)
The Children of Divorce by Andrew Root (Baker Academic, 2010)